D0898426

SUCCESSFUL
AFFILIATE
MARKETING
FOR MERCHANTS

FRANK FIORE

SHAWN COLLINS

que®

201 W. 103rd Street

Indianapolis, Indiana 46290

Successful Affiliate Marketing for Merchants

Copyright © 2001 by Que

International Standard Book Number: 0-7897-2525-8

Library of Congress Catalog Card Number: 00-109761

Printed in the United States of America

First Printing: April 2001

03   02   01   00   4   3   2   1

Trademarks

Warning and Disclaimer

Associate Publisher
Greg Wiegand

Acquisitions Editor
Angelina Ward

Development Editor
Howard Jones

Managing Editor
Thomas Hayes

Project Editor
Heather McNeill

Copy Editor
Megan Wade

Indexer
Chris Barrick

Proofreader
Harvey Stanbrough

Technical Editor
Bill Bruns

Team Coordinator
Sharry Gregory

Interior Designer
Kevin Spear

Cover Designer
Gary Adair

Layout Technicians
Heather Hiatt Miller
Stacey Richwine-DeRome

Contents

Foreword

By James L. Marciano

The affiliate marketing space has matured quite a bit since 1994, when the Olim brothers began their first affiliate program at CDnow. The 'buyweb" program revolutionized advertising and marketing on the Internet by shifting the "burden of response" from advertisers to content producers.

1996 saw the birth of affiliate solution providers – the software needed to track sales by Webmasters – with the introduction of LinkShare and Be Free. That same year, Amazon launched their affiliate ("associates") program, which became a prototype for others in the pay-for-performance industry to follow.

I'd consider myself one of the early adopters of affiliate marketing, and I didn't join my first affiliate program until mid-1997, when I was looking for incremental revenue for TheSquare. com, an executive recruiting firm that serves as the "talent agent" for a network of more than 50,000 alumni and students from the Ivy League and other top schools.

As I scoured industry publications and search engines for details on affiliate programs, the information wasn't always easy to find. What was needed was a search engine for affiliate programs, with ratings and details. I launched Refer-it.com in late 1997. Other affiliate directories quickly followed, including AssociatePrograms.com, CashPile.com, and ReveNews.com. In early 1999, I held the first Affiliate Solutions conference in NYC, where over 200 e-commerce managers, software companies, and Webmasters gathered to share best practices in the emerging affiliate industry.

By mid-1999, affiliate marketing emerged as the most cost effective way for marketing managers to acquire new customers. And by 2000, over three thousand companies and a million Webmasters had jumped on the affiliate bandwagon. As companies got focused on profitability, affiliate programs began to play a central role in their overall marketing strategy. Pay-for-performance marketing was no longer a cocktail party catchphrase, but a gateway on the "path to profitability."

As with any marketing program, affiliate programs don't run on autopilot. The successful merchants in affiliate marketing not only launch a program with best-in-class member agreements, commissions, and tracking software, but also manage and support their best performing affiliates for optimal results. Shawn Collins and Frank Fiore have done a tremendous job of packaging the industry's best practices so that you too can succeed in affiliate marketing.

About the Authors

Frank Fiore is an e-commerce expert and consultant, and author of e-commerce books entitled *Dr. Livingston's Online Shopping Safari Guidebook*, published by Maximum Press, and *The Complete Idiot's Guide to Starting an Online Business* and *e-Marketing Strategies*, published by Macmillan. He has been involved with e-commerce from its inception on the Net, and with his experience as an e-commerce expert and direct marketer of products, he knows e-commerce from both sides of the transaction. He is currently the Official Online Shopping Guide for About and has been interviewed for numerous TV and radio talk shows and print media on the subject of e-commerce and online shopping.

Shawn Collins is the affiliate manager for the ClubMom, the first free membership organization created exclusively to reward and celebrate moms every day. He is the publisher of *AffiliateManager.net*, speaks regularly at industry conferences, and is a columnist for *ClickZ.com* and *SAM Magazine*. Additionally, Shawn founded the United States Affiliate Manager Coalition and the Affiliate Webinar, as well as co-founding Affiliate Metrix, inc., a research, analysis, and benchmarking initiative for the affiliate marketing industry.

Dedication

To Lynne—my wife—I could think of no one better to be affiliated with for the rest of my life.—F.F.

For my wife, Vicky, a masterpiece of nature and the best ROI my heart will ever know.—S.C.

We'd Like to Hear from You!

As the reader of this book, *you* are our most important critic and commentator. We value your opinion and want to know what we're doing right, what we could do better, what areas you'd like to see us publish in, and any other words of wisdom you're willing to pass our way.

As an associate publisher for Que, I welcome your comments. You can fax, e-mail, or write me directly to let me know what you did or didn't like about this book—as well as what we can do to make our books stronger.

Please note that I cannot help you with technical problems related to the topic of this book, and that due to the high volume of mail I receive, I might not be able to reply to every message.

When you write, please be sure to include this book's title and author as well as your name and phone or fax number. I will carefully review your comments and share them with the authors and editors who worked on the book.

Fax: 317-581-4666

E-mail: feedback@quepublishing.com

Mail: Greg Wiegand
          Que
          201 West 103rd Street
          Indianapolis, IN 46290 USA

Conventions Used In This Book

Important text will be called out with a special typeface. For example, if you are instructed to press **Ctrl+C** or select a particular **menu item**, it will appear in **bold**. Web addresses and other text that you must type will appear in monospaced type. In addition, you will find special tips and advice in these sidebars:

Buzzwords

Every industry has its buzzwords. Affiliate marketing is no different. These tips will bring you up to speed on the terminology used in the text of this book.

Do

These tips will give you a quick summary of what the most important affiliate marketing DOs are in a chapter.

Don't

These tips will give you a quick summary of what the most important affiliate marketing DON'Ts are in a chapter.

The Internet is arguably the most important business phenomenon of the new millennium. But optimism for this new commerce tool has waned just as the new millennium has dawned. Companies know that e-commerce is an important part of their business, but customer acquisition costs have proven to be two, three, four, and in some cases, even ten times as expensive as acquiring a customer in the real world.

To make matters worse, investors began to pull money away from dot-com companies in the year 2000, and this withdrawal has meant less money for advertising. The end result is that dot-com companies are finding that they can no longer afford the high advertising cost of banner ads and sponsorships. In this new, frugal environment, online companies are looking for more than just brand exposure; they want to see a greater return on investments in ways that simple media buys could never deliver.

So an old idea is receiving more and more attention these days by companies faced with higher advertising costs, lower response rates, and unaccountable ad performance—and that idea is performance-based advertising.

Performance-based advertising promises to deliver increased brand awareness, lower customer acquisition costs, and increased sales. Because of these benefits, companies are flocking to this old but new breed of advertising. In fact, Forrester Research projects that performance-based advertising models will account for 50% of online advertising budgets by 2003, up from 15% in 1999.

Performance-based advertising is a broad term applied to both advertising and marketing and is known by different names by merchants and industry analysts: pay-for-performance advertising, cost-per-action advertising, revenue-sharing, referral programs, partnership programs, associate programs, syndicated selling, and the term commonly used by today's merchants—affiliate marketing.

It's hard to find an online merchant these days who does not have a link on her home page that reads "Join Our Affiliate Program." Companies are flocking to this new kind of marketing for good reason.

Be Free, a large affiliate solution provider, claims that its merchant companies earn between 20% and 35% of their total online sales through its affiliate sales channels. Further, Be Free merchants experience click-through rates 3–6 times that of traditional banner advertising, and receive tens of thousands of impressions—only paying for those impressions that generate revenues.

Surveys from Forrester Research have shown that affiliate marketing is one of the most effective traffic-driving techniques used on the Net today, beating out banner ads and direct mail. Because of this, affiliate marketing consultants have set up businesses that offer advice to online merchants, affiliate directories promoting affiliate programs have sprouted across the Net, and conferences focusing on affiliate programs have appeared to educate both businesses and Web site owners on the benefits of affiliate selling.

Why the popularity?

Look at it this way. You have a business and need to generate sales. One way—and one of the most popular ways—is to buy ads on other Web sites. Your banner ad placed on another Web site is viewed by thousands of potential customers. But there's no guarantee that the ad will generate an action, so you pay for the ad whether someone clicks on it or not. Wouldn't it be better if you paid only if the ad performed? That's the beauty of an affiliate program—you buy guaranteed performance. That is, you pay only when an action is performed.

The benefits to you as a merchant are obvious. Your business can use an affiliate program to increase sales, drive traffic, generate qualified leads, and extend the reach of your brand through your affiliate partner Web sites.

This sounds good for the merchant. But just how popular are affiliate programs with Web site owners?

Today, there are over one million Web sites on the Net that are participating in affiliate programs—and that number is growing every day. Affiliates who join a merchant's affiliate program not only earn revenue but also have the advantage of attracting additional visitors to their site who would be interested in the products or services offered. Some merchants offer content to facilitate sales and improve the caliber of their affiliate sites.

There's another advantage to an affiliate program. A merchant can easily target his or her offers to the right audience. You can target consumers with particular interests, knowledge, and spending habits, while paying only for the performance of your ad. This lowers your customer acquisition costs. In fact, the customer acquisition costs of an affiliate program are far less than any other means of marketing.

Now, you can look at affiliate programs as a way to get free advertising space on an affiliate's site. But that would be very shortsighted and would result in a less-than-effective affiliate program. In fact, that's one of the reasons so many affiliate programs fail. Affiliates should be seen as true marketing partners and an asset to your company—and should be treated that way. It's important to realize that affiliates, in many ways, represent your company, and their care and feeding—including educating them on your product or service and how to sell it—are important factors in a successful affiliate program. Their success will dictate the success of your program.

Other important factors that will determine the success of your affiliate program include proper affiliate tracking and accurate payments, a fair and clear affiliate agreement, targeted and timely offers, good promotional copy writing, ongoing communication with your affiliate partners—and most important of all—designing a program that creatively meets the challenges of affiliate marketing now and in the future.

In other words, affiliate programs are evolving away from a simple pay-for-performance advertising model and into collaborative commerce networks where the merchant and the affiliate partner are in business together. That's the future.

If this sounds like a lot of work—it is. Setting up and managing a successful affiliate program is not easy. Although some businesses claim that their affiliate program earns them up to 30% of their online revenue, achieving that kind of result takes a lot of creativity, planning, hard work, and management know-how.

If you have a product or service to sell on the Net, considering an affiliate program of your own should be at the top of your marketing to-do list. If you're ready to increase your revenue, reduce your customer acquisition costs, and extend your brand across the Net, this book will help. The material here will help you decide what kind of affiliate program is best for your business, show you the step by step how to design and build it, and then show you how to manage your affiliate program to increase revenue and brand awareness online.

PART I

What Affiliate Marketing Can Do for Your Business

What Is Affiliate Marketing?

Chapter Summary

Affiliate marketing has the potential to deliver increased revenues and brand awareness, and extend the shelf-space of your company's products or services. And here's the best part. You get all this exposure free and only pay when a sale is made or an action is taken.

If this sounds like the answer to your e-commerce dreams, you're right. That's the good news. On the other hand, it's a lot more complicated than it seems. In the world of the Internet, pay-for-performance means a different thing to Internet marketers. Internet advertisers place banner ads on Web sites to generate brand awareness, a click-through, a sale, or some kind of action. But Internet marketers see pay-for-performance as the basis of not just an advertising campaign, but a long-term marketing program.

Affiliate programs have become an invaluable part of marketing success for online merchants and are reshaping how business is being done over the Internet. By using an affiliate program, your company can place your brand name before millions of people through the Web sites or the e-mail marketing of your affiliates.

Here's the bottom line: An affiliate program is a win/win situation. Merchants gain the desired actions or consumer sales, and affiliates earn money. But affiliate marketing is not as simple as it seems. Having an affiliate program doesn't guarantee success. It takes hard work, know how, and a lot of time to make affiliate marketing work for your company. And it's all worth it, because affiliate marketing is becoming a central component of today's online company's operations and a cornerstone of its marketing strategy.

What a difference a year or so makes.

What was unimportant only 18 months ago is now deemed critical to the success of online businesses. In a not so surprising turn of events, dot-coms are now expected to show performance, revenue—and yes, profits! Whereas before it was rational to spend millions of dollars on banner ads, branding campaigns, and sponsorships with little or no return on investment, that type of marketing strategy is being seriously reconsidered.

If you listen to online marketing managers today, you'd think they'd just discovered that spending millions of dollars on TV, banner ads (see Figure 1.1), and Web sponsorships is not a cost effective way of acquiring customers and reaching profitability. Predictably, these marketing managers are diligently looking for new ways to get a higher return on their online marketing dollar.

This return on one's advertising investment goes for any online business—small, medium, or large.

Profitability, it seems, has become a trend. Proof of this is the recent boom in affiliate marketing. According to Affiliate Metrix (www.affiliatemetrix.com), 68% of all affiliate programs were launched in the year 2000. For a long time, there have been two camps in Internet marketing: the branding people and the direct marketing people. The branding people believed that it was all right to spend money without results as long as it strengthened a company's brand. The direct marketing people, on the other hand, held the position that if a company didn't make money on the money they'd spent, they would go out of business.

What's a Branding Campaign?

These ad campaigns have the purpose of building awareness of the company in the consumer's eyes. Nike's "Just Do It!" is more branding campaign than product advertising.

What's a Banner Ad?

A banner ad is an electronic billboard or ad in the form of a graphic image that comes in many sizes and resides on a Web page. Banner ad space is sold to advertisers to earn revenue for the Web site.

Banner Ad

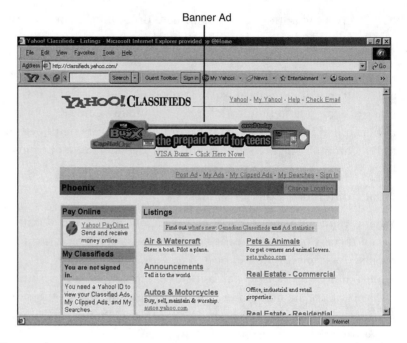

Figure 1.1
Banner ads can be placed anywhere on a Web page and come in all sizes. They are used for both brand awareness and as a call to action.

Although the camps seem to be in conflict, there is a new way where a business can do both. In fact, this new way is not so new at all, and it was an old-economy company that figured out the solution years ago.

Pay-for-Performance—Advertising Versus Marketing

Back in 1996, Procter & Gamble (P&G) (www.pg.com), one of the nation's leading traditional advertisers, was looking at the Web as a way to extend its reach and strengthen its brand with Internet consumers. But P&G didn't want to pay for ads that didn't perform. So in April 1996, P&G became the first company to move to a CPA (cost per action) advertising model by pressuring Yahoo! (www.yahoo.com) to accept a performance-based advertising plan that required the portal to be paid only when P&G's banner ads were clicked—and not on the basis of mere exposures. P&G knew that a click-through represented an active interest by a consumer in its advertising message, and were willing only to pay for that action when it occurred.

With the P&G campaign at Yahoo!, CPA entered the advertising lexicon and became an alternative to CPM (cost per one thousand impressions) advertising. Up until that point, an advertiser would pay for the number of impressions his or her ad would have. For example, an advertiser would pay $10 for one thousand impressions—or views—of his or her banner ad on someone's Web site. That would compute to one cent per impression. The advertiser would pay the Web site one penny every time his or her banner ad was viewed by a site visitor. Of course, many banner advertising campaigns cost advertisers up to $70 or more per one thousand impressions depending upon how valuable the viewers were and where the banner ads were placed on the Web site (see Table 1.1).

What Is CPM and CPA?

CPM stands for cost per thousand. An advertiser will pay for the number of times an ad is viewed on a Web site. On the other hand, when an advertiser enters into a CPA (cost per action) contract with a Web site, the company pays only for those people who click on an ad and take some kind of action, like buying something, filling out a form, or downloading a piece of software.

Table 1.1

| Frequency of Full Banner Ad Rates | |
Rate (CPM)	Percentage of Sites Offering
>$70	1%
70	2
65	2
60	3
55	5
50	9
45	6
40	10
35	10
30	13
25	15
20	17
15	6
10	2
5	1

Source: AdRelevance

In the beginning, CPM advertising paid off. The click-through rates for these banners was up to 10% or higher in some cases. Click-throughs are now below one half of 1%—and dropping—thus necessitating a re-evaluation of the cost effectiveness of CPM adverting and supporting John Wanamaker's (founder of John Wanamaker & Company clothing stores) oft-quoted lament that "I know half the money I spend on advertising is wasted, but I can never find out which half."

Unlike traditional uses of the CPM model—in magazines, newspapers, billboards, and TV—the unique nature of the Internet gives advertisers a way to actually track performance of ads on a one-on-one basis. Enter pay-for-performance advertising.

Pay-for-performanceadvertising uses two types of tracking methods—CPA and CPC. CPC is a pay-per-click program where the advertiser only pays each time a person clicks on his or her banner ad. CPA is a pay-per-action program where the advertiser pays only when a visitor clicks on a banner ad and performs a certain action on the advertiser's site, such as making a purchase, filling out a form, or providing his or her e-mail address.

In the world of the Internet, pay-for-performance means a different thing to Internet marketers. Internet advertisers place banner ads on Web sites to generate brand awareness, a click-through, a sale, or some kind of action. But Internet marketers see pay-for-performance as the basis of not just an advertising campaign, but a long-term marketing program. Thus the concept of affiliate marketing joined the e-marketers toolbox.

A Brief History of Affiliate Marketing

As the story goes, affiliate marketing all started at a cocktail party. Jeff Bezos, CEO and founder of Amazon.com (www.amazon.com), was chatting with a party guest who wanted to sell books on her Web site. This got Bezos thinking. Why not have the woman link her site to Amazon's and receive a commission on the books that she sold? Soon after, Amazon introduced the Amazon Associates Program. It was a simple idea. Amazon Associates would place banner or text links on their site (see Figure 1.2) for individual books or link directly to the Amazon's home page. When visitors clicked from the associate's site through to Amazon.com and purchased a book, the associate received a commission.

With that thought, Bezos created Amazon.com's affiliate program in July 1996.

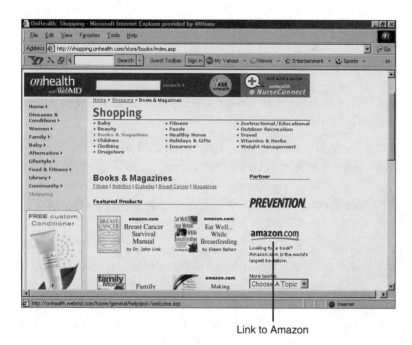

Link to Amazon

Figure 1.2
Amazon.com affiliates place a small graphic image promoting Amazon's bookstore on their Web page.

But Amazon wasn't the first company to initiate an affiliate program. According to Brad Waller, VP of Affiliate and Business Development for Epage (www.ep.com), the affiliate program for Epage started in April 1996. As documented in "The CDNow Story: Rags to Riches on the Internet," CDNow's affiliate program predates Amazon's by more than a year.

In November 1994, almost a full year before Amazon.com even launched its Web site, the venerable CDNow (www.cdnow.com) began its buyweb program. With its buyweb program, CDNow was the first to introduce the concept of an affiliate or associate program with its idea of click-through purchasing through independent, online storefronts.

It worked like this.

CDNow had the idea that music-oriented Web sites could review or list albums on their pages that their visitors might be interested in purchasing and offer a link that would take the visitor directly to CDNow to purchase them. The idea for this remote purchasing originally arose as a result of conversations with a music publisher called Geffen Records (www.geffen.com) in the fall of 1994. The management at Geffen Records wanted to sell its artists' CDs directly from its site but didn't want to do it itself. Geffen Records asked CDNow if it could design a program where CDNow would do the fulfillment.

Geffen Records realized that CDNow could link directly from the artist on its Web site to Geffen's Web site, bypassing the CDNow home page and going directly to an artist's music page. By linking Geffen Records to CDNow, the affiliate marketing format was born.

In this win-win advertising strategy, Geffen promoted and enabled the sale of its artists' discs online and CDNow actually sold the discs. Following this program, CDNow formally introduced the concept as "buyweb" in the fall of 1994. At first, it was simply a technology that allowed Web site owners, referred to as members, to link directly to an artist's page. Over time, the buyweb program grew. In 1994, CDNow had a dozen or so members, but no money changed hands.

By 1995 there were a few hundred affiliate members in the buyweb program. At that time, CDNow launched a revenue sharing program where it began to pay small commissions to Web site owners who used the technology. This gave Web sites the inducement they needed to join the program and provided them with an important opportunity to make money on the Internet.

CDNow created a methodology that enabled them to track purchases that online customers made and pay the referring Web sites 3% of the revenues from the discs that CDNow sold that were directly attributable to the links. The technology allowed CDNow to explicitly track when a visitor clicked through from say, the Geffen site, by encoding the Geffen name in the URL. Subsequently, the commission percentage was raised to 15%.

Participating Web sites were now able to add value for CDNow by recommending various compact discs to their site visitors that could be purchased on CDNow's Web site. The links that such sites placed next to their music reviews gave their visitors the option of effortlessly purchasing the reviewed disc on the CDNow site. The participating Web sites received value in the form of the commission paid by CDNow each time a visitor clicked on the CDNow link and purchased the highlighted CD.

This was the first affiliate marketing program on the Net.

From CDNow and Amazon's affiliate marketing programs came the beginnings of the affiliate programs we see today that have become a marketing staple of many online companies. Their popularity stems from the challenge of getting noticed among the hundreds of thousands of dot-coms on the Web. As the number of commercial Web sites continues to explode, the marketing problems of attracting targeted consumers to a particular Web site, making a sale, and then securing repeat visits, have become acute. Simple banner ads that just build and maintain a brand have become cost prohibitive, and their effectiveness has diminished over the years.

According to Forrester Research (www.forrester.com), banner ads had a click-through rate of 40% in 1994. By 1998, that percentage dropped to 1.5%. Today, banner ads return only a 0.5% click-through rate. Using banner ads on such sites as Yahoo! comes with few guarantees. There's no guarantee of visitors to your site, no guarantee of click-through, and in some cases, no guarantee of impressions. The only guarantee is that you will receive an invoice for that media buy.

What companies needed was a hybrid marketing program that delivered sales and branding—not just simple impressions. And affiliate marketing, with its performance-based model, fits the bill admirably.

Defining Affiliate Marketing

In your travels around the Net, you've probably run across a number of sites that are members of an affiliate program. You might have seen a CDNow or eToys (www.etoys.com) banner on some Web site enticing you to buy a CD or toy from these merchants. Or

A customer bounty is the amount paid to an affiliate partner for every new customer who is directed to a merchant in the affiliate program.

perhaps a text link with a line or two of advertising in a friend's e-mail message asking you to purchase a book from Barnes & Noble (www.bn.com) (see Figure 1.3). What all this means is that the Web site has joined a merchant's affiliate program and the merchant has agreed to pay a commission or *bounty* for every customer or prospect sent its way.

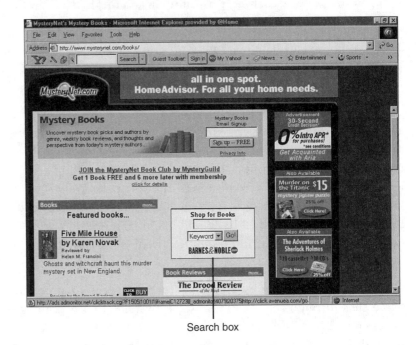

Search box

Figure 1.3
Barnes & Noble affiliates can place a search box directly on their Web page that visitors can use to search for mystery books on the Barnes & Noble site, then purchase them.

Affiliate programs have become an invaluable part of marketing success for online merchants and are reshaping how business is being done over the Internet. Affiliate programs are the great synergizer, combining marketing, advertising, and branding, and resulting in a company being seen and remembered by a host of potential customers. The more people who see a company's brand the better their marketing strategy.

By using an affiliate program, your company can place your brand name before millions of people through the Web sites or e-mail marketing of your affiliates. In other words, an affiliate program allows a company to reach new target markets and significantly expand its shelf-space and online presence. Affiliate programs provide increased revenue, a wider reach in the marketplace, and an increase in brand awareness that offers high return on investment and low operating costs.

The bottom line—an affiliate program is a win/win situation. Merchants gain consumer sales and affiliates earn money. With few marketing dollars a merchant can still establish a presence and earn a profit, as long as he or she recruits the right affiliates. In addition, an affiliate program is very scalable, and it allows you to be in control of your marketing budget by giving you total accountability and allowing you to control your marketing costs. Your affiliate program will grow with your company.

An affiliate program is really a simple concept. In a nutshell, an affiliate program is a referral-based marketing strategy where you increase your Web site's traffic and sales. You pay other Web site owners a commission or referral fee after one of their visitors is sent to your Web site and makes a purchase or performs an action. Affiliates provide the marketing, and your company fulfills the goods or services to the customer.

Here's another definition.

Jupiter Communications (www.jp.com) defines an affiliate program as a relationship between an online merchant (the company) and another Web site (the affiliate) in which the company pays the affiliate a bounty for each action generated.

You see, the beauty of an affiliate program is that you—the merchant—pay nothing up front. You only have to pay a commission or fee for a resulting action. Because the referring Web site—or the affiliate member—has a direct incentive to send customers to you, it will promote your product or service to its site visitors.

Making It Work

Buying performance from an affiliate site means paying only when someone takes some kind of action. For example, if someone clicks on your banner or text link on an affiliate site, you pay for that click. If someone clicks through to your Web site and makes a purchase, you pay a commission on that sale. Or if they click to fill out

What Is an Affiliate Link?

An Affiliate link is a piece of code residing in a graphic image or piece of text placed on an affiliate's Web page that notifies the merchant that an affiliate should be credited for the customer or visitor sent to its Web site.

a form, you pay for that action. You pay only if your ad performs. In addition, because you don't pay for the display of your banner or text link on your affiliate site until the ad performs, your brand is getting free exposure to millions of viewers.

The link on your affiliate site is coded with a unique ID. When a visitor to the affiliate's site clicks on the banner or text link, this is recorded and tracked by the merchant, thereby allowing the affiliate to be credited with the action. Your company only pays when and if the affiliate delivers the desired outcome. Your company does not pay affiliates for exposures based on page views, but only for click-throughs that result in actual leads or sales.

Here's an example.

Let's say you have an online business that sells videotapes. And let's say that the videotapes you buy cost an average of $25. An affiliate in your program gets a 5% commission on each videotape he or she sells through your site, which means that your company's cost per sale is only $1.25.

There's no cost per impression (free branding), because your company pays only for each sale. That's a lot better than CPM-based banner advertising where you would pay up front for impressions regardless of whether the banner generates 1 sale or 1,000 sales. As mentioned earlier, click-through rates on banner advertising have dropped to well under 1%, driving the cost per impression higher and higher with no guarantees of a sale or action on behalf of the consumer.

Let's do the math one more time. An advertiser pays a CPM of $35 for a targeted demographic. Consider an average click-through rate of a half of 1% and a 10% conversion rate (that is, the customer takes an action such as buying a $20 book). This means that the advertiser paid $70 for that new customer. Now tell me something—can your business model support that math? With the same performance metrics through an affiliate program that pays 10% on the sale, that new customer would cost $2!

Table 1.2 shows that affiliate marketing is more cost effective than banner ads.

Table 1.2

Banner Advertising	Affiliate Marketing (commission-based model)
If a company spends $20,000 for 2,000,000 banner ads *(assume $10 CPM)*	If a company gets $7,000 in gross sales
And receives 15,000 clicks to its site *(assume 0.75% click-through rate)*	And pays $700 paid to affiliates *(assume 10% commission rate)*
And gets 150 sales *(assume 1% conversion rate)* They receive $7,000 in gross sales. *(assume $50 average sale)*	And pays $140 in service fees to an Affiliate Tracking Company. *(assume 2% service fee)*
Company Spends $20,000	**Company Spends $840**
Company Sells $7,000	**Company Sells $7,000**

Source: Be Free.

Another key advantage to performance marketing is that an affiliate program lets you reach the right person, at the right time, in the right context. Affiliate marketing *is* targeted marketing. It lets you reach online customers in the places they are most likely to be spending time, by placing your contextual banners or links on sites that are in some way affiliated with your products or services.

The ability to target market is becoming more and more important for online businesses. A recent study by Cyber Dialogue revealed that 90% of online dollars are spent by 20% of online consumers. Finding that 20% will make or break your business.

A business normally pays top dollar for a prospect list targeted toward consumers who could potentially buy the products or services a company offers. Having an affiliate program is even better than buying a prospect list because affiliate marketing is a very inexpensive form of target marketing. A prospect list or mailing list is made up of people who have bought a similar product or service in the past. But when a consumer is referred from an affiliate site, that consumer is ready to take action right then and there.

What Is Targeted Marketing?

Targeted marketing is offering the right offer to the right customer at the right time.

Affiliates will join the affiliate programs that are most appropriate for the audience of their site, and when they market an affiliate program via their site or newsletter, they are delivering pay-for-performance target marketing.

A Forrester survey has shown that affiliate marketing is one of the most effective forms of online marketing (see Table 1.3). Surveys have also shown that a site with an affiliate program generates up to 30% of its sales as a result of its affiliate partners.

Table 1.3

Rank	Technique	Popularity	Effectiveness
1	Affiliate Programs	17%	4.3
2	E-mail to customers	77%	4.3
3	Public relations	45%	4.1
4	Television	30%	4.0
5	Outdoor	17%	3.7
6	E-mail (opt-in lists)	23%	3.5
7	Magazines	34%	3.4
8	Radio	32%	3.4
9	Direct Mail	30%	3.4
10	Sponsorships	34%	3.3
11	Buttons	55%	3.2
12	Banners	89%	2.8

Source: April 1999 Forrester Research. Effectiveness ratings represent average scores based on a scale of 1 (poor) to 5 (great).

It's interesting to note looking at Table 1.3 that the least effective form of marketing is the banner advertisement—the most popular one used today.

Affiliate Marketing Is Not as Simple as It Seems

Affiliate marketing sounds like a simple and inexpensive way to make a guaranteed sale. Right? Not necessarily. Simply having an affiliate program doesn't guarantee success. An affiliate program must be creative and timely. It takes time to implement, must offer competitive compensation, be able to educate affiliates to sell, and reward the best affiliates to keep them loyal to the program. Affiliate programs are not a marketing panacea. Successful affiliate programs require creativity, effort, focus, and, yes, money.

And what about the affiliates? How difficult is it for them to sign up for your program?

In reality, the process of becoming an affiliate is pretty straightforward. The interested affiliate simply reads your affiliate agreement, accepts the terms, and fills out a registration form on your site (or on the site of an affiliate solution provider). In most programs, the affiliate controls the content, creatives, and placement of your link, although there are some storefront programs such as vStore (`www.vstore.com`) that provide the total package by customizing a Web page with the look and feel of the affiliate.

So how popular is affiliate marketing?

In the bookstore category, Barnes and Noble.com had well over 100,000 affiliates by mid-1999 and, according to Giga Group (`www.gigaweb.com`), is adding 400–500 affiliates per day. But that's nothing compared to Amazon.com. At last count, it had over 500,000 Web sites in its popular affiliate program.

And it only gets better. By 2004, Forrester Research estimates that half of the projected $33 billion in worldwide online advertising spending will be performance-based. Jupiter Communications further estimates that 25% of Internet retail sales will be acquired through sites using the affiliate advertising model by 2002.

As you can see, affiliate marketing is rapidly moving into the mainstream of e-commerce and becoming an invaluable marketing tool for online companies. Small- to medium-sized online businesses that use affiliate marketing properly can gain more than an increased customer base. When they see an affiliate program on high-profile Web sites around the Net, consumers believe that a company is bigger and more established than it really is.

Be Free, one of the leading affiliate solution providers, encourages and facilitates closer relationships between its merchant customers and select, top-tier affiliates, whom it calls Performance Partners.

Performance Partners are primarily, but not limited to, sites that serve large numbers of shoppers (such as shopping engines and other shopping aggregators), and sites with large, loyal member bases, such as loyalty sites, rebate sites, and charity program sites.

For those companies that already have a large presence in e-commerce, an affiliate program is a strategy to help maintain that presence and position.

Affiliate Marketing Program Components

So what makes up a successful affiliate marketing program? The following are some basic components that a merchant should provide its affiliates, and components that potential affiliates should look for in a merchant's affiliate program.

First, and most important, are commission payments. You must decide whether you will pay affiliates a commission on sales only, or pay them by some other incentive. Here are your choices:

- **Pay-per-click**—An affiliate is paid per visitor they send, for example 1 cent per visitor it sends to your site.

- **Pay-per-lead**—An affiliate is paid if a visitor it refers submits certain information, for example joins mailing list or requests further information.

- **Pay-per-sale**—An affiliate is paid a percentage or flat rate for each sale it generates from visitors it directs to you.

Another thing to consider is to combine residual commissions with a per-lead or per-sale commission structure—commissions paid to an affiliate for subsequent purchases made by referred customers, or perhaps a higher commission on a first-time sale.

The next thing to consider is credibility. Does your site communicate a sense of confidence and security to your customers and potential resellers? Do you offer online, real-time stats for affiliate and sub-affiliate commissions, including traffic stats? Does your affiliate program receive positive reviews in the affiliate directories?

What Is Residual Income?

Residual income is income that is paid for all additional sales made at the merchant's site over the life of the customer.

Next on the list is the agreement. Do you have a fair and equitable contract for your affiliate members? Does it include language to ensure that you will only make substantive changes to the agreement "in good faith" with the affiliate?

Another important component is marketing resources. Will you regularly provide your affiliates with compelling, contextual content about your products and services? Will you give your affiliates market-tested text links, banners, sales letters, and testimonials?

And don't forget communicating with your affiliates. You must stay in touch with them on a regular basis, giving instruction and encouragement through newsletters and tutorials. An integral part of this is to foster a sense of community through regular chats, contests, and an e-mail discussion list.

Finally, there's customer service and support—and not just for your customers but for your affiliates as well. Be prepared to answer e-mail messages, faxes, phone calls, snail mail, and instant messages from your affiliates promptly and professionally.

Keep these basic program components in mind, and you will go a long way towards building and maintaining a successful affiliate marketing program.

The New Cornerstone

Affiliate programs have made a big impact on the landscape of Internet marketing and have swept through the Internet like wildfire. The affiliate program is becoming a central component in an online company's operations and a cornerstone of their marketing strategy. But we've seen only the first phase of this marketing approach. There are many changes and competitive improvements taking place now, and more are soon to come.

Michael J. Moody, President, Replicate-It.com, stated that everybody that is anybody now has an affiliate program. But they are just beginning to fine-tune their approach, and forward-looking program managers and marketers will need to adapt their operations to this ever-changing marketing strategy.

The first phase of affiliate marketing is aptly called the click and bye approach. This is currently the most dominant form of affiliate program on the Net today. It works like this: When a merchant's link is clicked on at an affiliate's site, the site visitor is whisked off to the merchant's site. In this model, the affiliate loses the traffic it painstakingly acquired.

This system worked well for companies such as Amazon.com, however, affiliates are becoming increasingly dissatisfied with the click-and-bye model and want to see more click-and-buy marketing models, where their visitors make a purchase but stay on their site. In addition, affiliates want to be credited with any and all sales in the future made by customers they referred to a merchant. There are programs now and in the works that address this affiliate concern that use pop-up windows and mini-stores, and customizes private label Web sites that keep both the sale and the visitor on the affiliate's site.

What Is Click and Bye?

This refers to the process of an affiliate losing the visitor to the merchant's site once the visitor clicks on a merchant's banner or text link.

Trends in Affiliate Marketing

Along these lines, a report from Forrester Research says that retail and media firms will increasingly share ownership of traffic, revenue, merchandising, and content to drive revenue and increase brand awareness. For the "New Affiliate Marketing Models" report, Forrester interviewed 50 retailers with active affiliate programs that have been in place for at least three months. On average, these retailers have more than 10,270 affiliates that currently generate 13% of total online revenues. Forrester stated that today's affiliate marketing programs would probably evolve from one-size-fits-all links to one of three models: syndicated boutiques (see Figure 1.3), e-commerce networks, or elastic retailers.

Syndicated boutiques will replace simple links at small content sites, featuring pop-up microstores that use automated merchandising and store-building tools to offer a small selection of branded products for purchase without leaving the content. The report says small niche sites will be able to convert customers on the spot through affiliation with brand names, and intercept new customers who elude advertising by offering bonuses to first-time buyers. An example of this type of model is Vstore.

Figure 1.4
Using Vstore's Build a Store technology, affiliates can create their own customized store on their site.

E-commerce networks, media and merchant sites can create new buying opportunities by combining exclusive content with relevant product offers. When an article generates interest, commerce networks can deliver a one-click buying experience from a known and trusted merchant who delivers the product, the report says. An example of this type of model is ePod (www.epod.com) (see Figure 1.4).

Elastic retailing evolves when merchants that target similar customer bases and offer complementary product lines create affiliations among themselves, the way commerce networks link strong content to commerce. Merchants will partner with complementary retailers to meet all their target customers' needs for advice, recommendations, and products. In sharing the cost of merchandising, retailers spend less per customer without changing their vertical economies of scale, the report says. Examples of this type of model are yet to come.

Here are some other trends that are, or soon will be, hitting the affiliate marketing scene, according to Moody.

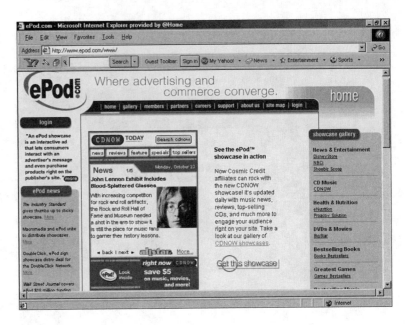

Figure 1.5
The ePod Showcase appears on an affiliate site and acts likes a small "shoplette" where visitors can buy products directly through the small shoplette window.

What Are Collaborative Commerce Networks?

These are networks of merchants and Web sites that work hand in hand as true business partners. Merchants treat their affiliates as sales and distribution channels worthy of any and all support that manufacturers would give to their resellers.

First, the terminology is maturing. Affiliates are being considered more and more as Web trading partners, and affiliate programs themselves are being seen as Collaborative Commerce Networks.

Although today, most affiliate programs allow an unlimited number of affiliates, this too is changing. Forward-looking program managers are recognizing that for network members to earn meaningful income, they will have to limit the total number of affiliates in the program. As a result, one can expect affiliate programs to begin limiting the number of their affiliates to those who are most likely to perform the best—a move toward quality and away from quantity.

Large volumes of affiliates may look good on paper, and surely investors love hearing about the large stable of affiliates acquiring new customers or members at a low rate. However, as you acquire more affiliates, you also increase the time that will have to be dedicated to activate these affiliates. The trend has shifted from quantifying affiliates to qualifying them. After all, what good is it to have 100,000 affiliates if only a fraction of those are generating results?

To succeed, you must have a strong pool of active, talented, and loyal affiliates.

Another trend is affiliate training. As affiliate programs continue to attract new Internet marketers, educating one's affiliates will become a top priority. One of the key items that must be offered is a quality training and marketing assistance program. According to Moody, Some of the most productive affiliate programs incorporate a "paint-by-the-numbers" approach to instructing their affiliates how to best market their products. These daily "to-do" lists are extremely helpful to new marketers and even provide a built-in discipline for the more experienced marketers. Increased emphasis on these programs and shared marketing tips from successful affiliates can be expected.

Personalization is catching on fast in affiliate marketing, where merchants are customizing messages to each affiliate's Web site. Instead of placing an ad link that promotes the merchant in general, merchants create ads or promotions about a specific product category or service that matches the interest of the affiliate's visitors. Following this tactic further, new technologies that can read a site visitor's cookies can direct personalized messages to individual users. Yo! (www.yo.com) and BSELECT from Be Free (www.befree.com) are two leaders in the personalization marketing space.

A growing adjunct to this targeted approach to affiliate marketing is the embedded commerce solutions of customized storefronts. This affiliate program model actually allows affiliate sites to set up their own private label store selling products that match their visiting audience. Another word for this type of program is *syndicated selling*—spreading thousands of shoplettes across the Web on affiliate partner sites. A good example of this syndicated selling approach is Pop2it (www.pop2it.com).

With syndicated selling, affiliate sites become true business partners.

We will also see more programs that provide an affiliate with residual income, giving the affiliate a revenue stream on all future sales from their referred customers, not just on the first one with the merchant. Sending a new customer to a merchant and only receiving a one-time commission will not give an affiliate the return it needs on the effort it puts into selling a merchant's product or service. Smart companies will figure a way to acknowledge the lifetime value of a customer and pay their affiliates a commission on all the customer's future purchases. Subscription-based products and services will be more suitable for residual compensation plans. One and Only (www.oneandonlynetwork.com), an online matchmaking and romance site, pays 15% of gross revenue (actual payout often approaches 40% when promotion payments are factored in) from new and renewal One and Only subscriptions.

Finally, there are ways to further increase an affiliate's revenue stream by building and managing their own prospect e-mail list. There are even affiliate programs, known as two-tier affiliate programs, that individual consumers can join where they can earn commissions on sales referred to merchants. In some of the new affiliate programs, a branded online storefront is not required at all! These are all promising developments in affiliate programs that show its flexibility, creativity, and on-going evolution.

Promises Come with Perils

Although promoting an online store through an affiliate program remains one of the most cost-effective means of marketing, several factors are restricting its growth.

First, many of the best niche sites are already promoting one or several affiliate programs. Successful affiliates, not wanting to have all their eggs in one basket, will work to establish relationships with three or four key affiliate programs. After all, it takes work on the part of the affiliate to promote a program. There is only so much time in a day and only so many resources that an affiliate site can devote to a merchant's program. The more merchants it has to promote, the less successful iyd programs.

For your program to make the cut, you'll have to have a very good revenue-producing—and unique—affiliate program to get these Web sites to replace programs they already have.

Another restriction to a program's growth is the choice of affiliates. Most would-be affiliates bring little or no traffic to a store. They offer low-traffic, amateurish sites with little content except banners to multiple affiliate programs. You must be selective in choosing Web sites to join your program. The old 80:20 rule takes on a greater exaggeration with affiliate marketing, as it becomes a 95:5 rule. Five percent of your affiliates will generate 95% of your program revenue.

Finally, as mentioned before, affiliates are tired of the click-and-bye model and want to have access to a better and more continuous customer revenue stream that they refer to merchants.

Though affiliate marketing is filled with promise for merchant and affiliate alike, merchants need to think outside the box with newer and more innovative affiliate programs, more tightly define their customer, identify the right kind of affiliates, create a desirable and rewarding program, and treat affiliates as true marketing partners. The concept of a collaborative commerce network will transform the nature of affiliate programs that we see today.

The Benefits of Affiliate Marketing

Chapter Summary

Talking sock puppets, imploring piggy banks, hamsters shot from cannons—are these any way to drive traffic to your eBusiness? Dot-com advertisers in the last few Super Bowls thought so—some of whom are paying the ultimate price of such ads by draining their corporate coffers of much-needed operating capital.

With customer acquisition costs running at unsustainable levels, tomorrow's eBusinesses must find more cost-effective ways to attract customers to their sites. One way to get a better ROI (return on investment) is to use affiliate marketing. Setting up a successful affiliate program can increase your shelf space, company visibility, and help you sell more products or services. Analysts also agree that affiliates are an important customer-retention tool for all segments of online commerce.

The types of products and services marketed through affiliates are nearly limitless and range far afield. Affiliate marketing succeeds when your company has a relationship with affiliate sites. Both you and your affiliates have a stake in making your offers sell, and with an affiliate program your marketing dollar is measurable, controllable, and returns a higher return on your investment than almost any other marketing vehicle on the Net today. Those companies that do not have an affiliate program right now are making an active mistake on a daily basis.

The total number of Web pages on the Net is rapidly approaching one billion. Many e-commerce companies have found that it takes a hefty marketing budget to be heard above this din. But cute million-dollar TV ads, multi-million–dollar flat-fee portal deals, and expensive banner buys that raise the cost of customer acquisition beyond what it costs in the real world have reduced the coffers of many e-commerce companies. All this is forcing many online companies to look for ways to reduce their marketing outlays and achieve a better ROI on the advertising they do place.

One way to achieve a better ROI is to use affiliate marketing to increase sales, drive traffic, generate qualified leads, and extend brand reach through relationships with affiliate Web sites. Companies can then target consumers with particular interests, knowledge, and spending habits, while paying only for the performance of their promotions.

The result is lower customer acquisition costs. If that is what your company is looking for—and what company isn't—then affiliate marketing is for you.

The High Cost of Customer Acquisition

Banner ads—the staple of online advertising—no longer deliver the click-through rates of just a few years ago. Average click-through rates have plummeted from their highs of 10% or more a few years ago to an average of less than 1% today. But that's not all. Customer acquisition costs have skyrocketed as dot-coms tried their hand at expensive media buys—both online and off.

A case in point is Pets.com (www.pets.com). This online merchant spent $27 million in 1999 to hype its company to consumers and another $2 million on an ad during Super Bowl XXXIV. Although traffic and sales went up on their site, the return on their advertising investment was poor. One month after their Super Bowl ad, Pets.com went public with less than spectacular results. Ten months after Super Bowl XXXIV, the company announced that they were closing down their operations.

And they're not alone.

What Is ROI?

ROI stands for Return on Investment. This is what all marketing managers want to see from the money they spend on their marketing and advertising campaigns. The higher the sales, the larger the number of shoppers, and the greater the profit margin generated by sales—the better the ROI.

According to a recent report by Shop.org (www.shop.org) and the Boston Consulting Group (www.bcg.com), pure play dot-coms shelled out $82 per customer acquired in 1999. This was double the amount all dot-coms spent in 1998 and at least six times what brick-and-mortar retailers spent in 1999 to acquire customers.

Another study by the Intermarket Group (www.intermktgrp.com) showed that some of the top e-commerce sites were paying a hefty premium for customer acquisition above what their brick-and-mortar cousins were paying. The study showed that Autobytel.com spent $20.40 to acquire a new customer; Amazon.com spent $27.60; Beyond.com $29.30; Priceline.com $32.30; and Barnes and Noble laid out $42.00. These are in comparison to brick-and-mortar customer acquisition costs of $10 or less. And other dot-coms fare no better (see Table 2.1).

Table 2.1

Acquisition Costs Are Climbing				
	Q1 99	Q2 99	Q3 99	Q4 99
theStreet	$113	$224	$168	$619
e*trade	$258	$286	$250	$362
EarthLink	$121	$126	$173	N/A
MindSpring	$21	$202	$324	N/A

Source: Jupiter Communications

Predictably, online marketing managers have become increasingly dissatisfied with banner ads and flat fee portal deals. These managers agree that they would invest more heavily in Internet marketing if only they could measure the return on their online investment. It's no wonder then that managers are seeking an alternative to the exposure-based advertising model that promises more than exposure and delivers actual sales.

Affiliate marketing is becoming more and more the marketing strategy of choice. Consider the following examples:

Art.com (www.art.com), using their affiliate marketing, determined a cost per acquiring a client as $15 each through their affiliate program verses $100 apiece using a broadcast medium and $30 a customer using banner ads. The company's president, William Lederer, believes affiliate marketing to be more effective than traditional advertising in acquiring new customers.

James Marciano, founder of Refer-it (www.refer-it.com) believes affiliate marketing is a "recession-proof marketing channel." "When the economy tanks, the CEO cuts the marketing budget first. The sales budget doesn't get cut. With these programs, you're out there already, making money for nothing." Jaclyn Easton, Web industry author and Los Angeles Times columnist, said at the 17th Annual Catalog Conference & Exhibition in June 2000 that the average cost of acquiring a new customer via e-commerce partnerships is $1.67 compared with $30 for a banner ad.

Finally, affiliate programs are relatively inexpensive and have helped level the playing field between big corporations and small companies by allowing companies to gain more exposure and online traffic.

Do

DO use an affiliate program to increase the shelf space of your product and extend the reach of your business.

Is Your Business Suited for Affiliate Marketing?

How would you like other Web sites to market and sell your company's products and services? And how would you like to pay the Web site only when their users buy your product or service or perform a task? Sounds like a marketer's dream, right? Well, it can come true with affiliate marketing.

Setting up a successful affiliate program can increase your shelf space, improve company visibility, and help you sell more products or services. You can sign up hundreds or even thousands of affiliates, and they will promote your product on their sites. And you reward them only if they can make sales. In effect, you get a powerful pay-for-performance sales force.

According to Netcraft (www.netcraft.com), there were approximately 7.5 million active web sites on the Net in July 2000. That's a pool of 7.5 million potential affiliates. In 1999, research from dot-com.com (www.dotcom.com) indicated that 80% of consumers registering a domain name did so for the first time. dotcom.com further indicates that by the end of the year 2000, 15.4% of American households are expected to own a domain name.

The same research indicates these consumers are building sites devoted to family and pets; clubs and organizations; photography; stamp and coin collecting; sports and trading cards; and, finally, computers and technology. Many of these consumers will be looking for ways to generate revenue to help pay for their hosting fees and perhaps generate some additional spare change. And many of these consumer sites are looking to join an affiliate program.

Because even the biggest affiliate program, Amazon.com, represents only 10% of the 7.5 million Web sites, you can see that a huge opportunity exists to build an affiliate program no matter what size your business. If you offer a service or product that appeals to a limited audience, you will find that these personal Web sites can form a critical basis for your company.

You must also remember that an affiliate program is a partnership. The better you can monitor your affiliates and the way they are promoting your Web site, the more your program will pay off. And the more energy you put into an affiliate program, building a close relationship with your affiliates and training them to sell, the better your program will be. And remember, as a merchant you enjoy the benefits of no-risk advertising, paying only when a sale is made. It's a great way to brand a product or achieve greater visibility across the Net.

Analysts also agree that affiliates are an important customer-retention tool for all segments of online commerce. In a recent report, Jupiter Communications estimated that if online merchants could increase their affiliate sales to 20% they could cut sales and marketing costs by 10%.

Want more proof? Nine of the top ten retail sites for August 2000, as ranked by Media Metrix (www.mediametrix.com) (see Figure 2.1), currently use affiliate programs. It shows that an affiliate program is a fundamental component in online success.

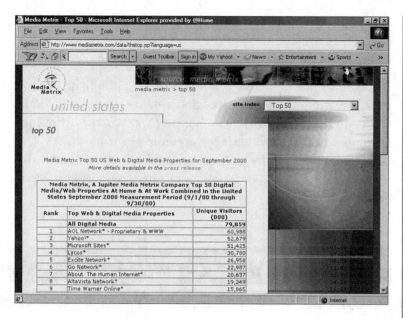

Figure 2.1
Media Matrix ranks Web sites on the amount of traffic they attract month by month.

You Can Sell Anything

There are thousands upon thousands of affiliate programs currently marketed by companies on the Net offering products and services, literally, from A (adidas.com pays affiliates to sell their shoes) to Z (Zmedia.com pays 40 cents each time an affiliate sends someone who subscribes to one of their newsletters).

The types of products and services sold through affiliates are nearly limitless and range far afield. In addition to the kinds of products and services you'd expect—books, magazines, videos, CDs, clothing, flowers, jewelry, office supplies, gifts, computer products, beauty, health, and fitness items, furnishings, and sports and recreation items sold through affiliate programs—there are many others that you wouldn't expect. For example, products that show the versatility of pay-for-performance marketing, such as long distance phone services, tickets to sporting events, security services, URL submissions, banner exchanges, classified ads, search engine placement services, Web design, Web hosting, singles ads, domain

What's Search Engine Placement?

There are many companies that will not only register your web site with the search engines but also will help you get a high placement in their search results. These are search engine placement companies.

names, groceries, contests, self help, marketing courses, and seminars. These are just a few of the vast number of products and services that can be sold through an affiliate program.

Of course, you can increase the success of your affiliate program by selling products and services that are, or soon will be, the hot sellers on the Net. Fall 1999 and Spring 2000 surveys from Jupiter Communications (www.jup.com) presented its study of U.S. e-commerce forecast by category (see Table 2.2). It showed that computers, travel, and entertainment categories would stay on top in the United States.

Table 2.2

United States E-commerce Forecast by Category			
	1998	2000	2003
Over 10% in 2003			
Software	8.6%	20.7%	48.9%
PCs	11.1	24.3	40.4
Peripherals	5.6	10.9	20.9
Air Travel	2.6	10.3	15.4
Books	2.5	6.3	14.3
Music	1.1	3.8	14.0
Event Tickets	0.7	2.8	12.5
Car Rentals	1.1	5.5	11.2
Videos	0.4	3.0	10.3
5% to 10% in 2003			
Hotels	1.7	4.6	9.8
Toys	0.3	1.9	5.6
Nutrition Products	0.0	0.7	5.1
Sporting Goods	0.3	1.1	5.1
Flowers	0.8	1.9	5.0

Table 2.2 (continued)

United States E-commerce Forecast by Category	1998	2000	2003
Less than 5% in 2003			
Tours	0.1	1.5	4.7
Consumer Electronics	0.4	1.5	4.7
Apparel	0.3	0.8	3.7
Personal Care	0.0	0.5	3.6
Medical Supplies	0.0	0.5	3.5
Cruises	0.1	0.7	2.8
Office Products	0.1	0.5	2.8
Specialty Gifts	0.2	0.6	2.5
Footwear	0.1	0.3	2.1
Furniture	0.0	0.1	2.1
Housewares	0.1	0.3	2.1
Movie Tickets	0.0	0.2	2.0
Over-the-Counter Drugs	0.0	0.2	1.9
Groceries	0.0	0.2	1.5
Prescription Drugs	0.0	0.1	1.5
Home Improvement	0.0	0.1	0.5

Source: Jupiter Communications

In April 2000 Forrester Research forecast European e-commerce by category (see Table 2.3). It showed that Europe's strong sellers are the same as those in the united States.

Table 2.3

	% OF TOTAL 2005 RETAIL
Over 10% in 2005	
Software	39%
Computer Hardware	36
Music	20

Do

DO understand that any product or service can be sold through an affiliate network.

Table 2.3 (continued)

	% OF TOTAL 2005 RETAIL
Books	15
Videos	13
Flowers	12
Event Tickets	11
5% to 10% in 2005	
Toys	9
Leisure Travel	9
Consumer Electronics	9
Sports Equipment	8
Apparel	7
Health & Beauty	7
Housewares	6
Autos	5
Less than 5% in 2005	
Garden	4
Groceries	4

Source: Forrester Research

But just because your product or service didn't make the analysts' cut doesn't mean you can't successfully sell it through an affiliate program (see Figure 2.2). If you take the concept of collaborative commerce networking to heart and truly build a targeted network of business partners, you can be successful selling your product or service across the Net.

Consider the following example.

Allan Gardyne runs Associate Programs.com (www. associateprograms.com), a top affiliate directory in which he also rates affiliate programs. He lists the top 10 affiliate programs (www.associateprograms.com/search/favourite.shtml) that are earning the most money for AssociatePrograms.com—and there isn't a commodity product in the bunch. The number one product for this site is a book by Ken Evoy entitled *Make Your Site SELL!*, which describes how to sell what ought to be virtually impossible to sell, and coming in a close second is *Make Your Knowledge SELL!*, showing you how to sell what you know on the Net. The number 10 best selling product is a service—Virtualis Systems. They offer high-quality Web hosting services.

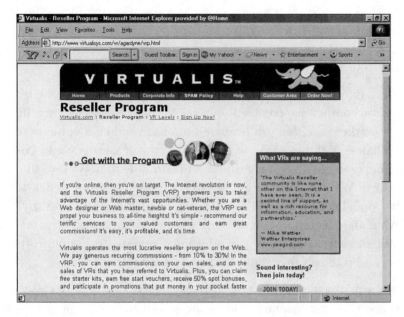

Figure 2.2
Affiliate programs are not just for selling products. Virtualis sells a Web hosting service through their affiliate program.

Plain and simple, almost every product or service online will be more successful if offered through an affiliate program. All this proves that you can sell just about anything through an affiliate program if you build the proper affiliate network.

Ask These Questions

So is your business suited for an affiliate program? Ask yourself these questions. If you answer yes, then your business can take advantage of this unique form of marketing.

First, look at your product or service. No matter how good your intentions towards building a marketing program, it's all for naught if there is no market for your product or service. If you're selling

Do

DO invest time and resources building an affiliate support team inside your business.

successfully from your own Web site, you should be able to sell it from others. And though you may think your product or service is the greatest thing since sliced bread, potential affiliates may think otherwise. Any good potential affiliate will be looking closely at your offer. Is your product or service a quality one? Is it priced competitively? Do they feel they can sell it to their site visitors?

Next, think about the program itself. Are you prepared to offer not only a good affiliate program for your business but also for you affiliates? The affiliate game has to be a win-win situation. Both you and your affiliates must profit from it.

Next, do you have enough margin in your product or service to offer a competitive commission rate? In today's competitive affiliate marketplace, are you prepared to offer residual income to your affiliates? Will they own the commission on all sales made by customers referred to your business and continue to do so into the future? Will you offer a click-and-buy program and not a click-and-bye one, keeping the affiliate's visitor on their site after the sale? What about offering a re-marketing program on behalf of your affiliates where they can gain additional revenue from the prospect list and referrals they build for you on their sites?

Will you invest in an affiliate manager—even a team, if necessary—whose sole responsibility is to create and manage your program on an ongoing basis while communicating constantly with your affiliates to keep them happy? Will you invest the time and effort in recruiting good affiliates and offer real-time statistics showing how many visitors your affiliates have referred to you and how much commission they are entitled to?

Finally, will you take the time to educate your affiliates on an on-going basis on how to properly market your product or service to their site visitors? Are you prepared to constantly offer new product or service promotions to keep your offer fresh on your affiliate sites?

If you answered yes to all these questions, then your business is suited to take advantage of the benefits of an affiliate program.

The Benefits of Affiliate Marketing

Here's a question for you. If you were looking to purchase a product, which would you be more likely to buy: the one you saw on a banner ad or the one that came highly recommended by a site that you already know and trust? Glenn Sobel, a top affiliate program consultant, says that this is "seeing your offer from a potential customer's point of view."

Affiliate marketing succeeds because, unlike traditional advertising where you buy space on a Web site, your company has a relationship with an affiliate site, and your affiliate links are in context with your product or service, rather than being in an ad slot. Because of this relationship, your marketing effort—being performance based—is enhanced. Both you and your affiliate sites have a stake in making your offers sell. Compare this to traditional ad buys and you will quickly see that affiliate marketing can be a more effective marketing vehicle.

In a nutshell, that's the prime benefit of having affiliates—they drive online traffic and they drive sales. Your marketing dollar is much better spent with a properly designed and managed affiliate program than on simple banner ads purchased on a Web site. With an affiliate program, your marketing dollar is measurable, controllable, and returns a higher return on your investment than almost any other marketing vehicle on the Net today.

Every online marketing manager is confronted with two sets of objectives, broadly characterized as customer acquisition and customer retention. We've seen that customer acquisition—generating initial traffic to a site and building an online brand identity—can be a very expensive proposition on the Net. By paying only for those customers that you acquire and getting free brand exposure to boot, affiliate marketing fulfills the first objective admirably.

Customer retention—keeping a customer over time—is also helped by your relationship with your affiliates. Although many of your customers acquired through your affiliates may buy directly from you in the future, you must remember one thing: An e-commerce site attracts visitors only when they're ready to purchase something. Your affiliate sites, being mainly content and community sites, will attract many more repeat visitors who go there for the latest information or to interact with others. That means that your offer will always be in front of your customers whether or not they go to your online store, thus helping you keep your customer over time.

Matching an offer to the site audience, by the way, is a key element of a successful affiliate program. In your attempt to grow your affiliate network quickly, signing up any Web site as an affiliate is not necessarily the way to go. You can greatly improve the success of your affiliate program by closely matching your product or service with the needs of consumers that visit your affiliate Web sites. That means you have to choose Web sites that provide the proper context and content, as well as those willing to aggressively recommend your product or service to their site visitors.

However, there is a caveat to this rule, and that is that you should not judge a book by its cover. Do not be overly anxious in disqualifying sites, especially those with a TLD (top level domain), because some of the most unlikely sites may have an ability to deliver your demographic. There are no hard and fast rules here. If you are baffled as to why a seemingly incongruous site has applied to your program, just fire off an e-mail to the Webmaster and ask how they plan to market your site.

Thus, an affiliate program is an answer for marketing managers who are being asked more and more today to justify their marketing budgets.

The Key Benefits

In April 1999, a Forrester Research survey stated that affiliate programs accounted for 13% of 1999 online retail sales, and this number is expected to grow to 21% by 2003. Jupiter Communications reports that affiliate programs account for 11% of the $5.8 billion of consumer transactions online, and they project that figure to grow to 24% or $37.5 billion in total sales by 2002.

These kinds of findings are numbers your business cannot ignore and point to a list of benefits that an affiliate program can provide your company. And what are they? There are several key benefits to having an affiliate marketing program.

- **You have the opportunity to create a powerful and effective marketing network for your product or service**—What other marketing vehicle can give you a network of Web sites referring high-quality purchasing traffic to your online store? In addition, this traffic is arriving on your site with a high recommendation from a trusted and known Web site that has a direct incentive to make sales for you.

  The merchants in Be Free's (www.befree.com) program make a good example. According to Be Free's statistics, merchants in their affiliate-tracking program earn between 20% and 35% of total online sales through their affiliate sales channel if they have over 2,000 affiliates. They experience click-through rates three to six times that of traditional CPM banner advertising and receive tens of thousands of impressions, paying only for those that generate revenues.

- **Using an affiliate solution provider like Be Free (www.befree.com), Commission Junction (www.cj.com), or Linkshare (www.linkshare.com), you can acquire measurable and predictable data to evaluate the ROI of each affiliate in your program**—Having the ability to track the performance of each affiliate allows you to determine what payments will be made to each affiliate based on impressions, click-through rates, completed forms, percentage scales, or any other performance criteria you want to offer. This gives you the freedom to design an exact program that fits your sales and marketing strategy and enables you to measure the success of both your own and your affiliates' marketing efforts in the short and long term.

- **Affiliate marketing provides you with risk-free advertising**—There are no upfront costs for placing your links on your affiliate's Web sites. You are advertising and getting brand exposure at no risk. You only pay a small percentage after you've made money—you only pay for results. Affiliate marketing is a very effective form of advertising. Compared to traditional CPM models and other online marketing options, affiliate program marketing is a highly profitable, very efficient marketing strategy.

What Is an Affiliate Solution Provider?

An affiliate solution provider will track a merchant's affiliate program, provide coded links to affiliates, and report to the merchant and its affiliates the number of impressions, click-throughs, and sales figures generated by the affiliate program. The larger affiliate solution providers will also make a merchant's program known to potential affiliates and provide the means for them to sign up.

Don't

DON'T treat your affiliate program as cheap advertising. An affiliate program is a marketing program and your affiliates are marketing partners in business with you.

- **Affiliate marketing focuses your management's attention on the development of a long-term marketing strategy, as opposed to short-term tactical media buys**—When your affiliates know your program is successful and they are getting paid when they refer sales to your business, your link is there to stay.

- **Developing relationships is the key to effective long-term online Internet marketing**—An affiliate program not only builds strong relationships with your affiliates, but with customers as well.

- **Affiliate programs are attractive to affiliates because they don't have to deal with inventory, customer service, questions, orders, or returns**—Affiliate marketing can be done from anywhere, affiliates can control almost everything, and their income potential is unlimited. They have the choice of which product to sell, which program to join, and whether or not they will stay with the merchant's program. Start up costs are virtually zero. All an affiliate needs is a computer, an Internet connection, and a Web site and/or opt-in list.

- **Analysts agree that affiliates are an important customer-retention tool for all segments of online commerce**—In a recent report, Jupiter Communications estimated that if online merchants could increase their affiliate sales to 20%, they could cut sales and marketing costs by 10%.

Are Affiliate Programs Just Cheap Advertising?

Affiliates are your partners in business and should be treated that way. And as partners they can either make your program a success—or harm it. Treating your affiliate as a source for cheap advertising will permanently harm your affiliate program.

Keep in mind that there are thousands of affiliate programs on the Net, all vying for the attention of affiliate Web sites. Each one is very easy for a Web site to join and just as easy to drop. But that's not all. Remember, you are doing business on the Internet, an interconnected network where news—good or bad—travels fast.

You must treat your affiliates like business partners. Educate them on your products, train them on how to sell, and keep in constant touch with them. You must also pay them well. To be successful, your affiliates need to be making money. If you're not writing lots of checks each month to your affiliates, your program is not a success.

If you don't pay enough they will not join. If you pay them late or not at all, they'll leave your program, telling as many other people as will listen that your program is a sham.

Keep Your Promises

A fairly well-established merchant selling toys changed its affiliate program midstream. Its affiliate program had been running well for some time. One of the reasons it was so successful was that the toy merchant agreed to pay not only on the first sale but all futures sales made by any customer referred to the toy merchant.

Then, suddenly, the toy merchant decided that rather than pay for recurring sales, it would pay only once for each new customer introduced by an affiliate. Instead of treating its affiliates as true business partners who helped build its brand across the Net, it took away the affiliates' hard earned efforts for a fair ongoing reward. No one at the merchant thought that this change in the relationship with the affiliates would amount to much.

They were wrong.

Like anyone on the Net, the affiliates had a voice. And they used it. Immediately every affiliate news site and directory reported what the toy merchant had done. In turn, other affiliates compared their toy merchant's program with others, showing that their competitors had a better compensation program and one that treated their affiliates fairly. The hard work that the toy merchant did and the equity it built up in the affiliate program was lost almost overnight.

The moral of the story is simple: Treat your affiliates as true business partners, treat them fairly, and focus on making them—not just your business—a success.

Don't

DON'T pay more than you can afford. It's better to start with a lower commission than to reduce it later.

Other Affiliate Marketing Uses

The pure merchant/affiliate sales model, where Web sites sign up for a merchant's affiliate program and earn revenue for themselves, is not the only affiliate model on the Net. Over the last two years, several companies have figured out how to use the affiliate marketing concept in new ways.

One model is a new type of affiliate site that pays its visitors for buying a merchant's products. Web sites such as Spree.com (www.spree.com) and ebates.com (www.ebates.com) (see Figure 2.3) do not provide a shopping site themselves but place links on their site to multiple e-tailers whose affiliate programs they are members of. When shoppers click through to the merchants' sites, the shoppers themselves receive a portion of the affiliate commission in the form of a rebate on their purchase. Spree.com and ebates.com collect the affiliate commission from the merchant and give a percentage back to the customer.

Figure 2.3
By joining merchant affiliate programs, ebates.com gives a portion of its commission back to the consumers who shop at its site.

So, instead of going directly to the online stores, shoppers can go to Spree.com or ebates.com to purchase and collect their rebate. The commission earned on the sale is a one-time event. If the customer goes directly to the merchant in the future to make a purchase, the affiliate site does not get this commission. So it behooves Spree.com and ebates.com to provide high-rebate incentives to shoppers to return to their site to make a purchase.

Rebates to shoppers range from 5% of purchases made on hard goods to as high as 25% at stores with high margin items like online greeting cards. ebates.com will also pay a small commission if shoppers refer friends who join the program.

A different take on this model plays to a shopper's altruistic nature (see Figure 2.4). GreaterGood.com (`www.greatergood.com`), iGive.com (`www.igive.com`), and ShopForChange (`www.workingforchange.org/shop`) allow consumers to shop online at major sites and then donate a portion of the affiliate commission the sites earn to charity. At ShopForChange, anytime a customer buys something from one of their popular merchants accessible through its site, it donates 5% of the purchase to a progressive cause. And at GreaterGood.com, consumers can shop at over 80 leading retailers and donate up to 15% of their purchases to support a cause that they care about—helping the homeless, preserving the environment, or supporting a local school. Visit `www.affiliatemanager.net/charity.htm` for a comprehensive list of charity sites.

Speaking of supporting local schools, new companies have formed using an affiliate program model for online school fund raising. A few years ago, a whole new industry using the affiliate program model was born when affiliate marketing and school fundraising converged to create online school fundraising.

Door-to-door sales, along with car washes, box top drives, and bake sales, have long been the fundraisers of choice for K–12 schools. But the recent explosion of online school fundraising companies has changed the rules of the game.

Don't

DON'T think that the only use for affiliate marketing is to sell products. Think outside the box and look for ways to apply the model to other business and non-business ventures.

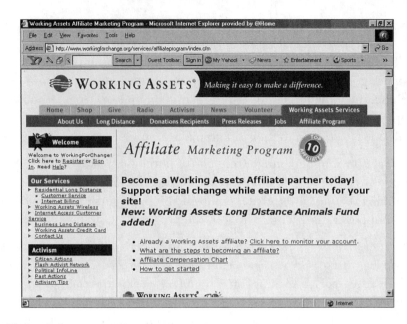

Figure 2.4
Affiliates that join the Working Assets Program earn revenue for the non-profit organizations they support whenever a consumer buys a product or service from their site.

It works like this.

A parent logs on to the school fundraising site, such as SchoolPop (www.schoolpop.com) or ShopForSchool.com (www.shopforschool.com) and chooses the school he or she wants to support. From there, links lead to participating merchants. When a parent makes a purchase from a participating merchant, a percentage of the sale is given to the school. The school fundraising companies take a cut of the sale but, they also negotiate special arrangements for the schools—affiliates—to receive a commission on each sale. This is a great deal for K–12 schools with little effort on their part.

Because of the current dangers of door-to-door sales by young children, these new programs come at just the right time. Visit www.affiliatemanager.net/school.htm for a comprehensive list of school fundraiser sites.

Although affiliate programs can come in a variety of flavors, we are only seeing the beginning evolution of the affiliate marketing concept. To quote Tim Choate, CEO of Freeshop.com, "For those people who do not have an affiliate program, it's critical for them to learn as fast as they can about what these programs can do, how they work, and how they function."

Become an Affiliate Yourself and Earn Income

Chapter Summary

Consider this: Joining an affiliate program, in addition to offering one, can be a big benefit to your company. Not only can you add valuable content to your site that will keep consumers coming back to you, but also your offers will be there in front of consumers whenever they are ready to buy.

Shoppers do not live on commerce alone. They go to the Web for information as well. By joining selective content affiliate programs, you can add free valuable content to your company's site—and get paid for it in the process. Why would a content site give you free information and pay you to do it? For the same reason you create an affiliate program—to acquire customers and increase revenue. So why not capitalize on your site traffic and gain additional revenue in the process? In addition to your company becoming an affiliate, it should be mandated that members of your affiliate team create their own sites and become affiliates so they can have a 360-degree understanding of the industry.

As the old saying goes, "What's good for the goose is good for the gander." Your affiliates—both content and community sites—are outsourcing their commerce to you, so why don't you outsource your content to someone else by joining their affiliate program and add value to your site? And here's the best part—you get paid for it! You can capitalize on your site traffic, offer valuable content to your shoppers, and gain additional revenue in the process.

There are a number of companies on the Web today that offer all kinds of content that could fit well on your Web site, and many of these companies will pay you to place their content on your site or link to their content from your site.

Why would they do this? For the same reason you create an affiliate program—to acquire customers and increase revenue. They do this by creating tiny content packages that you place on your Web site, and in return, you feed traffic back to their site. Their give-away content is a link back to full content hosted on their site. And here's the best part: This valuable content is FREE and there is no cost to join their affiliate program.

These affiliate programs come in many flavors, and there's a very good chance that one of them would fit your e-commerce site. You can find content sites that provide

- News of all types
- Articles on many subjects
- Web search services right from your site
- Local news, weather, entertainment, and events
- Sports and stock information
- Downloadable music, photos, and Webcasts
- Auctions
- Even consumer reviews and opinions

DO

DO join content affiliate programs to add valuable content to your site and earn additional revenue at the same time.

Quality content can help you attract potential buyers to your site, but quality content is a lot more expensive to create than most people realize, and maintaining a quality Web site is an even more expensive proposition. If you can reduce your content costs—and even make money doing it—the viability of your e-commerce site may come down to how well you can manage content costs. That's why joining content affiliate programs will help you add quality content to your site and get paid for doing it.

News and Features

If your eBusiness serves a local market, you could consider joining an affiliate program that offers local news, weather, entertainment, and events. AOL Digital City's affiliate program (`home.digitalcity.com/chicago/affiliate/`) (see Figure 3.1) lets you offer guides to local restaurants, clubs, attractions, live music, museums, art and cultural events, movies, and more. You just add one of its local content boxes to your site and every time someone clicks on that box, you get paid $.03.

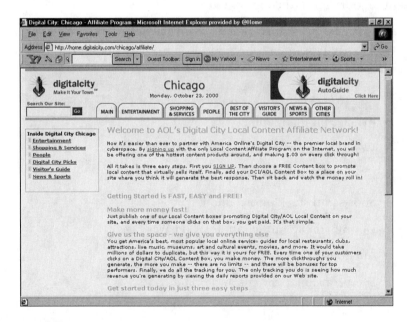

Figure 3.1
digitalcity.com offers local content for your Web site.

For more general news, affiliate programs from InterestAlert! and Strategy.com can fill the bill. InterestAlert! (`interestalert.com/remote/siteia/affiliate.html`) (see Figure 3.2) lets you put news headlines and summaries on your pages. Categories include top news stories, women's news, political news and commentary, sports news, a stock index, and a large variety of industry news. Your site gets paid $.0025 per paid view on the news pages they serve.

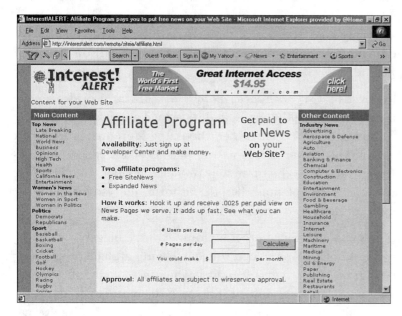

Figure 3.2
InterestAlert! lets you put news headlines and summaries on your pages from a variety of categories.

Strategy.com's affiliate program (`www.strategy.com/About/affiliates/Businesses.asp`) enables you to deliver information to your site to visitors whenever and wherever they are via Web, wireless, and voice.

By becoming an affiliate, you can offer your customers personalized finance, weather, and news information. When your shoppers subscribe to these services (co-branded with your logo and your Web site's look and feel) through your site, they can choose *what* information they want (earnings reports, local severe weather alerts, top world news, and so on), *when* they want it (if a stock moves by 12%, only when rain is in the forecast, Thursdays at 10 a.m., and so on), and *how* they want to receive it (via e-mail, mobile phone, pager, and so on). Your business receives 15% of the net revenue generated by your site and 5% of the net revenue generated by other sites you refer.

Another free news feed affiliate program is EchoFactor (`www.echofactor.com/affiliate.html`). If your company sells music, you can have a news feed on Britney Spears. If your company is involved with travel, choose a news feed on a specific city or destination. EchoFactor pays $2 for each news feed you place on your site.

Moreover (`http://www.moreover.com/associate`) provides breaking news from 1,800 sources, and it pays a commission every time you refer a new Web site owner who puts a Moreover headline Web feed onto his or her site. Moreover pays $1.30 for each unique visitor who completes the three-step Web feed builder, and $2.00 for each unique completion when the visitor is referred from the Moreover news feed on the front page of your site.

There's also an affiliate program for one of the biggest content providers on the Web. When you join About's affiliate program (`affiliates.about.com/index.htm`), you can take advantage of a wide range of quality content from over 700 of its expert guides. Each guide specializes in one area and provides in-depth information on his or her subject. You can link to an individual guide's content that is relevant to your company's interests. You can also add the ability for shoppers to search exclusively within your topic area, or search the entire About network. About will pay a standard rate of $0.01 for each qualified click-through from your site to About.

Some niche affiliate programs offer content as one of their linking options (see Figure 3.3). ClubMom (`www.clubmom.com`), a free membership organization created exclusively to reward and celebrate moms, makes a new article (with affiliate links) available to affiliates each month. Similarly, the One and Only Network, a matchmaking and romance site, offers a number of articles to affiliates that are integrated with affiliate links. These niche affiliate programs provide the valuable content to affiliates to improve the caliber of their sites and to reach a very defined-target marketing audience.

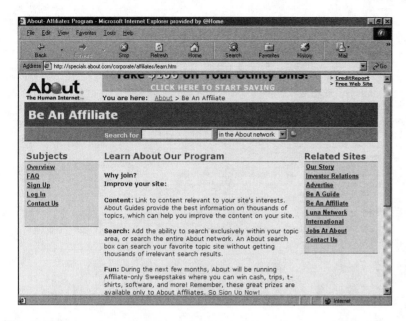

Figure 3.3
About offers affiliates access to hundreds of thousands of pages of content in more than 800 categories of information.

Web, Media, and Consumer Opinion Searches

There are several Web search affiliate programs that you can join to add a Web search service for your customers to use right from your site. Google's affiliate program (see Figure 3.4) (`www.google.com/affiliates/welcome.html`) provides one of the most advanced Web search technologies on the Net. Google has been ranked first for user satisfaction and loyalty among major search sites according to a recent NPD survey. Your company can earn $.01 for each Google search performed from your site. Go.com (`affiliate.go.com/`) has a similar Web search affiliate program. There are several types of content boxes to choose from. Each box integrates GO.com's quality content and services to create a powerful and unique online experience for visitors to your site. You earn $.015 per click.

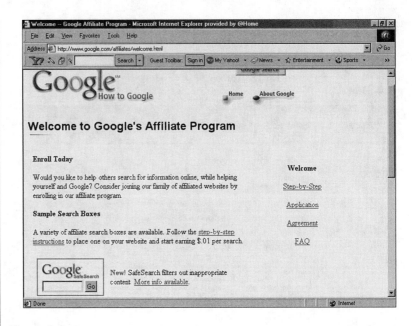

Figure 3.4
With Google's affiliate program, you can place its famous search service on any page of your Web site.

Alta Vista's program (`doc.altavista.com/affiliate/`) (see Figure 3.5) offers more than just a search service to your site visitors. Not only does it offer normal Web search capabilities right from your site, but your visitors can also search for up to the minute, breaking news from around the world, multimedia images, audio/MP3 and video files, and even stock quotes, stock news, research, and analyst opinion. In addition, your visitors can search local indices or search Web pages in their native language. Alta Vista has two payment programs. A Standard Program that pays $.02 every time a user clicks on its search box or uses any of the other available features from your site, and a Premier Program that pays $.04 per click.

If your e-commerce site deals in music, then one of these affiliate programs could fit well into your site offering. Liquid Audio (`www.liquidaudio.com/music/lmn/howlmn.html`) lets you integrate downloadable music easily into your Web site. It offers a large selection of secure, downloadable songs and provides all page and content hosting, all the tools, services and support for integration, and all customer support. Your visitors can search and browse through its catalog of songs, and your pages can be branded with your store logo. Your company nets about 25% of the retail price of the song.

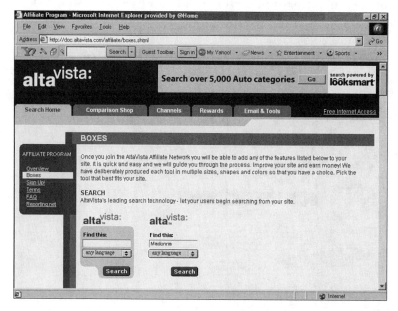

Figure 3.5
With Alta Vista's affiliate program, you can place its search services on any page of your Web site.

Global Music Network's program (`ap.gmn.com/`) (see Figure 3.6) not only offers downloadable music, but news headlines plus story extracts from music world, Webcast features that offer the latest in online streaming audio and video with a new Webcast featured every day, and features and photos of popular artists. You're paid $.05 each time someone clicks on a link to Global Music Network from your site.

Another entertainment affiliate program content provider is Boxerjam (`www.boxerjam.com/affiliate`), a game-show content site. Game show entertainment is hot right now, leading the ratings on TV, and is the number one reason new users are flocking to the Web. Boxerjam provides a game link that launches free games and chances to win thousands of dollars in cash and prizes from your site. One popular game is a puzzle called KnockOut! that offers original, new content each day. With games like Boxerjam on your

What's a Webcast?
WebCasting is the process of delivering media content—voice, film, video, or animation—on demand over the Internet.

site, you can increase traffic to your site and keep visitors coming back for more. As an affiliate, your company can earn $0.75 for every person who clicks through to a Boxerjam game or banner on your site, signs up for more fun, or plays a free game show at Boxerjam.

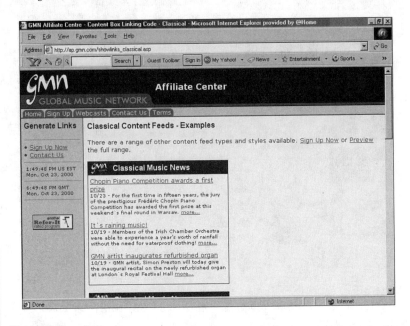

Figure 3.6
If you sell music-related products, Global Music Network's affiliate program would be a good addition to your site.

Another valuable service to offer shoppers at your site is Epinions (www.epinions.com/about/) (see Figure 3.7). Its free affiliate program lets you offer your visitors "word-of-mouth" advice that will help them make better buying decisions. You can easily build your own version of Epinions.com by adding Epinions content to your Web site. It can enrich your Web site's community as your users read and write opinions. It's a new program and it is offering affiliate sites an introductory revenue rate of $5 per thousand page views and $1 each time a new user signs up through your site and writes his or her first review.

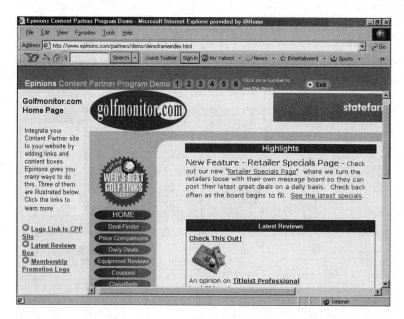

Figure 3.7

As an Epinions.com affiliate, you can place message boards from consumers on your site discussing the brand name products or services that you sell.

All-in-One Content Programs

Besides the affiliate programs already mentioned, there are three multiple-content programs that you can offer visitors to your Web site.

With CNET's program (`www.cnet.com/webbuilding/0-2633572.html`) (see Figure 3.8) you can get access to CNET's award-winning news headlines, price-comparison services, tech question and answer service, and the largest free software download library on the Internet. Each time you pass a user along to CNET, your company earns $.02.

When your company becomes an affiliate of Lycos (`www.lycos.com/affiliateprogram/`), you can choose one or more of its dynamic Lycos Network Content Boxes. There are several Content Boxes to choose from. Each contains useful information from around the Lycos Network and the kind of information that can help bring users back to your site. You can offer your visitors a general search service, a Safe Search for Kids service, and access to small business articles that help users run and build small business, in addition to sports scores, a people finder, stock information, software downloads, news, and TV listings. Your site can earn up to $.03 everytime someone clicks through.

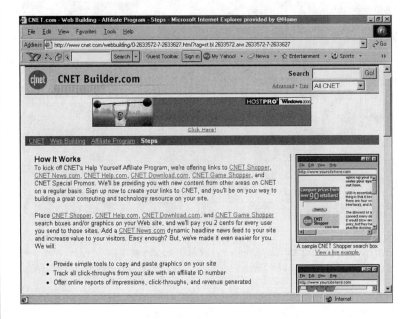

Figure 3.8
Add CNET's news headlines, price-comparison services, tech question and answer service, and the largest free software download library on the Internet when you join its affiliate program.

The affiliate programs from GoTo.com (www.goto.com) (see Figure 3.9) offer two affiliate programs that would interest any e-commerce site and are designed to increase your Web revenue and encourage repeat usage. They offer a Web search service that pays you $.03 each time your visitors search the Web from your site, and an integrated auction service search performed on your site, through which you can earn $7.50 for every 1,000 auction searches. The search results are customized and are integrated into your Web site.

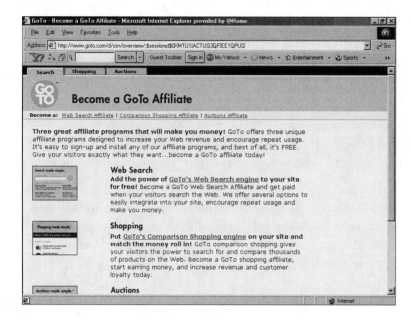

Figure 3.9
As a GoTo affiliate, your company gets paid each time your shoppers search the Web.

You can find other providers that pay you to place their content on your site in the affiliate directories listed in Appendix C. Since new directories spring up from time to time, you can also visit our live list of affiliate directories at www.affiliatemanager. net/directories.htm.

Have Your Affiliate Team Join Affiliate Programs

In addition to your company becoming an affiliate, it should be mandated that all members of your affiliate team create their own sites and become affiliates to have a 360 degree understanding of the industry.

The purpose here is two-fold. The affiliate team will have a better understanding of the issues affiliates face, and it will also have first-hand knowledge of the tools and resources needed to create a successful affiliate site.

The optimal affiliate site for a member of your affiliate team is one that is consistent with the theme of your own site. This way, the site will be able to gauge and test the effectiveness of your creatives, as well as join the competition and compare their performance against your program.

One example of this is BabyLounge (`www.babylounge.com`). BabyLounge is primarily a testing platform for ClubMom affiliate links, but it has also served to measure all other affiliate programs that appeal to the same demographic.

As you can see, pay-for-performance affiliate programs can work both ways. So, consider joining a content provider's affiliate program and reap some of the rewards of performance-based marketing yourself.

PART II

Setting Up Your Affiliate Program

Chapter Summary

Businesses don't plan to fail; they fail to plan. The time to establish an affiliate program and take advantage of this unique revenue-generating channel is now.

Affiliate programs offer a significant sales channel for your business. According to a poll by the United States Affiliate Manager Coalition (www.usamc.org), some merchants are generating more than 50% of their business from affiliate sites. Even if a more realistic figure is 10%–15% of total sales, what business wouldn't like to have 15% more sales? And with the cost of customer acquisition of other marketing and advertising methods at unprofitable levels, affiliate marketing can greatly increase the revenue of each marketing dollar spent.

When planning out your affiliate program, consider to whom you will be selling, what the needs of your affiliates are, what model you will choose, how you will track your program, how your affiliates will be paid and the terms of agreement between you and them. Also, it's important to remember that affiliate programs are not about technology—but about marketing. Affiliate consultants can also help plan your program and offer professional advice on how to quickly set up and run a successful affiliate program. Remember that affiliates are true business partners and should be treated that way if you are to have a successful and profitable affiliate program.

A ffiliate programs are hot. The number of online companies building affiliate programs is growing everyday. LinkShare, one of the top affiliate solution providers, reported that more than 10 million users clicked-through to affiliate sites from LinkShare member sites in the third quarter (Q3) of 1998 alone. LinkShare started the year representing affiliate programs for 70 e-commerce merchants, but by the end of Q3 1999 that number was up to 450. Other affiliate solution providers reported seeing similar growth with programs.

Be Free, another affiliate solution provider, reported that their merchants experienced over 338 million click-throughs from Be Free affiliates in Q3 of 2000. Further, the Be Free customer base of merchants has grown from 94 in Q3 1999 to 356 in Q3 2000.

"Affiliate marketing does the heavy lifting of the Internet," said Steve Messer, co-founder and CEO of LinkShare. "It is such an effective, profitable tool that in our view it has become an essential part of the infrastructure of Internet commerce."

And he's right.

At an affiliate marketing conference organized by the Institute for International Research (www.iir-ny.com) in July 2000, Art.com (www.art.com) showed a Cost of Acquisition Study their firm conducted. It compared various advertising media cost of acquiring customers versus the amount of revenue generated for every dollar spent. The results prove that among other things, affiliate marketing can drastically increase the return on investment (see Table 4.1).

Table 4.1

Art.com Cost of Customer Acquisition Study		
Promotional Method	Cost of Acquisition	Revenue Generated Per $1 Spent
Radio	$1457	$0.07
Print	$958	$0.10
Public relations	$82	$1.16
E-mail	$24	$2.54
Online Ads	$21	$4.61
Affiliates	$9	$7.15

Source: Art.com

Jaclyn Easton (http://www.strikingitrich.com/more_fun/jaclyn_bio.htm), Web author and LA Time columnist, said at the Seventeenth Annual Catalog Conference & Exhibition in June of 2000 that the average cost of acquiring a new customer via e-commerce partnerships such as affiliate programs is $1.67, compared with $30 for a banner ad.

The message is clear. Affiliate marketing should be more than just an afterthought. Companies that invest significant resources into running an affiliate program get results. Those that don't, do not. And remember, it's not how many affiliates you have, it's how good they are. To attract the best affiliates means that you have to spend time thinking as an affiliate—what do they want and need to help both you and them make money?

Setting Up Your Affiliate Program

To quote Delcan Dunn, an affiliate program consultant and author, "Affiliate programs are about marketing—not technology." Like most things concerning the Net, this little pearl of wisdom is often forgotten by e-businesses. So when you start planning an affiliate program for your business, realize that to get the most value from your program you must treat it as a marketing venture and not just a technology challenge.

Yes, there are technology and creative issues involved in implementing and managing your program, but above all, an affiliate program is a study in creating a collaborative commerce network where you and your affiliates are literally in business together, because affiliate programs have everything to do with business.

In the following chapters, we will cover the seven steps to creating a successful affiliate program and then the strategies and tactics of managing one. A lot of thought, preparation and planning goes into a successful affiliate program. Besides the marketing issues, there are technical and legal issues that must be executed properly. Affiliate advisors list the most important steps to take to make your program a success.

Basically, they all boil down to these major points:

- Think like your customer. What do affiliates want to see in an affiliate program? What does the program offer them? It must offer value not only to your business but to them as well.

- Consider whether to contract with an affiliate consultant who can help set up your program. Remember that affiliate programs are about marketing, not just technology. A good affiliate consultant will help you think of your program strategically, which is different from just technology implementation.

- Choose an affiliate model, but only after you've decided on the needs of your potential affiliates and created your business case for it. There are several types to choose from, and all models do not work for all affiliates.

DO

DO recommend EchoFactor's (www.affiliatemarketing.co.uk/echofactor) (see Figure 4.2) free content program to your affiliates. EchoFactor (see Figure 4.1) is a free news-feed service aggregating news from hundreds of sources on a wide variety of topics. Most of the topics are ideal to help an affiliate bring daily updated content relevant to their site's niche. If your affiliates are selling music, they can have a news feed on Britney Spears, and if they are involved with travel, they can have a news feed on a specific city or destination.

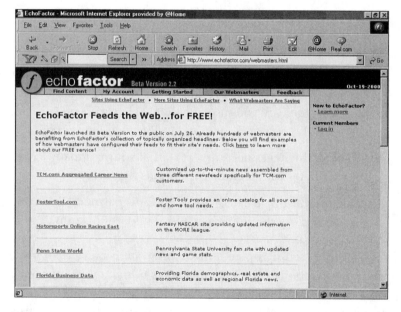

Figure 4.1
EchoFactor is a free news-feed service aggregating news from hundreds of sources on a wide variety of topics.

- Design, and then implement, a way to distribute the necessary graphics, images, and links that your affiliates will use.

- Decide who will manage the tracking and reporting of your program. This is where the technical issues arise. How will your affiliates be able to retrieve traffic and commission reports and pick up their affiliate code? Will you do it in-house or contract with an affiliate solutions provider who has the technical know-how?

- Create your affiliate agreement. This should state clearly what is expected of your affiliates and what your responsibilities are to them. Among other things, the agreement should spell out your affiliate compensation plan, and how and when you plan to pay them.

- Get the word out. Once a payment plan is established, your next step is to get the word out. Once your program is ready to go, you need to market it to potential affiliates. You need to develop a marketing plan that will attract affiliates—and not just any potential affiliate. You need to develop a set of criteria and an effective screening program to choose the affiliates that fit your program.

- Consider how you will train and educate your affiliates so they can effectively sell your product or service. What kind of support structure will you have for them? How will you communicate with them, how frequently, and in what manner?

- Establish the necessary support staff at your company to assist your affiliates with technical questions that arise.

- Affiliates must be treated as full business partners. Everything you do and say should reflect and reinforce this thinking.

As you can see, setting up an affiliate program is more than just an invitation to Web site owners to make lots of money selling your product or service. It takes hard work and a commitment to treat your program as a full marketing program—not just an advertising campaign.

Considering a Program Consultant

Before you begin planning an affiliate program, you might want to consider hiring a reputable affiliate consultant. Over the last few years and as affiliate programs have become more important to online merchants, a number of individuals have come forward offering professional advice on how to set up and run a successful affiliate program. Most consult with businesses that wish to establish an affiliate program, and many also advise Web site owners on which programs to join and what criteria to look for when joining an affiliate program. They offer their services to both merchants and affiliates alike.

A consultant can help get your company up and running quickly by knowing exactly where to list and announce your new program, how to promote it, how to make your program unique and get new affiliates excited, and how to generate a buzz around the launch of your program.

There are many companies and individuals that claim to offer professional affiliate program advice. It's always best to investigate both them and their claims, asking for references and following up on them. Though the following list of individuals is by no means exhaustive, here are some professionals that have been in the affiliate game for a while and whom you might consider contacting for their professional advice.

Glenn Sobel (`www.affiliateadvisor.com`) (see Figure 4.2) focuses on educating affiliates, consulting with merchants who have affiliate programs, and giving affiliate program recommendations for affiliate sites. His site is also a great resource for both merchants and affiliates alike. Sobel also specializes in helping companies write a win-win affiliate agreement that's fair to both merchants and affiliates. He has been a lead speaker at many affiliate conferences and is well respected by his peers and affiliate solution providers like Commission Junction (`www.cj.com`).

A prolific writer on affiliate programs and leading program advisor, Delcan Dunn (`www.activemarketplace.com`) has consulted with many well-known dot-coms, such as Pets.com, Ask Jeeves, OfficeMax, Travelocity, and others, helping them with their affiliate marketing programs. In association with his firm ADNet, he helps develop performance-based marketing programs for companies of all sizes.

DO

DO consider contracting with an affiliate program consultant. He or she can help you plan and execute your affiliate program. But also investigate him or her thoroughly and get references from companies he or she has consulted with.

Figure 4.2
Glenn Sobel is a well-know affiliate program advisor who has consulted with many companies about their affiliate program.

Other affiliate consultants to consider are Ola Edvardsson (`www.affiliatetips.com`), Ken Evoy (`www.sitesell.com`), and Corey Rudl (`www.marketingtips.com`). Edvardsson is a dynamic commentator and columnist who has helped companies across the United Kingdom and the united States achieve affiliate marketing success. Evoy has created a suite of solutions that advise merchants how to make good products that people need and want, how to build sites that sell effectively, and how both affiliates and merchants can attract targeted traffic to a Web site cost-effectively. Rudl owns four online businesses and consults for hundreds of clients, from mom and pop and home-based businesses to large multimillion dollar corporations. He specializes in showing small businesses unique and unconventional ways to promote their business on the Internet (see Figure 4.3).

Also, there are two dynamic and knowledgeable affiliate marketing consultants who have an intimate knowledge of Commission Junction and the industry as a whole. Keith Kochberg, formerly a merchant with Commission Junction, runs the boutique marketing firm, imarketing ltd (`www.imarketingltd.com`). Linda Woods, former resource programs manager with Commission Junction, offers an array of affiliate marketing services in her new incarnation as the Affiliate Goddess (www.affiliategoddess.com).

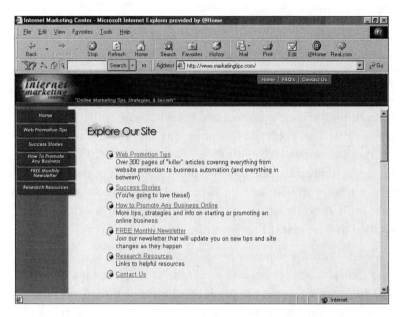

Figure 4.3
Corey Rudl consults from experience. He owns four online businesses.

If using an affiliate program consultant is right for you, remember that there are a number of affiliate and marketing consultants on the Net offering their services. These are just a handful. Additional consultants are listed in Chapter 11, "Managing Your Affiliates," and you can find a list online at www.affiliatemanager.net/ consultants.htm. Investigate consultants thoroughly and make sure that their approach to affiliate marketing meets your business objectives.

What Do Affiliates Want?

As affiliate programs on the Net mature, merchants are becoming more selective about the affiliates they choose. Likewise, potential affiliates are doing the same. Companies with successful affiliate programs become successful because they think like their affiliates. They plan their program from the affiliates' point of view. As in most business endeavors, what separates the successful companies

What Are Super Affiliates?

Super affiliates comprise that small percentage of sites that generate the lion's share of the revenue for your program. They are born marketers and are very successful with the affiliate programs they promote from their sites.

from the ones that fail is focus on the customer. And in this case, the company's affiliate is not only its business partner but, to a large extent, its customer as well. It pays, when planning your program to think like your affiliates.

And for good reason.

At first sight, building an affiliate network seems like an easy and inexpensive way to market your eBusiness. But don't let the simplicity of the concept fool you. First of all, the percentage of affiliates that sign up for your program and then become active in your network is quite low. Forrester Research says that the average affiliate program has about 10,000 affiliates. But only 10%–20% of the affiliate sites actually participate in the program—that is, those that actually place your affiliate link on their site. And of those 10%–20% of active affiliates only 20% of those are super-affiliates—those that produce the majority of the revenue for your program.

So why the vast discrepancy between affiliates that sign up and those that actually participate in a merchant's program? It could be chalked up to laziness or general apathy about their Web site. But these answers are too simple. Maybe it's because the merchant's program doesn't give affiliates what they want, and once they sit down to execute the program, they find out that it's not all that it's cracked up to be.

Thinking like an affiliate, what program elements and level of service would attract you (see Table 4.2)?

Table 4.2

What Affiliates Want
Be treated as a true business partner
A long term relationship
Good commissions or revenue generating potential
Access to the life-time value of the customer with life-time commissions
Restrictions on the number of affiliates in the program
Adequate communication with the merchant
Adequate training on the product or service

Table 4.2 (continued)

Good graphic and text links that sell
Adequate marketing support
Be part of a community with other affiliates
A good reporting and tracking program available for reports 24 hours a day
An honest and credible program with a credible merchant
Good service for customers sent to the merchant
clear and fair affiliate agreement with no hidden restrictions
Offers that are continuously updated and fresh
A wide selection of products to sell
Payments made on time

Source: Glenn Sobel

Let's take a more detailed look at what it takes to build a successful and profitable affiliate program from the affiliate's point of view.

True Partnership

Successful affiliate sites spend a lot of time and give up valuable screen real estate to promote a merchant's product or service. They want to know that all this time and effort is not wasted, so they are looking for affiliate programs that see them as true business partners.

Those merchants that see their affiliate program as just free advertising across the Net instead of building a true business relationship across a network will either attract poor affiliate partners or see their programs slip from favor. After investing both time and effort, affiliates expect a binding agreement with a merchant that doesn't give the merchant the ability to cancel the agreement and drop them on a whim. Affiliate programs are not short-term advertising campaigns. Good affiliate partners want to establish a long-term relationship with a merchant and benefit from all the advantages this relationship can bring.

DO

DO understand that affiliates are looking for a true partnership with your company. If you're not prepared to spend the time to build this kind of relationship, your affiliate program will perform poorly.

Affiliate program commissions are not about how much, but how long. More and more affiliates are interested in getting paid for the lifetime value of their customer referrals. They also want to keep their visitors on their sites and not shepherd their hard-earned traffic off to a merchant's site. They want to own the customers that they generate for the merchant. They don't want to refer a life-long customer to a merchant then get paid only for the first sale. Affiliates also look for residual programs that offer commissions where customers sign up for a continuous service that requires periodic, regular payments that the affiliate shares in.

Affiliates want to know that the product or service offer they are promoting is not being offered on thousands of other sites. Would it make sense for Burger King to open five stores on one block? Of course not. The same goes for affiliates. Affiliates want to join programs that are somewhat exclusive and that have restrictions on the number of affiliates it will have at any one time.

Adequate communications with the merchant is also on the list of affiliate wants. They want merchants who will communicate with them frequently, telling them what's new with their programs and how to better increase sales. They want to have all their inquiries answered promptly and betreated like a true business partner. And speaking of increasing sales, affiliates want to be trained properly on how to sell the products or services of the merchant. They need to know in detail the features, benefits, and target market—useful advice about maximizing their sales, and yours. It's in the interest of your business to help your affiliates succeed. And all this information should be available before they sign up for the program, not after.

Along the lines of communication, affiliates want to be part of a community where they can interact with other affiliates, gain support, and exchange ideas. Again, it's in the merchant's interest to foster support for their affiliates, yet many affiliate programs offer no community support. Community discussion boards offer an exchange of information between affiliates in addition to news and expert advice (see Figure 4.4). Merchants should provide this kind of communication opportunity and encourage affiliates to help and support each other.

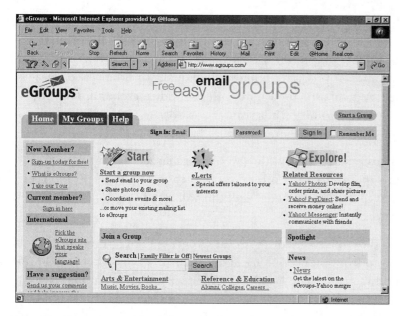

Figure 4.4

eGroups provides a service to any company or group that wants to establish a discussion list.

As a true business partner with access to the lifetime value of its customer, a merchant should provide the ability for an affiliate site to capture, build, and market to not only his or her current customers but to prospects, too. Affiliates want a program that encourages repeat business. The merchant could build a prospect database by having the affiliate place sign-up links on his or her Web site. The merchant would manage the database for the affiliate and market to it periodically with special offers through which the affiliate would gain additional revenue.

Finally, promoting a merchant's affiliate program sometimes requires an affiliate to divert traffic away from his or her site and towards the merchant's. If so, affiliates want to be properly compensated with a reasonable commission structure or referral fee to compensate for the lost traffic and the loss of future sales.

A Credible Program

The last thing an affiliate wants to do is damage his credibility with his visitors. In addition, an affiliate is looking for an honest and credible affiliate program from a merchant.

DO

DO offer affiliates ways to build a database of prospects from their site that can be later converted into customers and to make future sales from them.

DON'T

DON'T surprise your affiliates after sign-up with restrictions on payment. Be up front and clear on how and when you will pay your affiliates and post this information on your site. Affiliates will run—not walk— from programs that seem to have hidden restrictions on the sales or referrals they perform.

What's SPAM?

Spam is unsolicited e-mail. It's the junk mail of the late twentieth century. It clogs e-mail servers around the world and sucks up needed bandwidth on the Net, and it's the quickest way to create a bad reputation for you, your company, and your product.

If a customer referred from an affiliate to a merchant is unhappy with his or her purchase or service after the sale, the affiliate's credibility will suffer. Affiliates will be looking for not only a credible affiliate program, but also high-quality products and services to sell. A good affiliate will not offer shoddy merchandise, products, or services to his or her visitors or associate with merchants who offer poor service after the sale.

If customers feel that they were overcharged, received poor service or support, that the offer did not measure up to its promotion, or that they were scammed—all this will reflect on a merchant's reputation.

Credibility also resides with the program itself. Merchants should be up front on everything about their program. They should hold nothing back. The last thing affiliates want after signing up for a merchant's affiliate program is surprises, such as how they will be paid. Affiliates want to see a professional, considered, and detailed affiliate agreement with few or no restrictions on their ability to sell your and other merchant's products or services. The agreement should be posted on the merchant's site for all to read in simple, understandable language—no legalese—before the affiliate agrees to join the program.

The agreement should be fair with expectations on both side spelled out clearly.

Good affiliate partners will shy away from outright scams, deceptive or misleading promotional materials, or no clear examples of the merchant banners and links—or other means—for use on their site. A "too-good-to-be true" promotion of a program where affiliates are told they will make thousands of dollars overnight will attract sites that will do little to enhance your affiliate network.

Another consideration that affiliates look at is how the merchant treats spammers. The last thing a merchant or any other reputable affiliate needs is to have the reputation of the merchant's product or service besmirched by other affiliates in the program (or even by the merchant itself) for sending out unsolicited e-mails to every one who has an e-mail address.

Offers That Sell

Affiliates are looking for products and services that match the content of their site. They are looking for offers that are consistent with the theme of their Web site and the products or services should appeal to those who visit their site. After all, a parenting site would rather sell children's clothing, books, and toys than a Smashing Pumpkins CD. A site that does movie reviews would rather sell videos or DVDs than strollers. An affiliate that caters to Webmasters is looking for software programs, not gift baskets.

Affiliates need to cater to the wants and needs of their site audience.

They are also looking for programs that have good growth potential with an expanding product or service offering. Good sites work hard to keep their content fresh so they can attract return visitors. The same goes for the affiliate program they join. Affiliates want to offer products and services that keep customers coming back to see what's new and exciting. They don't want to join programs whose product offerings are a dead end, so affiliates will look for a merchant program that not only sells multiple products and services but also makes timely offers. Selling one product or service gives up a lot of valuable Web page space, so that product had better be highly profitable to sell. A merchant's program would be better accepted by affiliates if it sold a variety of products or service. Book, music, and movie stores are good examples of merchant programs where a variety of products can be offered. Clothing, sports equipment, and toy stores are others.

In addition, affiliates are looking for merchants who take advantage of the seasons or special occasions to promote their products. Christmas, Hanukah, Easter, Passover, Father's Day, and Mother's Day are seasonal events that affiliates can exploit to sell products to their visitors and keep their offers fresh. Birthdays and anniversaries offer other opportunities for fresh content.

Merchants who understand the need for this fresh content will attract the right kinds of affiliate partners.

DO

DO take advantage of seasonal and special events to create unique promotions that your affiliates can offer their site visitors.

DO

DO allow affiliates to purchase your product or service and apply their commission as a discount.

A Fair Program

For an affiliate, the revenue is what an affiliate program is all about. That's why they joined in the first place.

They will be looking for a fair program—one that adequately compensates them for their efforts. They want a high first-sale payout if they are working on a commission basis—then credit for all additional revues generated by customers referred to the merchant. Affiliates look at the reliability and frequency of payments a merchant's program offers. The sooner and more frequently affiliates are paid, the better. They also are looking for programs that are free to join. Any program that requires an affiliate to pay to join will almost certainly fail. In addition, and if they can, affiliates seek out merchants who offer programs that do not compete with them.

Affiliates feel that they are a key part of building a merchant's business, and being paid to help build the business of the merchant seems only fair. Offering two-tier programs that reward affiliates for both referring other affiliates to the merchant as well as for sending paying customers is a way for affiliates to cash in on the work they've done for helping build the merchant's business.

Affiliates will run—not walk—from programs that seem to have hidden restrictions on the sales or referrals they perform. Affiliates don't like high sales requirements for a fair commission or fee, unreasonable sales or referral minimums, or long periods before getting paid.

Reliability is another concern of affiliates. The affiliate programs that have a reputation for late or non-payment of commissions to Web site owners will not succeed. A merchant should explain clearly the payment process and when affiliates should expect their checks. Affiliates also need to know whether there is a minimum check that the merchant will cut.If there is a minimum payment, they should be told whether any processing fees will be applied.

Finally, affiliates expect to be able to buy a merchant's product or service themselves and apply the commission they normally would get to the purchase. That is, they want to buy the product or service at a discount equal to the commission they would normally earn.

An Uncomplicated Program

Affiliates are a busy lot. It's enough just to keep their Web sites fresh and up and running. So they are not looking for any more complications in their life. And that includes any affiliate program that they join.

In any program, affiliates must physically place links on their Web pages and/or e-mail. Any kind of links affiliates need to retrieve or any Web-based store design they must perform should be easy to find on the merchant's site and easy to place on their site. Affiliates do not want to hunt around a merchant's site looking for this material. There should be a separate place on a merchant's site—or the affiliate solutions provider site—where affiliates can easily and quickly retrieve this information.

Most important of all, affiliates want a simple way to retrieve reports on impressions (how many times their visitors have seen the merchant's product or service offer), click-throughs (how many times visitors click on the merchant's offer), the number of sales made or actions performed by their visitors and, of course, the revenue they have earned. These reports should be available 24/7 and be easy to understand.

The bottom line to all this is loyalty. If you want loyalty from your affiliates you need to show the same. Glenn Forde, affiliate account manager for i-traffic, concurred. Here's what he had to say:

"The best way to keep top affiliates loyal is to maintain a relationship with them. If you regularly communicate and form a mutual trust, that produces loyalty in the truest sense. Beyond that, ensure that the basics, including on-time payments, regular chances for bonus compensation, site promotions, and a variety of links, are delivered."

The secret to affiliate loyalty for the ClubMom affiliate program (www.clubmom.com/areas/corporate/affiliates.jhtml) came from a mantra on their own site: "ClubMom asks Moms what they want and gives it to them." After a callout in the ClubMom affiliate newsletter asking the affiliates what they wanted, they responded en masse, and it was interesting to see that they had quite a few common requests. They wanted monthly commissions, links directly to the registration page (not the home page), a community where they could interact with other affiliates and, most of all, they wanted a timely response when they had problems or questions. True to the mantra, the affiliates got what they wanted.

Woodrow Wilson once said, "Loyalty means nothing unless it has at its heart the absolute principle of self-sacrifice." That's what dedicated affiliates do. To a large extent they are sacrificing the time, resources, and energy to promote a merchant's program. They expect a lot in return.

Why Affiliate Programs Fail

For an affiliate program to work, it must be a win-win program for both the affiliate and the merchant. Glenn Sobel accurately describes what it takes to create such a program and what to avoid.

Affiliate programs are capable of simultaneous success and failure because there are two sides to the relationship. Seek to create a win-win (merchant succeeds and affiliate succeeds) relationship with your affiliates (see Table 4.3).

Table 4.3

What It Takes for a Win-Win Affiliate/Merchant
The merchant offers a credible product or service at a reasonable price.
The merchant handles back-end details correctly.
The agreement, commission, and tracking system used for the affiliate program are fair to all parties.
The merchant honors its relationships with its customers and affiliates.
The merchant provides the tools necessary for affiliate success, and limits affiliations to sites that make sense for its roduct or service.
The affiliates take reasonable steps to promote the merchant's products and services as part of their overall marketing efforts.

Source: Glenn Sobel

Additionally, it stands to reason that a merchant is going to fail when the affiliates fail. Obviously, if an affiliate is inactive, he or she cannot succeed. Ken Evoy, President of SiteSell.com (`affiliate.sitesell.com`), moderated a chat at Affiliate Webinar 2000 (`www.affiliateWebinar.com`) with the topic, "Why are so many affiliates inactive?" According to Ken, fewer than 1% of affiliates earn checks over $100 from any given merchant.

Ken boiled the reasons for affiliate failure down to five points:

- The average person simply does not know HTML (and never will)

- Search engine mastery is beyond most people

- Poor support/education/tools from some merchants

- Most affiliates are not willing to put in the work once it's clear that the affiliate model is not a "get-rich-quick" deal

- Most affiliates make fundamental mistakes, such as selling instead of pre-selling

Ken states that his top affiliates all pre-sell with great content, rather than SELL-SELL-SELL! In response to the mass inactivity of affiliates, Ken created Site Build It! (`buildit.sitesell.com`), as well as a free course, the Affiliate Masters Course, to help people overcome all the common barriers. Subscribe to it by sending a blank e-mail to `tams@sitesell.net`.

Review Your Competition

There's a good chance that when you visit your competitor's Web site you'll see those three little words that make marketing mangers smile—Become an Affiliate. In other words, because of its popularity, there's a very good chance your competitors have an affiliate program.

Scouting your competitor's program gives you a chance to see what they offer the same affiliates you are going to try and recruit. Before you even begin to plan, review their program, see what they offer, and see how you may be able to improve upon it.

DO

DO join your competitor's program. See what they offer, and see how you may be able to improve upon it.

Your first step is to find your competitor's affiliate programs. That's easy to do. Here are some good places to start.

First go to Associate Programs.com (`www.associateprograms.com`) (see Figure 4.5). Once there, either search for competitors by category or search by keyword to see what programs are offered in your market niche.

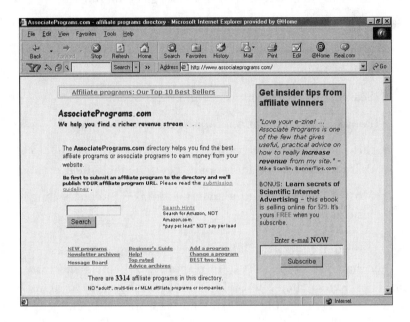

Figure 4.5
At AssociatePrograms.com you can search for competitors by category.

Another good site is Cashpile (`www.cashpile.com/active/cp/directory.cfm`) (see Figure 4.6). Using their directory you can find competing programs in your market category to obtain commission structure, number of affiliates, and program description to see whether your program measures up.

Some other good affiliate directories to scout out your competition are Associate-it (`www.associate-it.com`), Refer-it (`www.refer-it.com`), and ReveNews (`www.revenews.com`).

Figure 4.6
Another directory to use to search for competitive programs is at CashPile.

Once you've identified your competitors, create a spreadsheet to examine each competitor's affiliate program and evaluate the aspects of that program.

- **Financial**—How does your commission compare with your competition? Are you paying more or less? Does your profit margin allow you to offer the highest commission among your competitors? What is the minimum threshold the affiliate needs to earn before getting paid? How frequently do they get paid? Are there aspirational levels where affiliates can achieve higher levels of commissions?

- **Tracking**—How does your competitor track its program? Does it use an affiliate solution provider or track its program in-house?

- **Training**—What kinds of tips and tools are offered to the affiliates to help them sell the merchant's product or service?

- **Reputation**—Check out your competitor's reputation with affiliates. Sites like Affiliateadvisor.com (`www.affiliateadvisor.com`) (see Figure 4.7) give frank and direct reviews of affiliate programs, and Cashpile's Affiliate Voice (`www.affiliatevoice.com`) is an independent rating system that enables affiliates to voice their opinions about the programs they participate in. This independent rating system enables merchants to better understand how well their affiliate marketing programs are operating, and it provides affiliates with valuable information about a program before they sign up. AssociatePrograms.com operates an active discussion board (`webwizards.net/AssociatePrograms/discus/`) where affiliates post the pros and cons for affiliate programs.

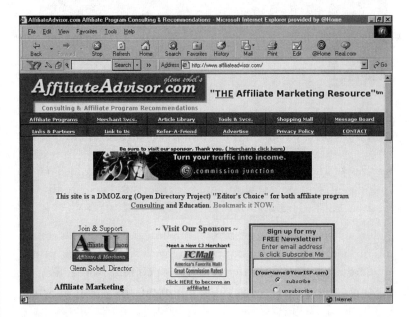

Figure 4.7
Affiliateadvisor.com gives frank and direct reviews of affiliate programs.

Finally, join your competitor's program. Because many merchants use the third-party affiliate solution providers, such as Be Free, Linkshare, or Commission Junction, you may not find out all you need about a competitor's program on its Web site. Usually all the details are on the third-party solutions site, necessitating that you join the program to see how it works—which, as mentioned previously, is a very good idea. By joining, you can see how easy it is to join and be placed on their affiliate mailing list, which announces program enhancements, incentives, or special offers to their affiliates.

The processes of scouting and joining the affiliate programs of your competition are ongoing. According to the Affiliate Metrix (www.affiliatemetrix.com) Merchant Report 2001, 68% of affiliate programs were launched in the year 2000. With the rapid growth of the industry, you must keep your eyes open, because the competitor who didn't have a program yesterday will probably have one tomorrow.

As previously mentioned, affiliate programs should be choosy about which affiliates are accepted into their programs. This is covered in more detail in Chapter 7, "Step Four—Choosing Your Affiliates." That said, it is imperative that all members of your affiliate team have their own themed sites in order to research the competition as affiliates.

Remember to create an overall plan for your program that meets both your needs as a merchant and your affiliate's needs as a business partner, keeping in mind the other programs you're competing with.

DO

DO open your program to affiliate opinion. See your program as your affiliates see it. Sign-up for Cashpile.com's affiliate rating system, AffiliateVoice (www.affiliatevoice.com). AffiliateVoice enables affiliates to voice their opinions about programs they participate in while allowing merchants invaluable feedback about their program.

Step Two—Choosing Your Program Model

Chapter Summary

Once you have your plan, the next step is to choose your program model. Affiliate program models come in many shapes and sizes. The more your program matches what's being offered on your affiliate sites, the more successful it will be.

You can affiliate with Web sites in two ways. First, by placing offers on your affiliates' sites that link back to your company servers where the sale is made, and second, via hybrid affiliate models. These models consist of Banner or Text Links, Storefronts, Pop-Ups, Imbedded Commerce, E-mail, and Two-Tier Programs. The most important objective of your program, of course, is to get customers to buy. That's why the creatives you use for your banners and links should be designed for that purpose and that purpose only. Putting in the time and effort to design good creatives will pay off handsomely in sales.

Finally, product endorsements from affiliates are one of the best ways to help sell your product to their site visitors. By providing pre-written marketing copy to your affiliates that they can place into electronic communications with their site visitors, you can both help your affiliate increase its revenue and add to your sales.

Affiliate programs come in all shapes and sizes. If someone has thought of a product or service to sell on the Net, it's a good bet that there's an affiliate program for it. And if you have a product or service that's selling on the Net, you too can sell it through an affiliate program.

In fact, selling it through your own affiliate program will help make it even more successful. Developing an affiliate program that creates a collaborative commerce network is one of the most powerful ways today to market online. Here's another advantage: A successfully developed and managed network of affiliate partner sites can make even the smallest business or an unfamiliar product on the Net competitive with other e-commerce offers. A network of partners extends your product's reach, increases your product's visibility, and produces additional revenue for your business.

Once you've decided on a plan and understand what you are looking for in a program, the next step is to choose a program model.

Affiliate Program Models

Affiliate programs models have evolved quite a bit since their inception. Over the last few years, affiliate marketing has evolved from the original prototype model that CDnow.com created and has spawned a variety of new and innovative models. Affiliate programs now work effectively for individuals, businesses, schools, and charities.

But in almost every case, the models that are seeing success are those that that are becoming evermore context-centric. That is, what's being offered to site visitors closely matches the content of the site itself. The idea is obvious. Place the product or service in context and more people will buy (see Figure 5.1). An affiliate site would have more success selling video games than lawn mowers on a site targeted to teenagers. It's presenting the right message to visitors in the right place at the right time. Whatever affiliate model you use, it must be content-centric to succeed.

What Is Context-Centric?

Context-Centric is matching your product or service offer closely to the visitors of an affiliate's site. Place the product or service in context (closely related to the content it's next to) and more people will buy.

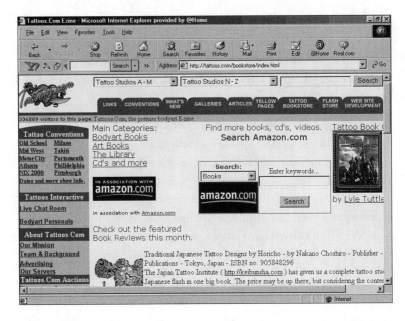

Figure 5.1
Tattoos.com is good example of placing product offers in context.

You can affiliate with Web sites in two ways—first, by placing offers on your affiliate's sites that link back to your company servers where the sale is made, andsecond, via hybrid models. The program models come in six basic types, and your company can offer any or all of them to potential affiliate partners.

They are

- Banner or Text Links
- Storefronts
- Pop-Ups
- Imbedded Commerce
- E-mail
- Two-tier Programs

Combined, they represent the different ways your business can generate revenue, generate leads, and acquire new customers.

Banner or Text Links

The oldest affiliate model is the banner or text link. Affiliates place a small banner, image, or text link on their site which—when clicked—sends the site visitor to the merchant's site (see Figure 5.2).

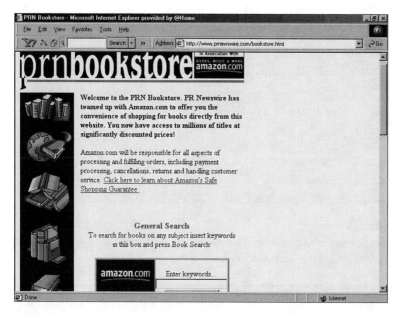

Figure 5.2
Pr News Wire is a good example of a site using affiliate banner links.

The banner or text link usually has the name of a company promoting what the merchant is selling. Amazon.com is a good example. A Web site might place a banner for Amazon on its Web pages promoting the fact that great books can be bought from Amazon. There would be some promotional copy on the banner to get the Web site visitor to click it (see Figure 5.3). When the user clicks the banner, it sends her to Amazon's site where she might buy a book. If the visitor buys a book, the affiliate site gets a commission.

Banners are not limited to products. Some financial institutions promote their different credit cards using affiliate marketing. NextCard at (www.nextcard.com) is a good example (see Figure 5.4).

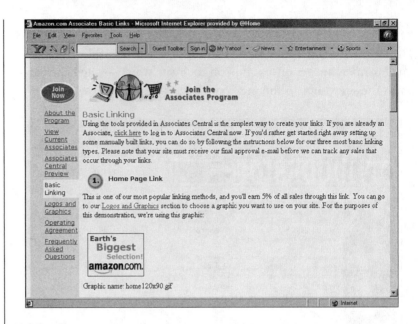

Figure 5.3
Amazon's square banner informs potential customers that Amazon has the earth's biggest selection of books.

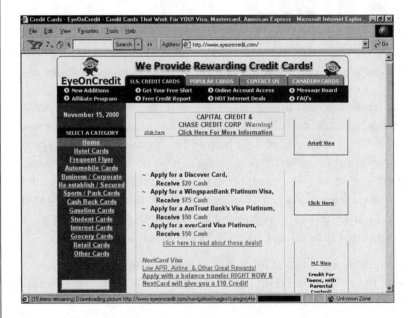

Figure 5.4
Unlike most affiliate programs that promote products, Nextcard uses affiliate marketing to promote a service.

Affiliate Web sites place a banner persuading visitors to apply for a NextCard Visa card at a very low percentage rate. When the user clicks on the banner, it sends them to the NextCard site where they can fill out an application. If the user is approved for a Visa card, the affiliate site gets a finder's fee.

Studies have shown that combining both a banner and a text description—especially a testimonial—produces better results than a banner or text link alone. This gives the viewer not only a graphic image but also a compelling reason to click it (see Figure 5.5).

Do

DO use a combination of both a banner and a text description—especially a testimonial—on an affiliate's site to increase the chance of a sale.

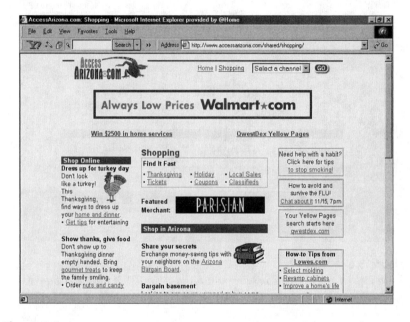

Figure 5.5
Access Arizona combines a graphic with text to promote a product.

There are other revenue models using banners that don't depend on commissions. Instead of paying a commission on products or services sold, you can offer Web sites a CPC (cost-per-click) affiliate program. In this method, Web sites earn revenue every time one of their visitors clicks through to your Web site. This method is especially useful for driving traffic to your site. Another model is CPA (cost-per-action). With CPA programs, affiliates earn commission every time one of their visitors clicks-through to your site and performs a task, such as filling out a survey form or entering a contest on your site. No sales are made, but your company can build up a list of prospects that you can market to in the future. Examples of pay-per-lead networks include WebSponsors (www.websponsors.com) and DirectLeads (www.directleads.com) (see Figure 5.6).

Figure 5.6
With DirectLeads, your company can build up a list of prospects that you can market to in the future.

The advantage to you is increased traffic to your site. The disadvantage to your affiliate is that he loses that traffic. These types of "click-and-bye" links, as discussed in Chapter 2, are frowned upon by some affiliates because there is no opportunity for residual commissions and there are no financial transactions. However, the CPC is guaranteed commission, and CPA deals typically convert at a much higher rate than the sales models. This makes the CPC and CPA models very attractive to many affiliates.

Storefronts

Though the basic e-commerce banners have been successful for online merchants, the results for affiliates have been negligible.

This is primarily because when a Web site's visitor clicks on an affiliate program banner, the visitor leaves the affiliate site to complete the transaction. The affiliate Web site loses the traffic that he has worked hard to acquire in exchange for the small chance that the visitor would actually complete a transaction at the online store and earn a commission.

As a result, affiliate Web sites like cost-per-click programs much more than banners. If a visitor clicks off their Web site, at least they have the guarantee of being paid for it. Similarly, cost-per-action programs are favorable to many affiliates because their traffic is more likely to convert to a commissionable action than it is in the sales model.

The storefront affiliate marketing model shows promise to revitalize the sales commission model. With the storefront model—or syndicated boutiques—visitors don't leave an affiliate partner's Web sites. With this model firms like vstore (`www.vstore.com`) provide Web server space and design templates to mom and pop Web sites that want to set up shop on the Net but don't possess the requisite technical know-how and resources to do themselves. Such firms pay their affiliates commissions on each sale generated through the storefront. In the storefront model, a Web site owner can actually create a complete online store that looks like it resides on his or her Web site.

The popularity of storefront affiliate programs is growing because—in the words of Roman Godzich, Director of Communities for vstore.com—"People are beginning to discover the difference between a 'pay-per-action' affiliate relationship and owning their own store."

Storefront companies sell no products themselves but offer the merchandise of many different merchants to their affiliate partners. In effect, they come between the merchant and the affiliate—working for the affiliate sites, not the merchants—by offering complete lines of merchandise built around the theme of each affiliate site. With this model, affiliate partners are offered a way to seamlessly integrate a complete online store, selling products in a variety of categories on their sites.

Do

DO consider incorporating models like storefronts and pop-ups into your program to e-commerce–enable affiliate Web sites and keep the affiliate's visitor on its site.

But as with any new technology, tread lightly and avoid putting all your eggs in one basket. In December 2000, Nexchange Corp., provider of the self-coined "Syndicated E-commerce" service, announced that it was closing down due to the company's inability to secure the financing necessary to carry it to profitability.

Although the Syndicated E-commerce concept promises to be a very important mix to any Web site's and retailer's revenue stream, unfortunately, it won't be Nexchange delivering on that promise. However, the technology is important and it will continue to be with us in a variety of permutations.

Why are these program models attractive to affiliates?

According to Forrester Research, building a Web storefront costs between $2 million and $40 million dollars, with another $2 million to almost $50 million in recurring costs. This is why storefront affiliate programs are so attractive to Web sites wanting to e-commerce–enable their sites.

Pop-Ups

Affiliate models that use storefronts keep the affiliate partner's traffic on its Web site. Its visitors never leave its site. With pop ups, visitors never leave the affiliate's PAGE. An example of this type of technology is ePod (www.epod.com) (see Figure 5.8) and IQ (www.iq.com). Both of these companies use a technology that offers products and services to Web site visitors through a small pop up widow. When a visitor comes to a Web site, he or she may see a small banner or icon advertising a product or service of an online merchant.

At first glance, some of the banners look like traditional affiliate banner links—they also offer ePods in a variety of sizes, including a double banner (468×120 pixels) and a baseball card (234×332 pixels). But instead of being whisked off to another Web site when the link is clicked—or even to another page on the existing Web site—a small pop up window appears with the offer inside. The original page still appears in the background, so when the visitor is finished reading the offer—or even completing a transaction—she is still on the Web page that she arrived on when the pop up windows closes.

Pop-ups do have their disadvantages, however. Because the pop-up window is small, there is a limited amount of space that you have available to present your offer and complete a transaction or task, or collect information.

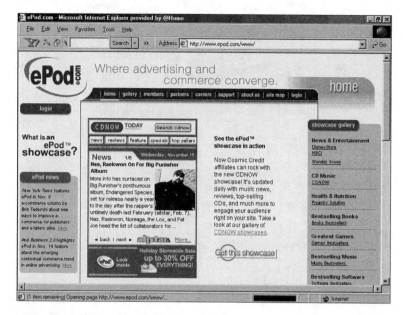

Figure 5.7
With ePod's affiliate program, Web sites can place complete e-commerce in the form of a pop-up on their site.

Imbedded Commerce—Boutiques

A more sophisticated form of a context-centric affiliate program is embedded commerce. This approach builds specialty "boutiques" for niche-market affiliates. All these programs have specialty pages designed for affiliates that carry only a portion of a merchant's product line. For example, Art.com (www.art.com) (see Figure 5.9) provides galleries populated with specialty art for a specific market niche.

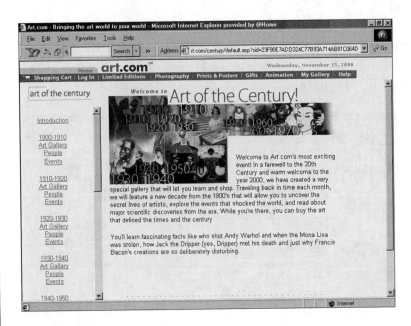

Figure 5.8
Art.com provides galleries populated with specialty art for a specific market niche to their affiliates.

Art.com provides a complete travel-oriented online print gallery. Another example of an embedded commerce boutique is eBags. com (`www.ebags.com`). Affiliates that run a site for business travelers can offer briefcases or computer cases, for example. eBags offers several vertical-market niches for affiliates, such as travel, school, fashion, sports, and outdoor recreation.

Another approach to embedded commerce is WebCollage. WebCollage (`www.webcollage.com`), a New York start-up, is offering a service to merchants who have affiliate programs that allows affiliates to embed parts of a merchant's e-commerce application right into their site. For example, instead of just offering a link to a travel merchant, affiliates can incorporate the travel reservations application itself directly into their site.

Eli Singer, WebCollage's chief executive, says their service also gives the affiliate the ability to customize certain aspects of the merchant's application to make it appear much more like it's a part of the affiliate's site. "Instead of sending a user somewhere else to access an application and losing that traffic, we decided that it made much more sense to bring the application to the user," Singer said.

Site59.com (www.site59.com), a last-minute travel service (see Figure 5.10), uses the WebCollage service to increase its reach and visibility across the Net by embedding its application in its affiliate sites.

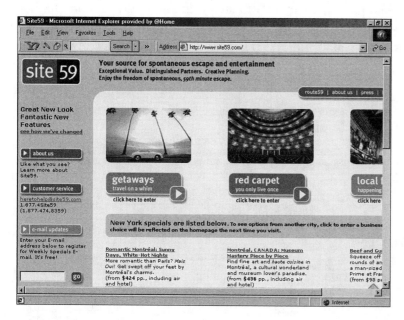

Figure 5.9
Site59 imbeds travel services that it gets through WebCollage.

E-mail

Many merchants with affiliate programs are focused solely on the activity that can be conducted on a Web site. But Web sites aren't the only places to conduct an affiliate program. Web sites can only generate a small amount of traffic and sales. Web sites are an important facet of affiliate marketing, but this passive method is neither the only, nor the most effective, method for optimizing the potential of affiliate marketing for your company.

Do

DO permit the use of opt-in e-mail lists by your e-mail affiliates. Be careful to monitor affiliates who use this strategy and include a provision against spam in your affiliate agreement.

Using e-mail, you can take a more proactive approach to affiliate marketing. Over the last year or so, e-mail affiliate programs have emerged as a significant player in the industry.

Barnes & Noble (www.bn.com) was the first merchant to use Be Free's (www.befree.com) B-Intouch program. With its MybnLink (see Figure 5.11) program, even individuals without a Web site could participate in an affiliate program by adding a link to their e-mail. With a service like B-Intouch, a merchant can make anyone with an e-mail address an e-marketer for their company.

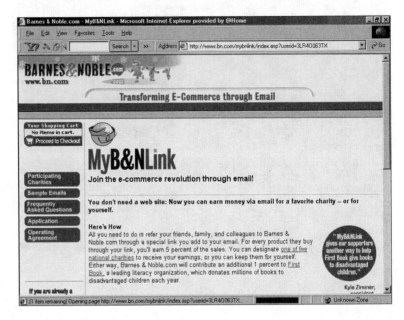

Figure 5.10
Anyone with an e-mail address can participate in the Barnes & Noble affiliate program.

It works like this:

When a person signs up to become a Barnes & Noble MybnLink program, they place a small snippet of code in the signature of their e-mail. This small piece of code calls the B-Intouch program from Be Free that automatically inserts a promotion for Barnes & Noble at the bottom of an e-mail message. If the recipient of the e-mail clicks through to Barnes & Noble's Web site and buys a product, the sender of the e-mail gets a commission.

What Is an E-mail Signature?

The signature option allows for a brief message to be imbedded at the end of every e-mail that a person sends.

It's quick, simple and easy. The merchant gets the sale and the e-mail sender gets a commission.

But why stop at text links in the signature field? With the growth of HTML enabled e-mail, complete images can be tagged at the end of mail messages, imploring the recipient to click the image offer for discounts or special deals on a product or service. It can also be used to direct the recipient to surveys and free offers where their e-mail address can be captured and then marketed to at some later date.

SuperSig (www.supersig.com) is an example of such a program. The SuperSig model enables the integration of interactive applications with e-mail and provides for the enterprise-wide implementation, management, and tracking of application-enabled e-mail.

And there lies another benefit to these e-mail affiliate programs. They're viral in nature.

Viral E-mail Marketing

The premise of viral affiliate marketing is simple. People love to show their support for their favorite products and will happily advertise them free. Look at all the brand names people wear on their clothes, or logos they stick on their car bumpers and rear windshield. And what about team sports apparel, such as hats, jackets, and T-shirts? So why not let individuals accessorize their e-mails with advertising messages too—and get paid for it!

That's the core of viral e-mail marketing—individuals acting as affiliates promoting a merchant's product or service offers.

With an estimated 3.4 trillion e-mail messages sent in 1999 (or 2.1 billion daily), you can see that an e-mail affiliate program is a powerful marketing device that can very quickly spread a merchant's offer across the Net.

Favemail is an example of this kind of e-mail technology (see Figure 5.12), and SuperSig is another. SuperSig (www.supersig. com) offers the ability for individuals to make money with their outgoing e-mail. But SuperSig (see Figure 5.13) also offers a way for individuals to personalize their e-mail message by including their

What Is Viral Marketing?

Viral marketing is the rapid adoption of a product or passing on of an offer to friends and family through word-of-mouth (or word-of-e-mail) networks. It is any advertising that propagates itself the way viruses do.

own graphics and pictures, stylized text, live opinion polls, quotes of the day, and information about whether or not they are online at the time.

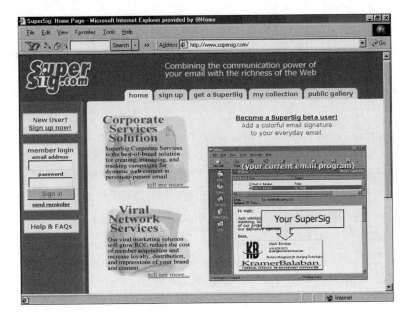

Figure 5.11
SuperSig offers the ability for individuals to make money with their outgoing e-mail.

Viral e-mail affiliate programs offer an easy entry for merchants wanting to promote products and services via e-mail while still maintaining the pay-for-performance benefits of affiliate marketing.

In addition to the formal affiliate e-mail programs, there is also a method known as *browser redirect* that allows affiliates to create a file that redirects a person to their affiliate link. This is especially useful for affiliates that wish to promote an affiliate program in their e-mail or text newsletter. The affiliate just has to go into the code and replace YOUR-AFFILIATE-LINK with the text link code from the merchant, then upload the page to its Web site.

With this method, affiliates can use a URL, such as `http://www.YOURDOMAIN.com/MERCHANT.htm`, in their e-mail or text newsletter, and all the people who clicked this URL would go to the merchant site through the affiliate link.

Here is an example of browser redirect code:

```
<html><head><meta http-equiv="refresh" content="0; url=
YOUR-AFFILIATE-LINK">
<title>Write some copy about the merchant here</title>
</head><body></body></html>
```

Two-Tier Programs

Amway (www.amway.com) built a retail empire using a multi-level marketing (MLM) business model. Friends and family would sign up to become Amway distributors, and in turn, sign up their friends and family to be dealers, who would then sign up their friends and family, and so on. When an Amway product is sold, the dealer gets a commission and every distributor/dealer up their chain—or their uplinks—gets a piece of the sale. Their multi-level marketing model proved very successful and has been copied thousands of times by Amway wannabes.

In the pay-for-performance space, affiliate marketers have created a similar model called the two-tier program. With a two-tier program, you are setting up a virtual sales force that's similar to the real world—manufacturer (your company), sales manager (the master affiliate), and sales person (second-tier affiliate). The master affiliate has an incentive to build his sales force (affiliates) and the sales force has the incentive to earn commissions and recruit other sales people so they can become managers (master affiliates) and have other people work for them.

There is a directory dedicated exclusively to two-tier affiliate programs, called the 2-Tier Affiliate Program Directory (www.2-tier.com).

Affiliate marketing has the potential to be even more effective when the two-tier model is part of the program. Two-tier affiliate programs can grow an affiliate program very quickly because they reward the affiliates for signing up additional affiliates. Basically, affiliate sites can sign up affiliate sites under them. When these second-tier affiliates make a sale, not only do they earn a commission or fee, but they also earn one for the affiliate—or master affiliate—themselves.

Do

DO expand your reach over the Net with a two-tier program, which can grow your affiliate program very quickly.

Here's an example: Let's say an affiliate joins a simple one-tier program. For every sale he makes, he gets a predetermined commission. So if your affiliate program paid a $20 commission on each sale an affiliate makes and he made 50 sales, his commission would be $1,000. Now let's say you offer a two-tier program, and the affiliate—a master affiliate in this case—has recruited 50 Web sites under him to sell your product, and your program pays $10 commission for each sale that the second-tier affiliates make under the master affiliate. And let's say that the 50 second-tier Web sites each make a sale. You would pay the same $1,000 to the master affiliate and an additional $10 commission per sale that his second-tier Web sites make. The master affiliate earns a total of $5,500—the $1,000 plus 50×$10. You can see the power and motivation that the two-tier program offers affiliates.

The advantage to the master affiliate is clear. He can receive continuous revenue from his second-tier affiliates virtually without any continued work promoting that specific program. But there are disadvantages too. The first is obvious. The master affiliate can "rest on his laurels," so to speak, and let his second-tier affiliates do all the work. That's a detriment to your affiliate program because your master affiliates are not giving their all promoting your product or service on their sites. They tend to spend more energy signing up second-tier affiliates as a means to generate revenue. If the second-tier affiliates also think this way, then your affiliate program will not be as effective.

While this drawback can harm your sales, another can harm your company's reputation. Two-tier programs can cause you to lose control of your affiliate program. Unscrupulous affiliates may use e-mail spam in an attempt to build the tier below them. These affiliates will send e-mails to thousands of sites with no regard to their content, offering your product or service to sell if they join your program under the master affiliate.

No one likes spam—especially Webmasters. If your affiliates attempt to build a second-tier program under them using spam tactics, you run the great risk of harming your product or service and the reputation of your company. One solution to this problem is to personally approve or disapprove any second-tier affiliate that your affiliates sign up. This is an optimal, but time-consuming approach to the problem.

Another approach is to deal with the offending marketers after the fact. AllAdvantage.com (www.alladvantage.com) has a multi-tier commission program. (This is not a two-tier affiliate program; it has multiple-levels. See Figure 5.14.) They also have a firm anti-spam policy. It states "If you spam, you are out—your account will be closed, your referrals will be lost, and you will be ineligible for a new account." They even post the spammers on their Web site.

Don't

DON'T harm the reputation of your product or service—or even your company. Don't allow your first-tier affiliates to expand their second tier by using spam tactics.

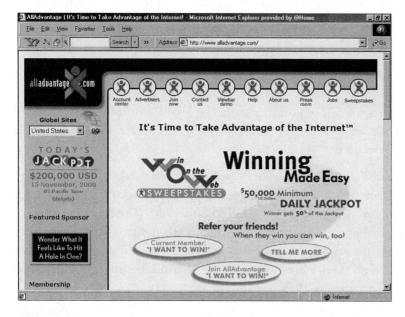

Figure 5.12
AllAdvantage.com is an example of a multi-tier commission program.

Another drawback to a two-tier program is communicating with the second-tier affiliates. Because they didn't directly sign up through your program, you can't capture their e-mail addresses. You need these to communicate and build a relationship with them.

Though a two-tier program can build your affiliate network quickly, the effort, time, and money that you spend dealing with the problems inherent in the system could be better spent rewarding existing affiliates

The Creatives

Affiliate programs are established to sell a merchant's product or service. So one of the most important objectives of your program is to encourage visitors to your affiliate's site to buy. After all, if you don't generate sales, all the work you do perfecting your product or service, establishing an affiliate payment model, choosing a program model, and creating a workable affiliate agreement is for naught.

And besides, if your product doesn't sell, you'll lose your affiliates.

So the upshot is that you have to be able to sell your offer. Do you know what it takes to encourage a visitor at your affiliate's site to take a specific action or encourage a sale? Put it this way. If you don't know how to sell your own offer you can't expect your affiliates to do it.

An affiliate program is only as strong as its weakest link. And that link in an affiliate program is the hyperlink from the creatives your affiliate places on its site that links to yours. The most important tools that you can give your affiliates are the creatives. These are the banners, buttons, pre-written text links, and pop-ups that they place on their Web sites. A successful affiliate program must provide a variety of these creative links.

At the very minimum, a good affiliate program should offer the following creative marketing materials to affiliates:

- Text Links
- Banner Ads
- Text/Banner Ads—Button Ads plus Text Commentary
- Ezine/E-mail Advertising Materials
- Storefronts/Mini-Sites
- Content

The Marketing Materials

Text links come first. You should supply affiliates with a half-dozen text links with marketing copy where the HTML is ready to cut and paste onto an affiliate's Web page. Here is an example of a ClubMom text link:

"ClubMom: Rewarding and Celebrating Moms - Every Day."

The words "Rewarding and Celebrating Moms - Every Day" are hyperlinked to the ClubMom Web site. The HTML code would look like this:

```
<TABLE width=400><TBODY><TR><TD>
<P><FONT face=Arial,Helvetica size=-1>ClubMom: <A
HREF="http://service.bfast.com/bfast/click?bfmid=26370742
➥&siteid=27415909&bfpage=click_here" TARGET="_top">Rewarding
➥and Celebrating Moms - Every Day</a><IMG
SRC="http://service.bfast.com/bfast/serve?bfmid=26370742
➥&siteid=27415909&bfpage=click_here" BORDER="0" WIDTH="1"
HEIGHT="1" NOSAVE ></FONT></P></TD></TR></TBODY></TABLE>
```

Next in importance are the graphic links. Keep them in mind when designing your banners and buttons.

First, according to Sandra Gassmann, President of Sage Marketing & Consulting (www.sage-marketing.com), the copy in the ads should coordinate with an affiliate's content. You may also group similar products into a large graphic called a storefront (see Figure 5.13).

Do

DO offer more than one type of graphic link to your affiliates. Develop four to six banners, buttons, or other graphic elements per offer.

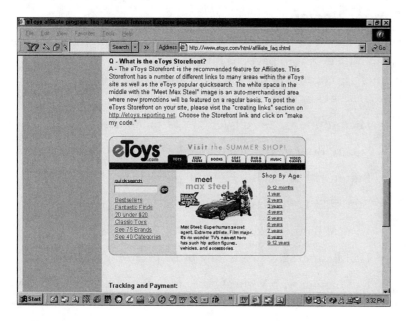

Figure 5.13
eToys offers its affiliates a complete storefront in a graphic.

Storefronts increase the credibility of the offer by presenting a selection of products in one place. Storefronts usually take up more real estate on an affiliate's Web site, but can be more effective than a simple banner ad (see Table 5.1).

Table 5.1 Which Links Attract the Most Click-Throughs	
Links to Specific Products	2.18%
General Text Links	1.80%
Storefront Links	1.43%
E-mail Links	1.31%
SearchBox Links	1.22%
Banner Links	1.12%

Source: eMarketer.com

According to Delcan Dunn, a good rule of thumb is to not offer more than 3–5 products in a storefront. Too many choices confuse the visitor.

Banner Design

Smaller than a storefront are banners. Like the storefront, they sit on an affiliate's Web page. As for sizes, the most standard sizes for banners, according to the Internet Advertising Bureau (www.iab.net), are

- Micro Button: 88 pixels long by 31 pixels high (88×31)

- Square Button: 125 pixels long by 125 pixels high (125×125)

- Button 1: 120 pixels long by 90 pixels high (120×90)

- Button 2: 120 pixels long by 60 pixels high (120×60)

- Vertical Banner: 120 pixels long by 240 pixels high (120×240)

- Half Banner: 234 pixels long by 60 pixels high (234×60)

- Full Banner with Vertical Navigation Bar: 392 pixels long by 72 pixels high (392×72)

- Full Banner: 468 pixels long by 60 pixels high (468×60)

Sandra Gassmann emphasizes the importance of the file size of the graphic. You should keep it as small as possible to allow for a fast download. Slowing the download time of an affiliate's site with intricate, fat graphics will not endear them to your program. The file size should be no larger than a few kilobytes (KB) for the small banners, no larger than 15KB for the largest banner, and 30KB for a storefront. A good rule of thumb is to keep most banners from 10–12KB.

Terry Dean, Webmaster for BizPromo.com (www.bizpromo.com), offers several techniques for banner ad design that have proven effective for marketing efforts:

- Use the words "Click Here" or "Enter" every time you design a banner. Tests have proven that these simple words can increase the click-through rate of a banner ad by 20%–30% without changing anything else in the banner.

- Animating your banners will increase click-through another 30%–40%. The key in using animation in your banner is keeping it small. The reason for this, of course, is the download time. If your animation file is too large, the viewer will not wait around to see it fully download. Try and keep your animated banner under 15KB. The way to do this is to keep your animation simple—maybe only one or two movements. Also decrease the number of colors in your graphic. According to Dean, a banner that may have been 15KB can often be decreased down to 3 or 4KB when you decrease the colors to 16 or 256 colors.

- Use an awesome, eye-catching headline in your banner. A pretty banner will not make buyers click through. You need a good headline to entice them to do that. According to Dean, a good technique to use is to keep the same headline on your banner ad that you have on your product page. When they click through the banner, they will come to see the same headline that sparked an interest in them in the first place.

- Use the word "FREE." It works when you use the word and then tell them exactly what they will be getting FREE (see Figure 5.16). Using the word "FREE" in virtually any headline will make your response rate increase dramatically. And

Don't

DON'T create graphical links that are so large they slow down the loading of your affiliate's site. Keep the image size small.

speaking of free, this is a good way to get consumers to use your product. Offering free trials, samples, or contests if they supply their e-mail address is a great way to get a potential customer to sell to in the future.

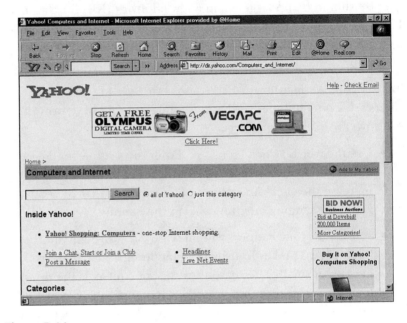

Figure 5.14
The VegaPC.com banner is an example of using the word "FREE" in their offer.

Do

DO join the banner Ad Discussion List (http://www.musictus.com/webmaster/bannerad.html). It focuses on strategies and results of advertising and pay-per-lead networks, banner exchange services, and commission based sales. The list encourages sharing of practical experiences between subscribers.

- Dean believes that a blue underlined text link will often increase your response rate. If you add a text link below your banners or in conjunction with a button ad, make sure the hyperlink is in blue (see Figure 5.17). When Internet users see blue underlined text, they know they are links. When you place your headline in this type of format, more people will realize that it is a link to another site. It will achieve a higher click-through rate.

The combination of a small banner button with some promotional text is an effective way to present an offer. Affiliates like this kind of hyperlink because the banner button can sit within the side bar of their Web page and not dominate it. Usually, to the right of the small banner button is text that describes the benefits of clicking on the banner button. The text is a link, the banner is a link, and by combining a visual with a short text description, affiliates can group a number of affiliate programs on a single Web Page. It is an effective method of offering more than one product on a page, without overwhelming the visitor or using a space-consuming storefront banner. Words explain what pictures can not and a picture tells a thousand words. Together, they make a potent advertising tool.

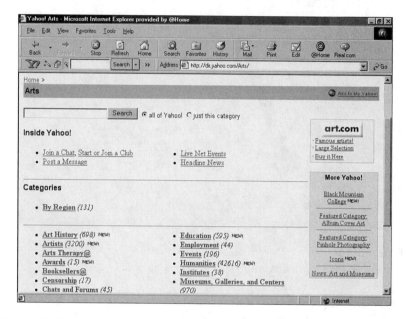

Figure 5.15
Yahoo! is an example of putting the hyperlink of Art.com's offer in blue.

- Another tip from Dean is that a blue border will give you a better response rate than any other color border for a banner. A detail this small may not seem like much but it does increase the clicks on your banner.

- It is often a good idea to use your company logo in the banner. Branding is important even if a viewer doesn't click on your banner. Placing your company logo on your banner helps produce a branding effect in people's minds. If you can't get a sale through your banner right then and there, you can at least build brand awareness on your affiliate sites.

Do

DO use your company logo in your graphical links. Branding is important even if a viewer doesn't click on your banner.

If you don't have the resources to do the creatives in-house, check out the services of BannerWorkz.com (www.bannerworkz.com) (see Figure 5.16), or you can look for a freelancer at places like elance (www.elance.com) and guru.com (www.guru.com).

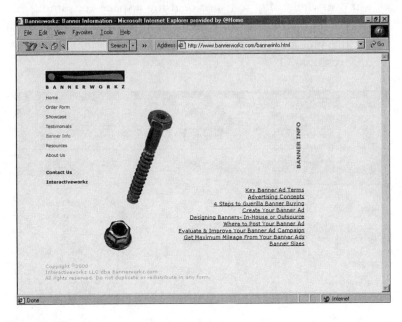

Figure 5.16
BannerWorkz will design and create banners for you.

One warning when you design your banners: Don't use cheap tricks to get people to click on your graphic. Never sacrifice your brand integrity for a cheap click. You're trying to build a relationship with a customer and your affiliate. Fake user interfaces are among the biggest offenders of those going after the cheap click. You've seen them—fake HTML or interactive-looking banners that don't work or operating systems warning boxes alerting you to a problem with your PC (see Figure 5.17). These types of banners degrade the credibility of your brand in the eyes of both consumers and your affiliates.

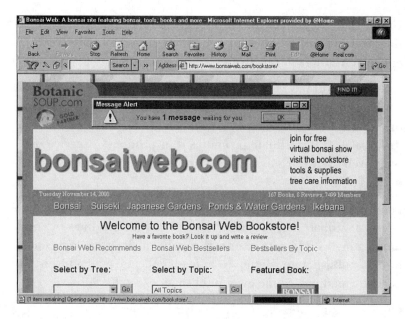

Figure 5.17
This is an example of trick banner that gives the impression that there is an e-mail message waiting for the user.

All in all, you have the responsibility of giving your affiliates the marketing tools to succeed by creating good sales and generating creatives, such as banner ads, endorsements/testimonials from affiliates, pictures of the product or service, and free reports.

Finally, remember that the graphics must give some indication to the viewer what type of products can be bought on the site. Appropriate linking increases sales.

Your text and graphic links should link to various pages, categories, or even individual products on your site. While linking to categories are okay, linking to individual products—when you can—is much more effective. For example, provide a cut-and-paste text link code that connects directly to one of your top-selling products instead of just to the main page of your Web site.

Endorsements and E-mail Copy

Graphic banners and text links are an important part of your creatives and how you present offers to potential customers. But make sure you don't assume that banner ads are the only way to go.

Don't

DON'T harm your offer or your reputation with cheap tricks that trick people into clicking on your banner links.

Do

DO ask for personal endorsements from the affiliate site encouraging their visitors to buy your product or service.

Graphic and text links are simple ways to link from affiliate sites to the products and services you sell, but there are other ways to entice consumers to buy from you.

One very good way is by asking affiliates for a written endorsement. Affiliates have a reputation and credibility with their site visitors—or else why do visitors come at all? You can use this credibility to make sales. If the affiliate promotes your product or service on their Web site, your sales—and your affiliate's commissions—will increase.

Finally, selling from an affiliate's Web site is not the only way to get sales. An affiliate can increase the sales of your products by communicating with his site visitors through e-mail. Many Web site owners publish a newsletter, or at least, collect e-mail addresses for periodic mailings. Some even publish an eZine for subscribers.

Opt-in e-mail is one of the most powerful tools of e-commerce trade. According to eMarketer.com (www.emarketer.com), on average, people receive 25 e-mails a day. They check their e-mail everyday, but they rarely go to a Web site everyday. A successful affiliate program rests on trust and credibility. Both of these can be built by your affiliates through the use of e-mail. If they write articles favorably recommending a product in their e-mails to their site visitors, sales will increase.

Why is e-mail marketing important? Studies have shown that people do not make a sale on their first viewing of an offer. It can take up to three or four exposures to an offer before a consumer makes a purchase. E-mail and eZine promotions to a qualified list follows up on the initial contact with repeated messages to buy. E-mail is the best means to conduct this kind of marketing, because the real power of e-mail comes in the endorsement in the e-mail from the affiliate. When an eZine or mailing list has been developed with a trust between the writer and the audience, the endorsement goes a long way to increase sales for you and commissions for your affiliate. It moves people from being strangers to being introduced to you and your products personally by your affiliate. The unfamiliar is replaced by a recommendation from someone they trust.

By providing pre-written marketing copy to your affiliates that they can place in their electronic communications with their site visitors, you can both help your affiliate increase his revenue and add to your sales. Also, be sure to provide your affiliates with the simple browser redirect code for marketing via e-mail.

Storefronts and mini-sites are great tools to offer to your affiliates that are not quite as savvy when it comes to Web design. Basically, both of these affiliate links are chunks of HTML that create a ready-made page for the affiliate. To achieve optimal performance, these affiliate links should be tweaked to fit the look and feel of the affiliate's site.

And of course, content is a fantastic creative marketing material for affiliates. It's easier for content and community sites to produce this sort of creative, but even if you do not have an editorial team in-house, you should produce some content for your affiliates. Affiliate content is most common in the form of an article that is integrated with affiliate links. For instance, a drugstore site might offer an article during allergy season on how to alleviate allergy conditions. This article would feature suggested products with direct product links.

Remember that affiliate programs and affiliate selling are not about technology—they're about marketing. That is why your creative materials are of upmost importance in creating a successful affiliate program. Scott Horst, Vice President of Marketing for Commission Junction, says "It is not enough to simply stick banner ads on a site and expect huge gains. It is about placement, context, marketing strategy and working together for optimal success."

Step Three—Getting the Word Out

Chapter Summary

Once you have your program model and your plan, your next step is to get the word out to potential affiliates about your program. Your task is to first craft a message that will get potential affiliates to sit up and take notice. Your message should clearly state the benefits of your program and how it differs from your competitors. Inform them how they can make money but provide a realistic revenue potential—even provide testimonials from existing affiliates if you have a program already in place. Show potential affiliates that you offer a fair, credible, and quality program.

Build your list of potential affiliates by using search engines, affiliate solution providers, and affiliate marketing directories. Consider whether you will ship internationally and state that to attract international affiliates from around the Web. In addition to the directories, use the affiliate announcement services available and consider an affiliate management consult to help with your program promotion. Don't ignore the power of PR to promote your program. Well-timed and targeted press releases will help promote your program with little cost.

Looking at the millions of Web sites that are potential candidates for your affiliate program and considering how to recruit them into your program can be discouraging. And then there's the fact that you must compete with thousands of affiliate programs that are already in existence. Building your affiliate base may seem like an impossible task, but like most things in life, a long journey starts with just the first step, and in the case of recruiting affiliates—several steps.

Building an affiliate network relies a lot on building momentum. In the case of small to moderate size businesses, image is everything. A small to moderate size business on the Net can gain more than an increased customer base with an affiliate program.

One result of an established affiliate program is the name recognition it supplies. Once a business name begins to appear on high-profile sites around the Net, users may begin to perceive the company as something bigger and more established than it really is. This image building has a multiplying effect that helps you recruit even more qualified affiliate sites. If you are a large business with an image of major standing on the Net, an affiliate program is a way to maintain that standing in the eyes of those who use the Internet.

But before you set out on your recruiting program, the first step is to craft the message that you will be e-mailing to potential affiliates. That is to say, why should a Web site join your affiliate program in the first place?

Step One—Crafting Your Message

When presenting your program to potential affiliates, your message should include the following value propositions:

- State the benefits of your program clearly and without hype.

- State clearly that you sell a quality product or service.

- State that your offer will fit well with the audience of their site.

- Show how your program compares with your competition.

- Inform them of your method of tracking their sales and earnings—how it's done and who will do it.

- State that by affiliating with you, their site will gain added credibility.

The most obvious benefit of your program to a potential affiliate is the ability for them to make money by simply referring their site visitors to your product or service (see Figure 6.1). Your message must be very clear—they will earn a specific commission or referral fee for each action their visitor takes. So at the very top of your message is the ability to make money.

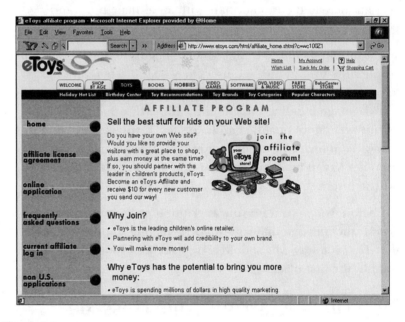

Figure 6.1
eToys has a good example of a one-page, easy-to-understand, direct message about their affiliate program.

Keep in mind that most people will see through hype, so don't promise that they will make thousands of dollars a day and be able to retire when they're 30. Provide a realistic revenue potential— and if you have a program already in place—provide testimonials from successful affiliates who have actually achieved the revenue numbers you say a hard working affiliate can earn.

Your next value proposition should state clearly that you sell a quality product or service within a quality program. A quality product or service does not include get rich quick schemes or multi-level marketing (MLM) programs. It also means that you have a program that will stand behind what you sell.

Having affiliate programs usually means that affiliates are selling the same products that you sell on your own Web site. That's the nature of the beast. But this is changing. Affiliate programs are in their infancy, and more and more variations on the program are appearing everyday. One example is the storefront and boutique affiliate programs like vstore, where the affiliate site can build a complete online store that looks like their own. Program, like vstore do not compete with their affiliate since they don't have a Web site that they sell from. Another example is giving affiliates exclusive product offers that you do not sell to shoppers that visit your site. If you can tell potential affiliates that you will, in some way, not compete with them, that will strengthen your message considerably.

The next element of your message should explain that your offering fits well on their site and would be of interest to a potential affiliate's Web site visitor. This in-context approach can show potential affiliates that your offering will add a valuable service to their site that will enhance the experience of current visitors to their site.

Show how your program compares with your competition. The more beneficial differences your program offers an affiliate, the more likely it will join your network. Summarize your competitor's benefits and show why your program is the best choice.

Another important element in your message is to tell potential affiliates how you track visitors and sales and the reports available to them. You want to make it clear that you have a program in place that records every resulting sale or referral and that the sale is credited to your affiliate member. In addition, if you offer a two-tier program, explain that the affiliate can earn a commission for each sale that results from the referral of an affiliate site that they recruit for you.

Do

DO craft a clear and concise message to use when promoting your program to affiliates. Don't hype your program with unrealistic revenue projections for the affiliate or promises of quitting their day jobs.

Do

DO keep your program competitive by watching for changes in your competitor's program. Determine the reason for his or her changes and how you can respond. Affiliates do shop around.

Finally, impress upon the potential affiliate in your message that by affiliating with your business they can gain added credibility for their site. If your program recruits quality affiliates and doesn't take the tack of building an affiliate network by piling them high and stacking them deep, you can tell potential candidates that they belong to an exclusive club, and that their site visitors will see this.

The key to a good message is telling a credible story. Give affiliates your qualifications as a business and explain the quality of your offering. Above all, watch the tone of your message. Stay away from any technical jargon—keep it simple, credible, and to the point.

Do

DO consider joining LinkShare's B2B affiliate network. If your company sells to the business community, you can create an affiliate program with sites that cater to businesses. LinkShare (www.b2blinkshare.com) has created an affiliate management program for companies that want to create and manage a B2B affiliate network (see Figure 6.2).

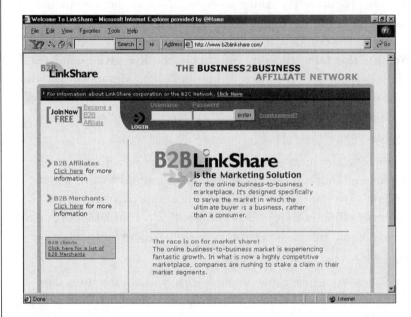

Figure 6.2
LinkShare offers an affiliate management program for companies that have a B2B affiliate network.

Also, keep in mind that potential affiliates can be generated in every part of your specific industry. Affiliates, while generally created in the business-to-consumer channel (B2C), may also be formed in the business-to-business (B2B) and consumer-to-consumer (C2C) channels.

Step Two—Building Your List

There are three prime ways to recruit affiliates. The first is to use the affiliate solution providers, the second is to register with the affiliate directories, and the third is to do it yourself.

But before you launch your affiliate recruitment program, there are some key points to remember. When looking at building your list of affiliate candidates, focus on three types of sites.

- Sites with their own domain name

- Sites that draw high traffic

- Sites that draw consistent or targeted traffic

Sites with their own domain name are far preferable to the free Web pages, such as Yahoo! GeoCities Pages That Pay (geocities. yahoo.com/home) and Lycos Tripod Commission Central (www.tripod.lycos.com). With the proliferation of low-cost domain registrars, a domain can be purchased for less than $20 per year. If a Webmaster is not serious enough to have his own domain, don't count on him to produce results for your program.

If your business has an established name on the Net and you are offering a product or service that appeals to a desirable demographic, you could have a decent chance of attracting Web sites with high traffic to your affiliate program. These are the Top 500 sites listed in Media Metrix (see Figure 6.3).

Unlike the high -traffic site that may draw one-time visitors, some sites draw a consistent number of repeat visitors because they fill a special or targeted need for the visitor. These are good potential candidates for your network for two reasons. First, they give the affiliate Web site a chance to continuously promote your offer to the same visitors and make a sale. And second, you can choose sites that can offer your product or service in-context, thus making a sale more possible.

Start with a list of 100 potential sites (10 dream affiliates and 90 likely to join your program) that you would like to form a profitable relationship with. Contact them, preferably by phone, but use e-mail if you can't find a phone number, and create a win-win strategy with them. Rather than aiming for tens of thousands of

Who Is Media Metrix?

Media Metrix measures traffic counts on all the Web sites and digital media properties on the Net. It regularly publishes the names of the Top 50 sites in the United States, the Global Top 50, and the Media Metrix Top 500 Web sites.

affiliates, which may look good on paper, focus on establishing business partnerships with highly targeted, segmented sites. After all, an affiliate is not just a place to advertise your business, but a business partner.

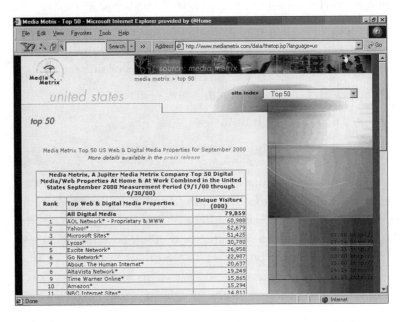

Figure 6.3
MediaMetrix tracks the top traffic-generating sites on the Web.

Keep in mind that while finding affiliate partners isn't as impossible as it seems, it does require an incredible amount of work.

Finding Affiliates

To find affiliates, start with your own site. You can promote your program to your current customer and site visitors who just may a have Web site that would fit with your program. The words "Join our Affiliate Program"—are being seen more and more on Web sites today. At the very least, you should do the same for your company's Web site. You should post your invitation to join your affiliate program on your home page and every navigational bar elsewhere on your site. This simple act alone can be a valuable medium for reaching Webmasters.

Do

DO place links on your Web site that say "Join Our Affiliate Program" or "Become a Partner" that directs visitors to your affiliate information page or pages. It's a free promotion strategy that works in recruiting affiliates.

And don't stop there. Plug your program in your e-mail signature, company newsletter, printed collateral, and even your invoices, e-mail signature, business cards, voice mail, and your signature in online forums and discussion lists.

Your next step is to use the search engines and Web directories to find potential candidates. How? By thinking like your customer. Find out where your customers like to go and you'll find your best affiliates. Here's how.

The bane of most search engines on the Net is that they return hundreds, even thousands of results that may have little to do with what you are specifically looking for. For example, search for the latest Madonna CD, type in the word Madonna, and a search engine will return a list of sites about Madonna, Madonna fan clubs, Madonna fashion, Madonna posters—and of course, the names of Madonna CDs. You might get lucky and even see a site in the listing where you can actually buy the Madonna CD you are looking for.

Do

DO link back to your affiliates from your site. Whereas this might not be possible for merchants with a large number of affiliates, you might consider doing it for some of your best affiliates. Linking them from your site will direct additional traffic to their site, and is a nice way to show your best affiliates how you support them. Amazon does this from their site (see Figure 6.4).

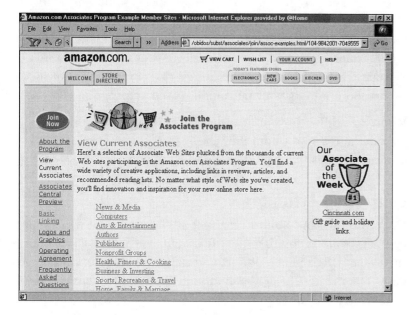

Figure 6.4
Amazon links to its affiliates from its site.

You can use this inefficiency of the search engines to find sites that would be good candidates for selling your particular product or service. Let's take the Madonna CD example. Suppose you had an online store that sells CDs—Madonna CDs included. And suppose you wanted to recruit affiliate sites to sell your CDs. You can use the search results to target potential affiliate sites that could sell Madonna music from their site to their "Material Girl" visitors.

If you enter the name of a Madonna CD in the search engines and get the same results as before, you have a ready-made list of affiliate site candidates. Some good search engines to use for this recruiting strategy are Goto.com (`www.goto.com`), DirectHit.com (`www.directhit.com`), and Google.com (`www.google.com`). You can use this strategy for any key words that you have placed on the pages of your own Web site. The sites that index well for your own keywords are the sites you want to target.

Another trick is to use AltaVista.com (`www.altavista.com`) to find targeted affiliate sites. Let's say you're selling pet supplies and are looking for sites that target pet owners. Spend some time thinking about who your competitors are in your market space. Let's say it's Petsmart.com (`www.petsmart.com`). In the AltaVista search bar, type **link:petsmart.com**. You'll get a list of hundreds of sites that link to Petsmart.com. From there, you can quickly compile a list of sites to e-mail about joining your pet supplies affiliate program.

If you are adding to your affiliate program, simply visit your best affiliates and see to whom they are linking. Sometimes they link to other great sites that would be a perfect match for your program.

Contacting Affiliates

Once you find and build your list of affiliate candidates, it's time to contact them. As you first identify potential affiliates, enter their site name, URL, e-mail, phone, and a short description into a database. Then write a brief e-mail to send to each site. This is how ClubMom writes its:

> "I just reviewed [their site name], and I really liked [write a couple of complimentary sentences about their site]. You've done a great job."

Do

DO use the affiliate Webrings to find affiliates. Go to Yahoo's Webring directory (`dir.webring.yahoo.com/rw`), type in the words **affiliate program**, and a list of Webrings will appear. All the sites in these Webrings are participating in or discussing affiliate program marketing.

Then attach to the e-mail a short version of the message you crafted in Step One. Make sure you personalize the e-mail with a name if you can, and if not, with the name of the Web site. Start with 100 e-mails at first, and then add about 50–100 per month. If possible, make a phone call to all the potential affiliates—this is far more effective than sending an e-mail. In order to determine the most desirable sites, rank them according to the 3 T's (Top Sites for High Traffic, Targeted Traffic from Search Engines, and Top Level Domains (TLDs) for Niche Traffic) (see Table 6.1).

Table 6.1

The 3 T's of Affiliate Recruitment	
Top Sites for High Traffic	Media Metrix Top 500 sites
Targeted Traffic from Search Engines	Sites that place at the top in search engines for your keywords
TLDs for Niche Traffic	Content and community sites with a good domain name

Step Three—Registering with Directories

Once you've done your best to hand pick and contact your best affiliate candidates, it's time to turn to the affiliate directories. They have already spent the time, effort, and advertising dollars to attract Web sites interested in joining an affiliate program to their sites. These visitors can be yours if you list your program with these directories.

The affiliate directories are like specialized Yahoo!s. There are 20 or so main directories and as many smaller directories to register with. They consist of two types:

- Affiliate Network Directories—or Affiliate Solution Providers

- Affiliate Marketing Directories

There is a complete list of these directories in Appendix C, "Affiliate Directories."

Affiliate Solution Providers

The first type of affiliate directory is that of the affiliate network or affiliate solution provider. These networks actually administer your program and provide the tracking and reporting features you and your affiliates need. Your company pays this middleman a fee to handle the tracking, sign-up, and payments for each referral or sale of your affiliates. The advantage of contracting with one of these network directories is that they invite Web sites to visit their site and view the stable of merchants with affiliate programs in their own network and allow them to join (see Figure 6.5).

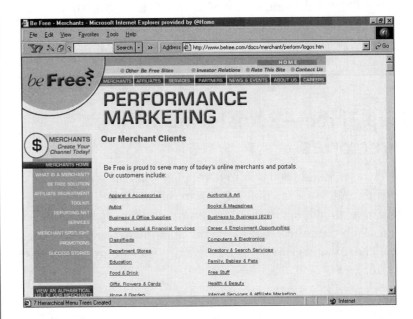

Figure 6.5
Be Free lists all the merchants whose affiliate programs they manage.

If you contract with one of these solution providers, they will list and even announce your program to their network of Web sites. Using this shotgun approach, your company can recruit and sign up volumes of affiliates a week! The disadvantage is twofold. First you have to contract with a solution provider, and some will not let you join another solution provider's program as long as you are with theirs. This can present a problem if you want to have access to more than the potential affiliates the solution provider can offer, or if you want to run two programs side by side to see which one gives the better results, offers the better tracking and reporting program, or even which program your affiliates prefer to work with.

The shotgun approach of these solution providers also can be a disadvantage. You will receive hundreds, even thousands of sign-ups a week. Even though some of these programs have an auto-approval feature, you do have the option of turning that feature off and personally approving each request for sign-up. But let's be realistic. If you plan to personally approve each request in order to keep your program targeted to the right affiliates from the hundreds you may receive each day, you had better have the staff and resources to do it. As you can see, this could be quite time consuming.

If you use a solution provider, you have two choices. Either build your program on quantity, with most of your network performing below average, or shoot for quality and hand-pick your affiliates from the pool of candidates that the shotgun approach will produce. With some of the affiliate solution providers, you can pay a fee to have them manually review the applications to your program.

The biggest and most popular affiliate solution providers are Be Free (www.befree.com), Commission Junction (www.cj.com), and Linkshare (www.linkshare.com). You can find others in Appendix C. These and other solution providers are reviewed in Chapter 9, "Step Six—Tracking Your Affiliate Program," to show how each of their programs work.

If you decide to contract with one of these solution providers—and even if you don't—your next step is to register with the dozens of affiliate directories dedicated to affiliate marketing. Whether you submit your site yourself or use a submission service, be sure to check back periodically. Over time, categories expand and change, and you want to make sure your program is listed in the proper category so it can be found.

Because of the popularity of affiliate marketing, new affiliate marketing directories pop up almost every day (see Appendix C). The good news is that submitting your program is free. There is nothing to join. The key directories to start your registration process with are Associate-it.com (www.associate-it.com) (see Figure 6.6), AssociatePrograms.com (www.associateprograms.com), CashPile (www.cashpile.com), and Refer-it.com (www.refer-it.com).

Figure 6.6
Associate-it is one of the top affiliate marketing directories to register your program with.

Another very good directory to list your program with is ReveNews (www.revenews.com). Besides being a directory of affiliate programs, ReveNews (see Figure 6.7) also hosts a series of discussion lists for affiliates that you could use to find potential recruits for your program. You can also get the latest news on who's doing what in affiliate marketing—especially about your competitors. Another directory not be overlooked is MakeMoneyNow.com (www.makemoneynow.com).

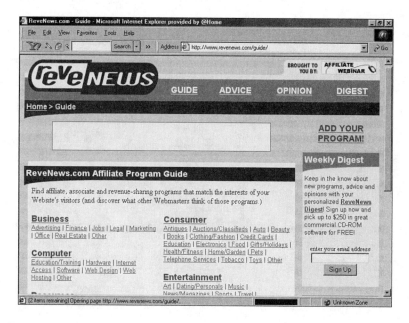

Figure 6.7
ReveNews hosts a series of discussion list for affiliates that you could use to find potential recruits for your program.

The number of affiliate marketing directories has grown to such an extent that there are now directories specializing in specific market niches. For example Woo Doggy! (www.WooDoggy.com) lists affiliate programs that offer free content. If you offer a two-tier affiliate program, make sure you register with the 2-Tier Affiliate Program Directory (www.2-tier.com) (see Figure 6.8).

Keep in mind that although there is no charge to be listed in these affiliate marketing directories, you are not automatically listed when you submit your request. The directory's editor reviews just about all the affiliate programs submitted to the directory. He or she makes the final decision on whether to list your program.

How to Get Listed

You should try to be listed on as many of the affiliate marketing directories as possible. But with the increased popularity of these directories, many of them are becoming quite selective about whom they choose to list on their site. As a result, it's very important that you submit and present your program in the correct manner.

Do

DO use AffiliatePromote (www.affiliatepromote.com). Its site contains a comprehensive listing of affiliate program directories and other resources to help you promote your affiliate program. Check out the resources and directories there to announce your program to the affiliate directories.

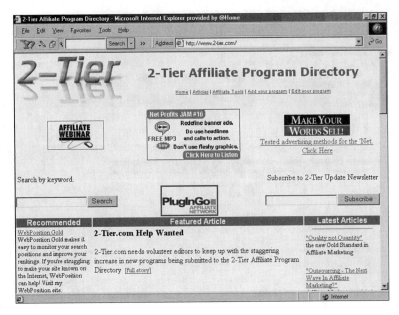

Figure 6.8
Register with the 2-Tier Affiliate Program Directory if you offer a two-tier program.

Neil Durrant, founder of Affiliate-Announce (www.affiliate-announce.com), the original affiliate directory submission service, suggests how to increase your chances of getting listed in these directories. Although each directory will have its own admission policies, most will not accept sites that offer adult content (pornography), multilevel marketing schemes (MLM), or any program paying commissions on more than 2-tiers or levels. A few even restrict gambling sites.

Durrant notes that a lower priority is often placed on most pay-per-click programs. Some directories will still accept your pay-per-click program listing, but be prepared for a higher rejection rate than for a pay-per-lead or pay-per-sale program. It is wise to follow their submission process exactly. With new affiliate programs being created every day, the editors are very busy reviewing submission after submission, and if you have ignored the submission policies, the chances of your request being filled could be nil.

Durrant offers six tips to increase your chances of being listed.

- **Make sure your program is ready**—Make sure you have all the aspects of your program established and ready to go. This means your sign-up form is working, your tracking and reporting system is in place, and your affiliate agreement is finished and ready to be read by potential affiliates.

- **Create an Affiliate Information Page or Pages**—Both the directories and potential affiliates need to know exactly what your program offers. Create a page or pages where they can find out what kind of program you have, how they get paid, and how you will help them promote your product or service (see Figure 6.9). Also, even if you've signed up with one of the affiliate program solution providers who provide a co-branded sign-up page on their site, this is not enough. You still need to have an affiliate entry page that details your program and the benefits to affiliate partners.

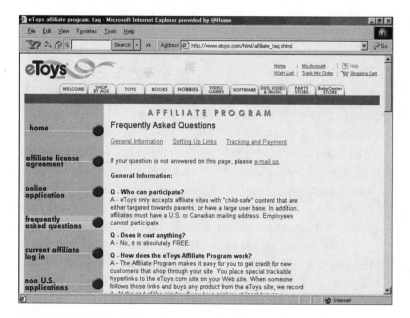

Figure 6.9
eToys has a good example of a set of Frequently Asked Questions that clarify their program for new affiliates.

Your affiliate information page should include a description of your product/service, your commission and payment terms and the conditions of payment, a link to your home page, and your privacy policy.

- **Do Your Homework**—Review the directories before you submit. Get a feel for how they list programs. All provide a drill-down directory of category selection and some also offer a keyword search. Find the category that best suits your program and, if available, submit to that category on that category page. A good trick is to think like affiliates. How would they search for a product or service to sell on their site like yours? You'll notice that headings can have more than one meaning so be careful with your choice of categories. Just because you're in e-commerce, make sure that you are selling e-commerce services. If you're selling a product or service to the consumer, a shopping category would be more appropriate.

  Also, be careful about entering your program in a directory that also lists two-tier programs. If you have a two-tier program, list your program under the products you sell—not the way you plan to pay affiliates. Register your two-tier program at a two-tier directory, like the 2-Tier Affiliate Program Directory. Why? One of the most cost-effective ways of adding affiliates to your team is to set up a multi-tier affiliate program and let affiliates recruit for you.

- **Prepare Your Submission Data**—Take time to plan out the information you want to submit. If you are asked for your URL, and if your only option is to provide one address, submit one of your affiliate's information pages. You will be asked for a program description. Often you are limited to just 255 words, so you need to get your message across accurately and briefly. At the very least, make sure to mention the product or service that you are selling, the commission or referral fee you will be paying, and any unique or competitive features of your program. And this is important—don't hype! Affiliates are not dumb. Neither are the directories. Don't make wild, unsubstantiated promises to affiliates. Do that and you seriously risk having your listing denied.

  You may also be asked for a list of keywords or phrases. Again, think about how potential affiliates will search for programs like yours. Choose the keywords or phrases that they might use.

- **Don't Play Tricks**—An editor, not a computer, reviews all submissions. What may work with the Internet search engines will not work here. So don't bend the rules. The editor will catch you and refuse your submission. Don't name your program "aaa1music" in an attempt to get top billing in the directory. Spend your creative energies offering a great program the directories will love and promote for you.

- **Submit Your Data**—This is where the rubber meets the road. After your data is prepared, you're ready to start submitting. Check your list of directories you are going to submit to and read over each of their submission polices carefully. Follow them to the tee. Cut and paste your data from a saved file in Notepad when filling out their submission form. This will save you a lot of time when submitting to multiple directories.

Keep these pointers in mind, and your chances of being accepted for listing in the affiliate marketing directories will rise accordingly.

International Directories

The first W inthe WWW stands for World. That means your program can and should have a world-wide presence and be marketed to potential affiliates all around the Web. Whether your business is U.S.-based or overseas, affiliate marketing can work for you. Many foreign countries are adding affiliate programs to their marketing agenda.

The first country, outside of the United States, to embrace affiliate marketing was the United Kingdom (UK). There are at least six different affiliate networks directories available to submit to, not to mention the international expansion of several existing U.S. networks. TradeDoubler (see Figure 6.10) (www.tradedoubler.com) is a UK directory that also operates throughout Sweden, Norway, Finland, Denmark, Germany, France, and Spain. They claim to be the leading European provider of performance-based marketing solutions and affiliate programs.

Do

DO register you affiliate program in international affiliate directories if your company sells internationally. This will expand your network even further.

Figure 6.10
TradeDoubler is a UK directory that covers most of Europe.

Another UK directory, ,ukaffiliates.com (www.ukaffiliates.com), has opened recently along with a similar directory called MagicButton.Net (www.MagicButton.net), ,which currently operates out of London, with designs on Scandinavia, Spain, France, and Germany.

Finally, the U.S.-based networks have established a presence abroad. Commission Junction now has offices in Amsterdam, Oslo, Hong Kong, and London to serve both non-U.S. affiliates and U.S. merchants with affiliate programs. CJ now offers its site in multiple languages, while making payments to affiliates in their own local currencies. Be Free is also playing a role in the international arena. Be Free has opened offices in Paris and the U.K., and has enticed several European merchants into joining its network.

Affiliate Program Announcement Services

If you're thinking that recruiting affiliates one by one and evaluating and submitting to affiliate directories seems like an incredible expenditure of time, you're exactly right. Setting up and running a successful affiliate program is hard work. But there is some help on the recruiting side. You can spend weeks tracking down affiliate directories and submitting to them one by one—or you can use one of the affiliate announcement services. One of the first and largest is Affiliate-Announce (`www.affiliate-announce.com`) (see Figure 6.11). For a small fee it will ensure all your directory submissions are completed promptly and professionally while you concentrate on looking after your affiliates and building your business.

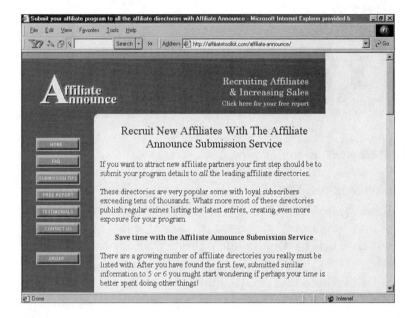

Figure 6.11
For a small fee, Affiliate-Announce will ensure all your directory submissions are completed promptly and professionally.

Affiliate-Announce will submit your program to over 40 of the leading affiliate directories quickly and painlessly. This will save you hours finding the directories, checking their individual submission policies, and processing their online forms. In a little more than the time it takes to submit your affiliate program to any one of the directories, Affiliate-Announce collects the same information for submission to about four-dozen sites. A real human manually submits each listing for only $79. A similar service is Affiliate Broadcast (`www.affiliatebroadcast.com`). For $59 they will submit your program to over 30 affiliate directories (see Figure 6.12).

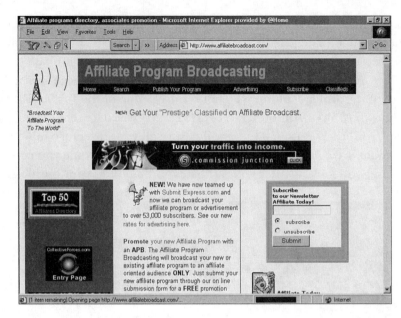

Figure 6.12
Affiliate Broadcast will submit you program to over 30 affiliate directories.

Although not affiliate directories, two other sites should be considered to announce your program. Marketing-Seek.com (`www.marketing-seek.com/articles/submit.shtml`) lets you submit a written article by you to their Web site to promote your affiliate program. Your name, e-mail address, URL, and photograph are listed with your submission. A similar site is the ConnectionTeam.com (`www.connectionteam.com/submit.html`). By submitting your original content and adding your name to the article, you can earn name recognition and traffic (see Figure 6.13).

Step Three—Newsletters, Discussion Groups, Mailing Lists, and Other Promotional Strategies

Directories aren't the only way to get the word out about your program. Another strategy for locating potential candidates is using the discussion groups, eZines (electronic magazines), and e-mail discussion lists.

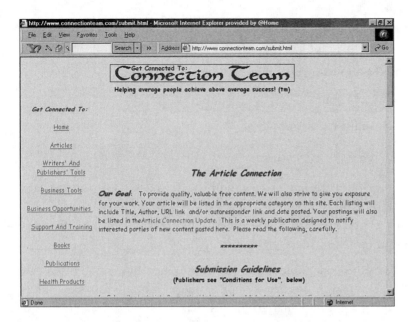

Figure 6.13
You can gain recognition for your program by submitting articles to ConnectionTeam.com.

According to Internet Marketing Center's Corey Rudl, "Newsgroups are one of the largest, untapped online resources. Hundreds of thousands of people read newsgroups on a daily basis, and tens of thousands of people participate in them daily." First go to Deja.com (`www.deja.com/usenet`), type in the words **affiliate program**, and view the list of discussions. You will find that many affiliates hang out on these discussion boards that you may want to recruit for your program. Be warned that newsgroups are not the place for posting blatant advertising. Abusing your newsgroup audience with blatant advertising will result in minimal and even negative responses that could harm both your program and your company's reputation.

Done right and as a member of your niche-specific group, you can post regularly to gain credibility within the community. You can ask questions to obtain affiliate marketing feedback from group participants and offer your site resources and affiliate program when they apply. Most discussion groups allow you to attach a signature to your posts. If not, include your name, title, e-mail address, and your program URL in the body of the message. By posting to the

What's an eZine?
eZine is short for electronic magazine. Some eZines are simply electronic versions of existing print magazines, whereas others exist only in their digital format.

discussion groups and including your signature, you can enhance the visibility and the credibility of your affiliate program.

The best newsgroups where affiliates hang out are

- alt.business
- alt.business.multi-level
- alt.html

Many of the affiliate program directories have their own message boards with varying levels of activity. Visit `www.affiliatemanager.net/boards.htm` for a list of the affiliate program directory message boards.

You can use the same approach with eZines and e-mail discussion lists. Discussion lists are groups of people who discuss a common topic by sending e-mail to the list that is then sent to all others on the list. Search for eZines and discussion lists that cover affiliate programs at Listz.com (`www.listz.com`) (see Figure 6.14). Another good place to search for affiliate-related mailing lists is at Yahoo! Groups (`www.yahoogroups.com`) (see Table 6.2).

Figure 6.14
You can find affiliate discussion list at Listz.

Table 6.2

Affiliate Related Discussion Lists on Yahoo! Groups
Affiliate Programs
Affiliate Programs for Newbies
Affiliate Programs for Webmasters_New Ezine

A good strategy to follow before you post to a newsgroup or discussion list is to lurk for a while. Get the feel of the list. See what they are discussing and what problems they have. Then join the discussion looking for ways to announce your program in a way that solves one of the list member's problems or answers a question.

Affiliate newsletters are another good source for promoting your program. AssociatePrograms.com has a very good newsletter that goes out to affiliates and to get a positive mention there will help you recruit affiliates. Cashpile also has a newsletter and it is also offered in an HTML format. Visit `www.affiliatemanager.net/newsletters.htm` for a list of affiliate newsletters.

Another useful, yet underused technique for recruiting affiliates is to trade for them.

It works like this. Find another merchant with a non-competitive product or service to sell and throw in a short endorsement for his or her program in your newsletter to your affiliates. The other merchant does the same. This is a free and effective way to grab some quality affiliates. The affiliates acquired through newsletter plugs are likely to be active, because they made the effort to read an affiliate newsletter. Another co-marketing idea is to trade affiliate lists. Send an e-mail blast to your respective affiliates with a message dedicated to promoting another merchant's program.

Step Four—Contracting Out Your Recruiting

If you don't have the time or resources to create a team dedicated to promoting your affiliate program, you might want to look at contracting out the recruiting job to an outside agency. There are several to choose from.

Don't

DON'T post blatant advertising or promotional messages on newsgroups. This would be considered spam and could damage both your product or service's credibility and your company's reputation.

Start with AffiliatePeople.com (www.affiliatepeople.com/) (see Figure 6.15). If you want to advertise your affiliate program both online and off line, they can create a comprehensive media-placement campaign. They also can help your company obtain placement in affiliate directories, provide ongoing directory maintenance, and find and sign-up high-performing affiliates targeted for your company. There are several other companies that do the same (see Table 6.3).

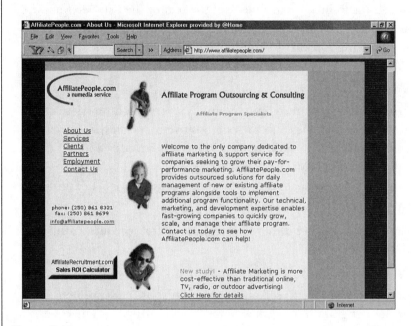

Figure 6.15
AffiliatePeople.com can help advertise your affiliate program both online and off line.

Table 6.3

Affiliate Recruiting and Management Agencies	
Affiliate Performance	www.affiliateperformance.com
Alliance Builder	www.alliancebuilder.com
Carat Interactive	www.carat-na.com
E-Base Interactive Inc.	www.ebaseinc.com
eComm Works	www.ecomworks.com
FlightPath Marketing	www.flightpathllc.com

Table 6.3   (continued)

Affiliate Recruiting and Management Agencies	
greater than one inc.	`www.greaterthanone.com`
i-traffic	`www.i-traffic.com`
LinkProfits	`www.linkprofits.com`
Mass-Transit Interactive	`www.mass-transit.com`
SK Consulting	`www.skconsulting.com`
TargetMarket Interactive	`www.tmi-la.com`
Vizium	`www.vizium.com`

Outsourcing companies outside of the United States include AffiliateMarketing.co.uk (`www.affiliatemarketing.co.uk/consulting.htm`), DVisions Limited (`www.dvisions.co.uk`), simplesiteUK (`www.simplesiteuk.com`), as well as ukaffiliates.com (`www.ukaffiliates.com`). These companies are all located in the United Kingdom.

Consider this suggestion before signing a contract with one of these services. If you are going to pay another organization to recruit affiliates for you, try to tie its payments to results. Pay the affiliate recruiting service not on how many affiliate sites they sign up, but on how many of them place your links on their pages. For example, tie the recruiting service's compensation to an action, such as paying the service only if and when a recruited affiliate makes one or two sales, or when a certain number of click-throughs are performed from an affiliate's site. This way you should be able to get a higher quality of affiliates for your program. It may cost you more than just paying for quantity, but it can be worth it for the quality of affiliates you get. For the most up-to-date list of companies for contracting out your program, visit `www.affiliatemanager.net/outsource.htm`.

Step Five—Using PR and Advertising

Up to now, you've seen ways of promoting your program that are free or of little cost. But if you have money to spend, you can advertise your program on the affiliate program directories, affiliate marketing sites, in eZines, and sponsoring newsletters. The

Do

DO try to get a pay-for-performance agreement when contracting out to an affiliate recruitment service. Make their payment rely on not how many affiliates they sign up, but on how many of them place your links on their pages.

directories will sell banner ads to merchants to advertise their programs. Associate-it.com, AssociatePrograms.com, CashPile, and Refer-it.com sell a variety of advertising packages on their sites as well as e-mail blasts and newsletter spots.

Another source for paid advertising to attract affiliates are the free Web page or homesteading sites like Yahoo! GeoCities Pages That Pay (`geocities.yahoo.com/home`) and Lycos Tripod Commission Central (`www.tripod.lycos.com`) (see Figure 6.16). While these services will give you access to millions of Web site owners in their network for a fee, the kinds of affiliates that you may recruit can fall far below the quality of affiliates you need to make your program a success.

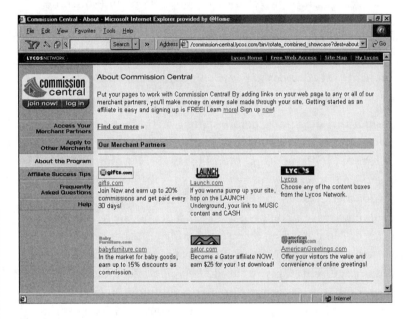

Figure 6.16
Lycos' Commission Central will present your affiliate program to the hundreds of thousands of Web sites they host for a fee.

Do

DO promote your affiliate contest or sweepstakes free on CashPile's Merchant Special Promotions Page (www.cashpile.com/active/announce.cfm). Simply fill out a short form and submit your special promotion to be considered for display.

Another promotion strategy that has a cost—but one less than advertising—is Public Relations, especially press releases. Done right, you can get thousands of dollars worth of free advertising for the cost of sending out the right kind of press release to the right media outlets. The cost can be a little as a hundred dollars to send the release over the news wires, and some are even free (see Table 6.4).

Table 6.4

PR News Services on the Net	
PRWeb www.prWeb.com	Free press release distribution service that distributes your news through the Web and e-mail.
Internet News Bureau www.newsbureau.com	Send your release to 4,500 journalists. Single releases are $250 each.
IMEDIAFAX www.imediafax.com/	An Internet-to-media fax news distribution service that allows you to customize your own target lists and fax press releases anywhere in the world 24 hours a day for 25 cents a page.
BusinessWire www.bizwire.com	Distributes your news with photos and graphics for as little as $300.

The secret to PR is relevance. If you want your press release to be picked up by the media that's announcing your new affiliate programs or any new developments that take place, like how many affiliates you have, how successful they are, or how fast your program is growing, you must make it timely and relevant. Announcing just another affiliate program these days is no news at all. But if you can show that your program is different in some way, then you have a chance of seeing it promoted both online and off line, which can attract potential candidates to your program.

Good PR requires cultivating a relationship with the press. Cry wolf too many times with releases that are not relevant or deemed important, and when you do have a good story to tell the press will ignore you.

Another tip is to make your press releases short and to the point, no more than one page long. Make your ground-shaking announcement, send it to the right media outlets, and don't pester them with follow-up phone calls. If they feel it's worth doing a story on, they will.

Follow these five steps of program promotion and you should have a large stable of affiliate candidates to choose from. The next step, of course, is the actual choosing.

Step Four—Choosing the Right Affiliates

Chapter Summary

A good, effective promotion strategy will net you thousands and thousands of affiliate sign-ups. But quality—not quantity—guarantees a successful program.

Accepting applications sight unseen is not the best way to acquire quality affiliates in your program, but it's the most feasible given the staffing constraints for most affiliate programs. Affiliates must be chosen carefully, just like any business partner. Look at the content of their site, their traffic, and especially the image they portray to visitors. As affiliate partners of your business, their image will be your image.

Stay away from those sites that stack program upon program on their Web site with no original or useful content for visitors or those that try to sell everything to everybody. Selling to everyone is selling to no one. Five percent of your affiliate sites will generate 95% of your revenue from the program, and 1% will be your best revenue generators. This 1% comprises your super affiliates. Find them first, then learn how to evolve your other affiliates into them. Finally, don't ignore your non-participating affiliates. There are reasons why they sign up for your program but do not place your links on their sites. It could be the lack of information you provide to build enthusiasm and trust in selling your product or service.

You've done all you can to attract potential affiliate candidates to your program using the strategies in Chapter 6, "Step Three—Getting the Word Out." You now have hundreds, probably thousands, of Web sites all expressing interest in joining your affiliate network.

Do you automatically approve all of them and place them in your program? If it is at all possible, you should manually approve your affiliates, but this is a slippery slope, because affiliates want and expect instant access to links when they apply to your program. If you use all the strategies in Chapter 6, many of your candidate sites will come from what Marcia Kadanoff, chief marketing officer of IQ.com (www.iq.com), calls the "drive-by" model: Someone at a Web site drives by the merchant's site or visits one of the affiliate solution providers or affiliate directories and picks up the latest and greatest affiliate program offered by a merchant. Here's the problem with drive-bys. According to an affiliate survey conducted by Refer-it.com, 54% of Web sites that joined a program either were not sure or definitely did not add a link after joining a program. That is to say over one half of those who want to join your program will sign-up, and then never put you on their Web site.

That's why affiliates must be chosen carefully, as any business partner would. It's much better from both a management and cost perspective to have a few hundred-quality affiliates than thousands of non-performing affiliates that are a drain on your program's resources.

Know the Affiliate Types

Every successful business transaction has two important elements— make the right offer and make it to the right prospect. In affiliate marketing, that means choosing the affiliates that match your offer. Affiliates come in all shapes and sizes but fall into four general categories: the super affiliates, the up-and-comers, the onesies, and the untouchables. They're explained in the following sections.

The Super Affiliate

The best type of affiliate partner is the super affiliate. These affiliates make up a very small part of your network but are the backbone of your program. They drive 99% of your revenue or referrals. Super affiliates have a number of things in common. First, they are high traffic sites and their traffic matches up well with your offer. They also take an active part in promoting your program on their site and to their visitors. They write endorsements, provide useful content, offer helpful advice, and find creative ways to integrate your links and graphics into the content on their sites. Super affiliates can also provide you with valuable ideas and tips you can pass on to your other affiliates.

Up-and-Comers

Up-and-comers have content that matches your offer and a large number of visitors that match your targeted customer base. Although they do not generate the types of revenues that super affiliates do, they do show that kind of potential. With a little training and education on your product or service, they could join the ranks of your super affiliates.

Onesies

Onesies might be low-traffic sites but do provide a degree of revenue and visibility for your program. These are normally sites that focus on small, original-content or community niches, such as sports, movie, or rock stars, or other areas of interest, or community sites that host discussions on specific topics (see Figure 7.1). Their revenue may not be high, but they do provide a steady stream of sales and referrals. They will earn one (maybe) check from you per year, hence their name.

Untouchables

The last type of affiliate—and the ones to avoid—are the untouchables. These sites will typically have little or no original content nor host any kind of community interaction. Most are simple one page Web sites that stack several banners or links one on top of the other on their Web page. They have no content—just banners and text links. There is no attempt to promote a particular program, and the Web site hopes to generate revenue from visitors who may click on one of the links. These sites are naturally drawn to pay-per-click programs, so if you have one, be very careful to avoid these types of affiliates. Also, based on the sites that have been determined to be perpetrators of affiliate fraud, the untouchables seem to be the biggest perpetrators.

Figure 7.1
Manux is an example of a niche Web site catering to a special audience.

Acquiring the Super Affiliate

Affiliate programs are about marketingnot technology—about partnerships, not cheap advertising. You are building a reputable, effective extension of your sales force and must choose business partners whose Web site operations have similar practices and standards as your own. Yes, you should start your affiliate program as soon as you can, but it pays to start slow. Why? First of all, for every capable and well-chosen site you are on, the volume of your business will increase. Second, you need to be deliberate in choosing the best affiliate you can.

You can acquire your super affiliates in two ways—find them or mold them from your average affiliates. First, though, you need to know what makes a super affiliate, where do you find her, and what are her needs?

Besides being in the top 1% of your revenue-generating affiliate sites, how do you recognize super affiliates and what makes them so successful? First of all, a super affiliate is a very good e-mail marketer. A super affiliate has built a large database of people using an opt-in e-mail list or newsletter. He uses this list to market the products and services of the affiliate programs he has joined. As soon as he is informed of a new promotion, the super affiliate sends out an e-mail to his subscribers informing them immediately of the new offer. In a way, the super affiliate probably knows what works in affiliate marketing better than you do. Super affiliates have learned that they must take an offer to the customer, not wait for the customer to visit their site.

The downside to e-mail marketing, of course, is the potential for spam. Check with the affiliate who plans to use e-mail marketing and make sure he uses opt-in lists. Another way around this problem is to provide a way for affiliates to sign up subscribers to your list. That way you know that the people have signed up voluntarily. You could pay the affiliate a few cents for each e-mail subscriber directed your way. This not only helps curb spam, but also offers a way for affiliates that do not do e-mail marketing a chance to use this valuable promotional vehicle.

Another indication of a super affiliate is her interest in testing different ways to offer a product or service. She has a knack with words and is a born marketer, knowing the value of testing to determine what message wording works and what does not. And if you offer a two-tier affiliate program, you'll probably find that super affiliates use them. They love to groom the sub-affiliates under them to help them earn revenue for themselves and their sub-affiliates.

One powerful strategy that many super affiliates use is the Affinity Shopping Portal. Think about this: What's the greatest challenge to an affiliate site trying to sell the same product or service as

Do

DO insist, but not require, that affiliates purchase your product or service. If possible, ask them to write about the product from their first-hand knowledge. This way, the affiliate becomes a respected, credible source of reliable information.

other affiliates in your network? She needs to find ways to set herself apart when offering your product or service. That's exactly what some super affiliates do.

The Specialized Affiliate

On the Net, content is king. And the more the content is targeted to a specific consumer group, the better. Some very successful super affiliates have discovered this and put it to use in some very creative ways. They either earn big commissions or referral fees by dedicating themselves to one program or set up an Affinity Shopping Portal.

A good example of a super affiliate dedicated to one affiliate program is Over-the-Counter.com (www.over-the-counter.com) (see Figure 7.2). It was created as a means for people to purchase embarrassing drugstore items online, such as pregnancy tests (www.over-the-counter.com/pregnancytest.html), gas-relief products (www.over-the-counter.com/gasrelief.html), and adult diapers (www.over-the-counter.com/adultincontinence.html). The Over-the-Counter.com site is an affiliate of Drugstore.com (www.drugstore.com) and subdivides the merchant's pharmaceutical products into separate categories, then creates a targeted site to sell them.

An affiliate site can subdivide categories for almost any program that offers a wide variety of products from a merchant. If you sell books, CDs, movies, toys, clothing, and so on, you can identify affiliates who would make great candidates for the different categories of the products you sell and help set up a focused Web site or storefront. In a way, vstore does this seamlessly for their affiliates.

Another prime example of a super affiliate dedicating a site to one program is the American Web Ventures Network (www.awvn.com). Jeff Belton created his first singles personals site in 1995, and is now the top associate in the One & Only Personals Network (www.oneandonlynetwork.com) where he generates as much as $23,000 per month in commissions with no advertising cost, no employees, and only part-time effort.

What's an Affinity Shopping Portal?

One type of super affiliate will join a number of affiliate programs that are compatible with each other and focus on a particular product type or service. A good example is Over-the-Counter.com (see Figure 7.2). It subdivides an affiliate merchant's pharmaceutical products into separate categories, then creates a targeted site to sell them.

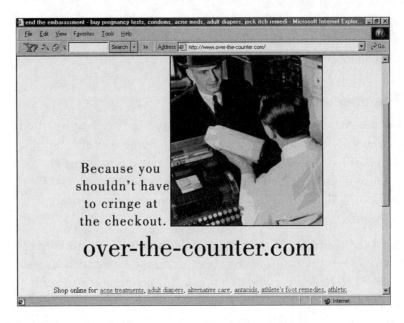

Figure 7.2
Over-the-Counter.com has been very successful in taking one merchant's affiliate program and dividing it up into specialized niche sites.

Shopping Portals

Affinity Shopping Portals are another strategy that super affiliates use. A quick look at their sites show that they have aggregated many different affiliate programs under one roof and targeted the non-profit niche, offering consumers a way to help their schools or causes that they would like to support. In Chapter 2, "The Benefits of Affiliate Marketing," we talked about these other uses for affiliate programs. Schoolpop (www.schoolpop.com) (see Figure 7.3) and ShopforSchool (www.shopforschool.com) identified the niche of school fund-raisers. The school fund-raiser sites enable parents, family, and friends to help their K–12 school when making online purchases.

These sites donate a portion of their commission to the school of the buyer's choice. In a similar vein, other sites have sprung up to facilitate donations to causes and charities when consumers make their online purchases. A good example is GreaterGood.com (www.greatergood.com).

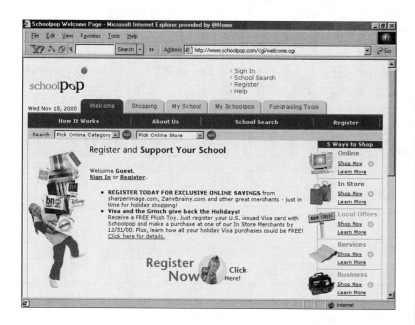

Figure 7.3
SchoolPop is an affinity program that uses a number of affiliate program to offer products an services to its members.

Treating the Super Affiliate Right

As for the special needs of the super affiliates, once identified, they should be treated differently from your other affiliate partners. For one thing, the super affiliates in the ClubMom affiliate program frequently request customized reporting by e-mail or fax in addition to the standard reporting system set up for the network. Also you should communicate personally with each super affiliate when there is a new promotion or offer, even sending him or her the new code instead of having him or her retrieve it from your site. The nature of the super affiliate is to take immediate action on any new promotion, so it's worth the extra effort of contacting them personally.

Keep in mind that the supper affiliate may demand a higher payout rate than what's standard in your program. If not handled properly, this can cause problems with your other affiliates. A safe way to deal with this is to create a fair compensation method as your standard plan, then add performance levels that pay higher as they're reached. Your super affiliates should have no trouble reaching these higher performance levels.

Affiliate Discussion Boards

So where do you find these super affiliates? The answer is go where they go. And where they go is to the affiliate marketing discussion boards on the Net (see Table 7.1).

Table 7.1

Affiliate Marketing Discussion Boards	
AssociatePrograms.com	webwizards.net/AssociatePrograms/discus/
CashPile	www.cashpile.com/cashcorner/index.cfm
iBoost	www.webdesignforums.com
ReveNews	www.revenews.com/opinion/

Before you post a message to these boards, remember that posting blatant advertisements for your program will not be tolerated, and will put your program and company in a bad light. Post well-thought-out messages in response to questions asked by the board's participants. Make sure that you have a signature at the end of each post that plugs your program. This kind of promotion is acceptable. For a frequently updated list of affiliate message boards, visit www.affiliatemanager.net/boards.htm.

Sometimes the question is not necessarily how to find the super affiliates, but rather how you can help them to find you. In an attempt to bring merchants and super affiliates together to create a relationship, BeFree created its Performance Partner Program (www.befree.com/docs/partners/performance) (see Figure 7.4). BeFree offers eligible performance partners (super affiliates) special products and services on behalf of participating merchants.

Another way for super affiliates to find you is the Affiliate Webinar. CashPile.com and the United States Affiliate Manager Coalition (www.usamc.org/) teamed up to present the first Affiliate Webinar (www.affiliatewebinar.com), which was an affiliate marketing seminar conducted entirely online to bring affiliates and merchants together (see Figure 7.5).

Do

If you use BeFree as your affiliate solution provider, DO encourage your affiliates to join BeFree's Performance Partner Program.

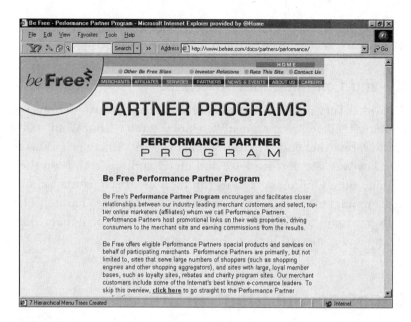

Figure 7.4

BeFree brings merchants and super affiliates together to create a relationship with its Performance Partner Program.

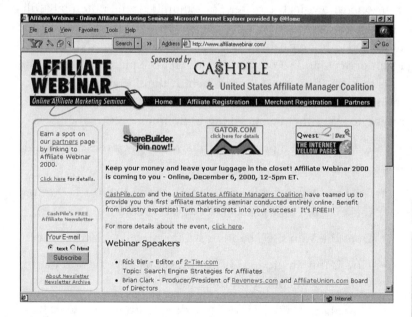

Figure 7.5

Affiliate Webinar brings affiliates and merchants together through an online seminar.

Super affiliates are an invaluable part of your program, and the special care and feeding of them is well worth the effort.

Up-and-Coming Super Affiliates

The other very important level of affiliate partners are the up-and-comers. Affiliate Advantage, a Web-based service from WebPartner (www.webpartner.com), helps merchants with affiliate programs to spot key Web site performance and merchandising trends on their affiliate sites. Online merchants can then use this information to develop ways to increase revenue from their affiliate channel. This is a very useful tool for identifying, tracking, and micro-managing the up-and-comer affiliates to bring them to the super affiliate level.

Choosing the Right Affiliates

When you've received an application from a Web site, visit it. Look it over and see what it offers and what audience it's directed at. Look at its content. Are the site owners trying to reach anyone and everyone who visits their site? For example, is the potential affiliate offering visitors search engine placement AND credit card applications AND phone cards AND long distance service AND pre-paid legal services, and so on, and so on? Get the picture? Declan Dunn calls this the "flea market" approach. If the site sounds like this, then your products or service will be offered to everyone—and selling to everyone means selling to no one.

When you evaluate a potential affiliate site, keep these points in mind:

- See what type of visitors the site is trying to attract. Do they make an attempt to reach a targeted audience?

- Does the Web site's content synergize well with your offer?

- How is the site design? Is it professional? Would you want your offer to appear on their site?

- How about traffic? How much does it attract? Little traffic may bring few sales or referrals.

- Do you ship internationally? If not, don't accept international affiliate sites.

Let's look at each point in detail.

Think of yourself as a visitor to the site. Does the content satisfy the need of a person who has chosen to come there? Does the Web site's content synergize well with your offer? You must select affiliates that complement the products or services you are selling and would be of interest and relevance to their site visitors. This helps ensure that site visitors are pre-qualified, which will result in a higher conversion rate than would normally be the case. A site with targeted traffic provides a targeted customer prospect.

This is a necessary prerequisite for contextual merchandising. Contextual merchandising is simply placing targeted products near relevant content (see Figure 7.6). Can you place your offer next to content that is relevant to your product or service?

What Is Contextual Merchandising?

Contextual merchandising is the strategy of placing a product or service offer within the context of the Web page—for example, placing a link to buy a book that is being reviewed on a Web page.

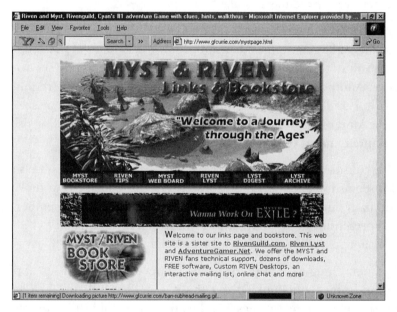

Figure 7.6
The Myst & Riven site combines content on those games with an Amazon bookstore focusing on RIVEN Books and hints and solution guides.

For example, if you're selling videos, does the potential affiliate offer movie reviews, a fan club, or articles on the cinema industry? If so, they can link directly from a movie review to the exact video that you sell. For example, Linkshare's Outpost program allows someone to create a link based on SKU number. The same goes for books, music, computers, or just about any other commodity item sold on the Net.

Another reason to seriously look at content sites is because that's where the majority of Internet users go when they go on the Net. And because content is the prime reason people go online, good content sites make the best type of affiliate partners. Because content sites generate a significant amount of traffic, contextual merchandising can provide both you and your affiliate a good revenue opportunity.

vstore capitalizes on contextual merchandising with their affiliate program. Affiliates can choose from a list of products the kind of store they want to have on their site. With the large amount of products available, any affiliate site should be able to match their content with products to sell.

Look at the site design itself— in particular, the graphics. If a site has lots of large graphics that slow down the loading of the site, visitors will not stick around—and, consequently, not wait to see your offer. Another thing to look for are plug-ins. Does the site require a visitor to download a plug-in to view some cute message or see some kind of flashy presentation? If so, chalk up another lost visitor and a missed opportunity for a sale.

Also consider the site's image. How professional looking is the site? If it seems too amateurish or doesn't reflect the image of your company and the products you sell, don't approve it. Remember, it is representing your company. Its image can be construed to be your image.

The next thing to consider is traffic. Suppose you have a site application from a good-looking site, but it says it has little traffic. Little traffic will bring fewer sales or referrals. You should still consider it as an affiliate. As you will see later, one of your responsibilities to your affiliates is to help them market your product or service by showing them how to promote their site on the Net. If you will not accept a site with a certain amount of traffic, then say so on your affiliate information page before they sign-up.

What's enough traffic? Some affiliate consultants say a Web site needs at least 500 unique visitors a day to earn a decent revenue from an affiliate program. If they have a very targeted audience, this number should suffice. But numbers alone aren't enough; a Web site needs to build trust and credibility with its site visitors. That's done with community. You should certainly target sites with this sort of traffic volume, but also strive to bring your affiliates with less traffic up to this level.

Has the site made an attempt to build a community of users that would be useful for building up a prospect list of potential buyers? Has the site built up an e-mail opt-in list offering a newsletter to its visitors? Research has shown that Web sites that build opt-in e-mail lists and communicate with their subscribers are pretty aggressive marketers and will do better than other affiliates in generating revenue and leads. The more of these elements a site has, the better the chance you have of making sales or referrals from it.

Also consider whether or not you will ship internationally. There is no reason to have affiliate sites that target visitors from other countries if you do not plan to ship internationally. Again, you should state whether you would accept international sites on your affiliate information page.

Finally, when evaluating a potential affiliate's application, don't limit yourself. For example, if you sell travel packages, don't accept just travel-related sites. There are many Web sites that are enamored with a city or geographical area but are not, in themselves, travel sites. These sites would make good affiliates because visitors would like to know how to buy travel packages to those destinations or even travel merchandise to use when they go. If you sell women's jewelry, look for Web sites devoted to women or women's fashion. Think creatively about potential affiliates, even if at first glance they don't seem to fit your perceived network (see Table 7.2).

Do

DO look for affiliate sites that offer community interaction. Original-content sites make good affiliate partners, but so do community sites where people come to interact—especially if it's over a specific subject.

Table 7.2

Possible Affiliate Partner/Offer Partnerships	
Children or Parent Sites	Arts and Crafts
Retirement Sites	Beauty and Health
Liquor Sites	Cigars
Internet Service Providers	Computer Products
Personal Calendar Sites	Flowers, Gifts, and Greeting Cards

Table 7.2   (continued)

Possible Affiliate Partner/Offer Partnerships	
Society and Culture Sites	Museum Stores
Leisure Sites	Show and Sports Tickets
Accounting and Legal Sites	Office Supplies
Special Event Sites	Party Supplies
Support Group Site	Health and Pharmacies
Travel Destinations	Accident and Disability Insurance

What's an Impression?

Every time a Web page is displayed to a viewer, that is called an impression.

The 80:20 Rule

Vilfredo Pareto, born in 1848, was an Italian economist and sociologist known for his application of mathematics to economic analysis. He was the person who came up with the 80/20 Principle, also known as the *Pareto Principle*. His 80:20 Rule has often been applied to affiliate programs, basically stating that 80% of affiliate activity is generated by 20% of the affiliates. The reality is that 95% of affiliate activity is generated by 5% of the affiliates. That is to say, the largest part of a business' success relies on a small fraction of its clients. It is well known that 10% to 20% of affiliate members will place a banner or link on their site and wait for click-throughs. They may get many people to see the banner or link—or click on it—but deliver no sales. On the other hand, 5% of affiliate members will actively promote their affiliation with a company through articles, Web pages, and newsletters devoted to their product. And though their number of impressions may be low, their click-throughs bring a higher percentage of sales.

If 5% of your affiliates will generate 95% of your activity, only 1% of your affiliates will be your best affiliates. The 5% are made up of your up-and-comers, and the 1% consists of your super affiliates. Onesie affiliates account for the remainder of the activity. If you use all the strategies outlined in Chapter 6, you will generate thousands and thousands of affiliate candidates. But which is better? To have thousands of affiliates in your program, or to shoot for hundreds that will generate the best results for your program?

Which would you rather have? Quantity or quality? I strongly suggest the latter.

Activating the Non-Participating Affiliate

With enough work, you can even change your onesie affiliates into up-and comer affiliates or even activate affiliates that have signed up for your program but have not placed your links on their site.

So, what are the reasons why many affiliates sign up for your program but don't put up your links on their site? Neil Durrant of Affiliate Marketing.com in the UK suggests you consider the following:

- Are your instructions clear?

- Are your banners and text links properly designed?

- Does the Affiliate understand your product or service's benefits?

Your affiliate's problem may be as simple as the linking instructions—the "how to" you send just isn't clear enough. Are your instructions clear, and do they make sense? Remember that many of your potential best-performing sites are not maintained by programmers, or even those who know a lot about coding a page in HTML. Make your instructions for placing your linking code on their pages simple and easy to understand from a non-programmer's point of view. Drop the techno-jargon and speak in everyday language.

The second question you need to ask yourself is whether banners and text links are properly designed. Will they provide the response they are designed to give? Are they designed to sell or just to promote your company image with a simple logo—a corporate billboard, so to speak? Do you offer a nice variety of links, both graphical and textual, both general and for specific products, and in different shapes and sizes?

Finally, have you given the new affiliate a clear list of your product or service's benefits and merchandising and marketing tips (see Figure 7.7) that the affiliate can use within the copy of his site to promote your offer and monetize his site traffic?

Don't

DON'T make the mistake of assuming that just because an affiliate has a Web site they understand the ins and outs of Web programming. Keep your set-up instructions to the new affiliate free of techno-babble.

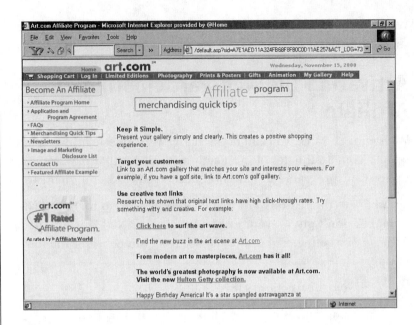

Figure 7.7
Art.com gives merchandising tips to its affiliates to drive sales.

Initial Contact with an Affiliate

Declan Dunn advises that you put together a quick-start guide that goes out to each affiliate when they join your program. But instead of sending out a single welcoming e-mail, the quick-start guide should be sent out in seven easy-to-understand parts at different intervals. I remember, when I was a precocious metals and currency broker years back, using the same technique with my customers. Unlike stocks and bonds that were mostly understood at the time, prospective customers for commodities, such as precious metals and currencies, needed more education before they could make a buying decision. SI would send out a multi-part information packet over a period of several weeks, educating them on how the metals and currencies could be used as an investment vehicle.

Why split these mailings? First of all, I found that regular communications built up familiarity and credibility. It would do the same for your new affiliates. The multi-mailings also break a lot of important and detailed information into manageable chunks and helps keep the affiliate motivated and believing in your program, which is crucial over the first few weeks.

A useful tool for this process is the auto-responder. The auto-responder allows you to send a series of personalized messages with the affiliate's name and a specific subject included the e-mail. Using an auto-responder like the one from AWeber Communications (www.aweber.com) (see Figure 7.8) allows messages to be set-up so they are sent at pre-determined intervals. Take time to create a useful series of e-mails that teach the new affiliates how to implement your links, offer merchandising tips, educate them about your product range, and offer general affiliate tips and advice with links to helpful resources. And here's an important point to keep in mind. Make sure you allow the affiliate recipient to opt-out of your mailing at any time by including the opt out information in each e-mail.

Another useful technique is to publicize the earnings of your top 5, 10, or 20 affiliates in your series of e-mails. This demonstrates to your inactive affiliates that others are making real money—and that they can, too.

Sometimes it's not just an inactive affiliate's laziness that's to blame for poor performance. If could be that she was not given the necessary information to make activation a more distinct possibility. When you send out your activation e-mail to the affiliate, write to her as an individual with a reference to her site—don't just send out a dry, corporate e-mail with a lot of promotional hype telling her what to do. Offer help and advice and invite the affiliate to contact you if she needs help.

What's an Auto-Responder?

An auto-responder is an e-mail feature that automatically sends an e-mail message to anyone who sends you a message.

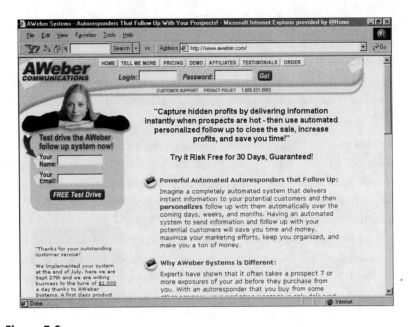

Figure 7.8
AWeber Communications offers an auto-responder program made for affiliate programs.

Here's an example of the activation e-mail that is sent to new ClubMom affiliates:

> Dear <<FIRST_NAME>>:
>
> Welcome to the ClubMom Affiliate Program! As an affiliate of ClubMom, <<SITE_NAME>> will enjoy the benefits of partnering with the top Mom site on the Internet. We are committed to providing our members with a variety of tools and resources, and we're pleased to have you join the team.
>
> GETTING STARTED
>
> You can start referring new members (and earning commissions) today. Just go to our affiliate site at `http://clubmom.reporting.net` and you'll find everything you need, including a variety of ClubMom banners, text links, mini-site code, e-mail code, and content to place on your site.

COMMUNITY

We've started up a group where our affiliates can communicate with each other to share ideas and strategies, interact and learn how to earn higher commissions. Just go to `http://groups.yahoo.com/group/clubmom-affiliates/join` to sign up for this group.

QUESTIONS?

If you have general questions, please refer to our FAQ at `http://www.clubmom.com/corporate/affiliates_faqs.jhtml`. If you cannot find your answer there, e-mail `scollins@clubmom-inc.com` and I will get back to you within 24 hours.

Thank you for joining the team—and here's to a lasting, creative, and profitable relationship!

Sincerely,
Shawn Collins
Affiliate Manager
ClubMom, Inc.
200 Madison Avenue, 6th Floor
New York, New York 10016
tel 646.435.6513
fax 646.435.6600
`http://www.clubmom.com`

P.S.

If you are interested in getting your site ranked better in the search engines, go to `http://www.usamc.org/sesebook.htm` to download my free E-Book, Search Engine School.

You should be very personal and accessible when you are recruiting affiliates, and this should stay consistent after the affiliates have joined your program.

Chapter Summary

Unlike a simple advertising contract that merchants sign when placing ads, the binding agreement between you and your affiliates is much more complicated. It should be written in everyday language and detail the legal and monetary responsibilities that you have to your affiliates and those your affiliates have to you.

Unfortunately, most affiliate agreements miss important points, including what, how, and when the affiliate is paid; how their performance is tracked and reported; issues of copyright and trademark protection; and any marketing and promotion assistance you plan to offer the affiliate. Because of the popularity of affiliate programs, many in the industry are trying to make them more credible and professional. To this end, you should consider participating in the Affiliate Union, which is organized by affiliates hoping to establish minimum acceptable standards for merchant agreements and to devise a certification program for merchants.

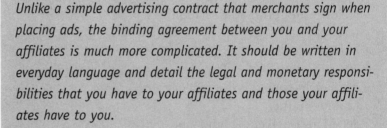

One of the most important elements of your affiliate program—and one often overlooked—is the affiliate agreement. Although agreements exist for every credible affiliate program, many of them miss covering important points. Affiliates are quite aware of the benefits of your program. After all, those benefits are portrayed in your marketing materials and promoted on your Web site. But they also know that it's the affiliate agreement that reflects the elements of your program that both you and the affiliate agree upon.

Thought must be put into such things as revenue percentages, tracking and reporting procedures, payment schedules, and the boilerplate issues of copyright and trademark protection. The agreement must also cover any marketing and promotion assistance you plan to offer the affiliate, any exclusivity clauses (such as the right of rejection for unsuitable sites) or non-compete clauses, and how and where your banner and text links will be placed on the affiliate's site.

Remember that the agreement has the final say as to how your relationship with your affiliates will operate. So, a lot of thought has to be put into drafting your agreement so that it not only reflects your program and how it operates but also creates a long-term and mutually beneficial relationship between you and your affiliate partners.

Affiliate Union Certification

As affiliate programs become more and more popular, those in the trade are seeking to make them more credible and professional. To this end, the Affiliate Union (`http://www.AffiliateUnion.com/`) was established (see Figure 8.1).

The "Affiliate Union" is an ongoing series of planning discussions between affiliates, merchants, and affiliate technology providers aimed at developing both a "certification standard" for affiliate merchants and the organization to implement those standards.

It would be good for you to see the current thinking on a standard for affiliate company policies and agreements before writing your own.

What's an Affiliate Agreement?

An affiliate agreement is the terms between a merchant and an affiliate that govern the relationship.

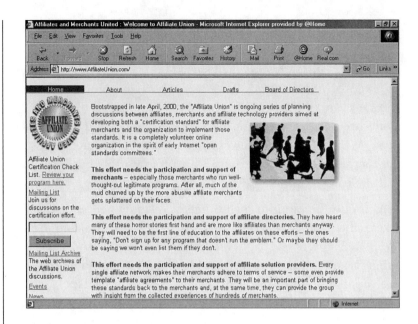

Figure 8.1
The Affiliate Union was organized by affiliates hoping to establish minimum acceptable standards for merchant agreements.

Do

DO keep informed of the progress of the activities of the Affiliate Union. You should monitor and even participate in the Affiliate Union's merchant certification process and make sure your program is in line with their recommendations. Affiliates could be comparing these certification elements to your program some day.

The Affiliate Union has consulted with a variety of affiliate merchants and is seeking feedback from them while designing a standard that could provide a basic benchmark for policies governing affiliate-merchant relationships rather than to dictate procedures. When the process is in place, it will be very easy to be certified by the Affiliate Union, and no doubt Affiliate Union certification will be a selection factor for Web sites wanting to join your affiliate program. You can see an annotated version of the current working draft for merchant criteria and operational guidelines, by the Affiliate Union Board of Directors, at www.affiliateunion.com/drafts.html.

The Elements of an Affiliate Agreement

The affiliate agreement is a legally binding contract between you and your affiliate partners. It is the reference of last resort for disputes between a merchant and an affiliate. So it is the responsibility of your affiliates to read and understand your agreement before they sign up, and your responsibility to make the agreement clear and understandable. That means cut out the legal jargon to a reasonable extent (after all, it is a legal document to be drafted by a lawyer). Write your agreement in easy-to-understand language. Most of your affiliates will neither have a legal background nor have access to legal counsel. If your agreement is easy to understand and organized in a logical manner, more affiliates will join your program.

Your agreement may make or break the number of Web sites that sign on to your program. If your agreement is steeped in legalese and is difficult to understand, they might pass on your affiliate program and go on to the next. In fact, many affiliate consultants who run Web site directories are counseling Web sites to do just that.

So just what are the elements of a good affiliate agreement? They break down into basically two types—legal issues and monetary issues.

The legal issues are

- Enrollment and Acceptance Criteria
- Exclusivity Clauses/Affiliate Conduct
- Banners and/or Text-Linking Criteria
- Vendor Responsibilities
- Affiliate Responsibilities
- Trademarks and Copyrighted Criteria
- Customer Data Considerations
- Confidential and Proprietary Information
- Affiliate Web Site Content
- Term of the Agreement
- Boiler Plate Elements such as Indemnification, Independent Investigation, Limitation of Liability, and the Relationship of the Parties Involved

The monetary issues cover

- Compensation Rates—Commissions and Referral Fees
- Escalating Commissions (if any)

- Reporting and Tracking
- Payment Schedule
- Residual Income (if any)

Cover these elements in your affiliate agreement using easy-to-understand language and you will lay the foundation for a long-term and mutually beneficial relationship between you and your affiliate partners.

Legal Issues

Most affiliate programs focus on the money. After all, an affiliate program is all about generating revenue for both you and your affiliates. But there are several legal issues that must be addressed before the money issues are detailed in the agreement.

The first of these is your affiliate enrollment and acceptance criteria. Here are some points to keep in mind when writing this section.

Enrollment, Exclusivity Causes, and Conduct

Inform the Web site applicant that when he signs up for your program it is only provisional. His acceptance in your program depends on a number of factors that you should include in this section of your agreement. State that you must first see his Web site. That means it must be live.

The agreement should say what types of sites will be accepted and what types will not. You want to keep your affiliate network professional looking and within cultural norms, so you should reject any site with adult (sexually explicit) content or sites that promote violence, discrimination, or engage in illegal activities. You should also reject any sites that appear to be banner farms, or do not seem to provide original content or a compelling reason for people to visit. While you're looking at their content, make sure the site is not violating any intellectual property rights.

With regards to affiliate conduct, be sure to include an anti-spam policy, as well as grounds for termination. There should also be a mention that the Web site agrees not to add content that violates

Do

DO inform affiliates what site content and affiliate behavior is and is not acceptable to join and remain in your affiliate program. If you do not want an affiliate to participate in a competitor's program, state it clearly in your agreement.

this section of the agreement after they are accepted in your affiliate network. This should also be mentioned in an Indemnification Clause in your agreement that holds your company harmless against any and all claims, lawsuits, damages, and expenses that occur because of the affiliate's content or conduct.

Finally, you might want to consider an exclusivity clause that prevents an affiliate from placing competitive programs on his site. For example, if you sell music CDs, you can stipulate that the affiliate cannot place a competitor's links on his Web site. On the other hand, you should also mention in this section that you are not restricted from adding sites to your network that compete with your affiliates. Note that the term *exclusivity clause* is a dirty word to affiliates. Rather than mandate that your affiliates be exclusive, craft your program to be beneficial to affiliates so they would not want to promote the competition.

Linking Criteria

Speaking of links, your next section of the agreement should deal with affiliate responsibilities to the program. The biggest and most important one is the placing of links on their site. In general, you should insist that the affiliate place only your banner and text links on his or her site. You should not give authority to affiliates to create their own banners, buttons, or graphics. And you should prohibit their hosting of your images on their servers. If a promotion ends and the affiliate is hosting the image on his server, you will not be able to remove the expired promotion from his site. You should also prohibit affiliates from including actual price information on their Web sites to avoid problems with price fluctuations.

The only exception to this rule—and it should be stated in the agreement—is permission to add testimonial text under or near your links. Even this should be under the condition that the affiliate runs the copy by the affiliate manager to ensure that the testimonial is accurate and truthful. The affiliate also must be told that he is responsible for the proper maintenance of the links around his site. That means the affiliate should be checked periodically to make sure the links work. Your linking procedures should be detailed on your Web site—what the linking code is, where to get it, how and where to place it on the affiliate site, and so on—and

What's a Linking Code?

Linking codes are the lines of HTML code affiliates use to put links on their Web sites. Affiliate solution providers often provide a tool that enables affiliates to simply copy the code for an affiliate link and paste it into their own HTML pages.

your agreement should reference them. The affiliate should also be specifically prohibited from making any warranty, representation, or other statement concerning your products or services.

A good general rule of thumb here is that the main objective of your company is to restrict the involvement of your affiliates to generating revenue for your business. They should not be communicating directly with customers about order status, customer service, and product availability and pricing.

Intellectual Property and Proprietary Information

When you give permission to affiliates to display your banners on their site, you are placing your brand in their hands. It pays to add an intellectual property clause to your agreement.

Don't

DON'T let affiliates change or modify the graphics provided by you. Your graphic links reflect your brand and should not be changed to suit an affiliate's site.

It should be stated that your company is providing a limited license to the affiliate to display your logo, trademark, and promotional materials. This is your brand and you want to ensure that the affiliate displays it properly. Affiliates should use only pre-approved graphics available from your Web site or from your third-party solution provider. The affiliate should not be allowed to resize or otherwise modify your graphics. So protect your brand and trademarks with this clause.

In addition to your trademark, you will be exchanging valuable confidential and proprietary information with your affiliates. For example, your company will most likely provide affiliates with information about impending product releases to give them time to prepare for the new offers. You may also provide your affiliates with proprietary software or code to integrate with their Web site. If this is so, you should forbid affiliates from disclosing or disseminating the information to outside parties.

Customer Data and Relationships

Even though the affiliate is recruiting customers for your company, the customers and the data collected in the process belong to you. Affiliates are an extension of your sales force and as such, are sales people. Affiliates do not own the customer data anymore than your sales people would. This does not mean that your affiliates would not benefit from building a customer or prospect list off their site visitors. This can still be done, and your company can market to this database and share any revenue generated with your affiliates.

So your affiliate agreement should state that all customer data generated by the affiliate for the purpose of your affiliate program is the sole property of your company. Of course, this section should be written to allow for affiliates to maintain their own customer lists that pertain only to the affiliate Web site and not your particular program.

It would be a good idea to incorporate into your agreement a relationship of parties provision to prevent future affiliate claims about the nature of their relationship with your company. You don't want your affiliates to give the impression that they are somehow a part of your business. Legally, they are acting on your behalf and not as a division or department of your company. The relationship of parties provision disclaims the creation of any agency, joint venture, partnership, or any other entity not stated in your agreement.

Indemnification, Disclaimers, Limitation of Liability, and Miscellaneous Issues

Your agreement should cover the boilerplate issues that are necessary in every agreement of this type. An Indemnification clause should be included, holding your company harmless against any and all claims, lawsuits, damages, and expenses that arise. The terms of agreement should be stated, including a termination clause as to when, how, and under what circumstances a relationship with an affiliate can be terminated. Any and all disclaimers should be included as clauses in the agreement, making no expressed or implied warrantees with respect to your affiliate program or any products or services sold through the program.

A limitation of liability clause should also be included, protecting your company against any indirect, special, or consequential damages or loss of revenue arising in connection with your agreement or program. And finally, your agreement should include the legalities of where the agreement will be governed and how disputes will be resolved.

So much for the legalities. Now on to really important issues.

Don't

DON'T forget the indemnification, disclaimers, or limitation of liability clauses in your agreement. These protect you from any illegal actions of an affiliate who is acting as a sales agent on your part.

Monetary Issues

No matter what kind of promotion you do on your Web site and no matter what you tell potential affiliates about the kind of money they can make in your program, it's the sections on payment in your agreement that dictate what you will pay your affiliates, how they will be paid, when they will get paid, and how you plan to track their sales and/or referrals for payment.

This is the section of your agreement that will get the most scrutiny by potential affiliates and should be made as clear as possible. The payment provisions should contain no gray areas of understanding or hidden tricks. Be up front and totally explicit about your payment policy. As a merchant, realize that contracts designed to cheat your affiliates will doom your program in the long run.

Remember, just because you explain your payment structure in your promotional materials doesn't excuse the fact that you must have a payment clause in your agreement. Affiliate agreements have legal consequences, and the legal agreement should be treated as such. That said, be sure you can maintain the payment structure outlined in your agreement. It's far better to err on the conservative side and start with a low commission than to cut the commission amount after the program has launched.

Do

DO explain your payment structure in detail in your agreement. It's not enough to have explained it in your promotional materials. What you pay affiliates and how and when you pay them has legal consequences.

Compensation Rates and Payment

Your agreement should clearly define what you will pay your affiliates and whether you are paying per sale, per click, or per action taken. A lot depends on your capacity to pay. Most affiliate commissions and fees are set low because the products sold by the merchants have a slim profit margin. You can't pay what you don't have. If you are stuck with paying a low commission rate or fee and your product is bought infrequently, it might be hard to build your affiliate network. Services and home-brewed products fare better with affiliate programs because the profit margin is much higher and the merchant can afford higher payout.

Once you've set your payout structure (see Chapter 10, "Step Seven—Paying Your Affiliates"), you need to define what is commissionable and what is not. You must state whether you will pay only per session, or track the customers sent from your affiliate site and pay the affiliate if the customer buys later at another time. A session is defined as one continuous visit from the consumer, and if the consumer leaves your site, the session is over.

The payment clauses in your agreement should determine the scope of the compensation given the affiliate and the compensation rates paid on different products (you might offer some products at a higher compensation rate because they are on sale or offer a higher percentage for more expensive items). The agreement should also make provisions for any charges or credits that will be deducted prior to payment. Typical deductions include amounts collected for sales taxes, duties, and shipping and handling. If applicable, you might deduct for credit card fraud or bad debt.

And most importantly, any returned product from customers should be deducted from the affiliate's check after the product has been returned.

Finally, you should state when affiliates should expect payment. Payment schedules are largely up to your discretion. Although some merchants pay their affiliates quarterly, it is highly recommended that—to stay competitive—you pay affiliates on a monthly basis.

Do

DO explain any and all provisions for any charges or credits that will be deducted prior to payment in your agreement. Affiliates need to know exactly what they will be paid for and what they will not. Typical deductions include amounts collected for sales taxes, duties, and shipping and handling— even credit card fraud and bad debt.

You might want to consider delaying payment of the first check for 60 days, and then pay 30 days thereafter, establishing a 30-day delay. The 60-day delay before first payment gives you a chance to evaluate the new affiliate. The 30-day delay after that gives you a chance to handle product returns if any and deduct them from the affiliate's next check, as well as for processing (approving commission vouchers, cutting checks, mailing, and so on). If you outsource your affiliate commission payments, you will have to take into consideration the time it takes for your payment to clear, because the affiliate solution provider or other third-party will begin to cut your checks.

Escalating Commissions

If you plan on giving incentives to affiliates by paying a higher compensation to those with higher sales, then it should be stated clearly in the agreement. You should state what the higher rate is and at what level of sales the higher rate will apply. This is known as the super affiliates clause.

Don't hide these higher rates and how to reach them. If your affiliates discover that some affiliates are receiving a higher compensation than others and they don't know why, they will feel you are playing favorites and this will harm your program.

Your next consideration is a minimum payment clause. Here's why. Do you want to write checks out to affiliates for a dollar or two? Not very cost effective. So setting a minimum payment clause and making it clear to affiliates is good business sense. It's common for merchants to set minimums in any payment period for administrative convenience. For example, if an affiliate earns less than $25 in any payment period, the amount will be rolled over into the next payment period.

On the other hand, don't encourage or sign up Web sites that have little ability to meet your minimum payment. If you feel you must have these low-performing sites, either lower your minimum payment or a have strict traffic requirement for your affiliates.

Reporting and Tracking

Do

DO name who will do the tracking and reporting for your program. If it's not your company and you are using a third party solution provider, name that provider in your agreement.

How and when you track and report an affiliate's statistics should be included in your affiliate agreement. You should explain to your affiliates whether the tracking and reporting is done in-house using your own software or is outsourced to a third party. If outsourced, that third party should be named.

You should say what you will report and when. Will you have a real-time reporting mechanism, or will there be a time delay—say 24 hours—before reports are posted? Will you track and report impressions, click-throughs, orders, shipped orders, number and amount of sales, products sold, and deductions for returns? Will affiliates find these reports on a Web site, or will they be e-mailed or faxed to them? All this information must be in your agreement. Your agreement should detail the method of tracking as well as the required chain of events that will trigger an affiliate's right to compensation.

And what about repeat sales? If you offer affiliates the chance to earn revenue from visitors outside of the initial visit to your company Web site, will you track that? This should be stated in your agreement, too. And if so, how long will you track the visitor—30 days, 60, 90? It must be stated in your agreement. Any repeat-sales or residual income should be stated and explained in the agreement so that it is understandable by the potential affiliate.

Finally, you should have a provision in the compensation clause disclaiming any responsibility for payments relating to an improper link on the affiliate's site, and technical problems that would cause downtime of your tracking program that would affect your affiliate's compensation. Your agreement should disclaim any express or implied warranties relating to the operation of the affiliate network and should also limit your liability to the total amount of revenue generated by the affiliate Web site.

Delivery of the Affiliate Agreement

There's a sticky legality here that you as a merchant must consider—the delivery of the affiliate agreement and how and when the affiliate agrees to it. In legal terms, you must ensure that the manner of delivery of the agreement does not hamper its enforceability.

The easiest way to avoid this issue is to mail a printed version to the affiliate for signature. But this is the Information Age! Many things are done electronically. Today, agreements are agreed to by simply pressing the "Submit" button after a very long Web page that contains the agreement (see Figure 8.2). But take care. Just linking to another Web page that contains the agreement outside of the registration process could cause problems. The best solution is to include the agreement as a required page in the registration process, requiring the affiliate candidate to agree to the terms and conditions of the agreement before moving on with the registration process.

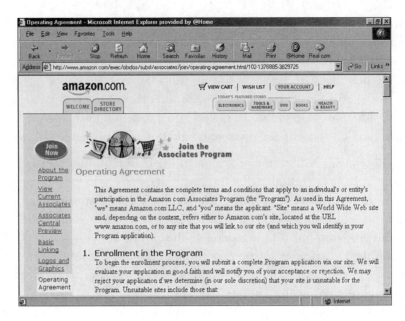

Figure 8.2
Here is an example of an online affiliate agreement from Amazon's associates program.

Do

DO send a copy of the agreement via e-mail to the affiliate after she signs or agrees to its terms. This reminds the affiliate of her program responsibilities and gives her a copy for her files for reference.

To be safe, you might even consider sending the agreement to the affiliate via e-mail after registering so she has a copy in her possession.

Also, you should make your agreement available for view to potential affiliates on your Web site or on your affiliate solution provider's Web site before they even begin the registration process. A good place for that would be on your Affiliate Information pages.

In any case, delivering your affiliate agreement in this way will help prevent any legal disputes with your affiliates later.

A Sample Agreement

So how do we bring all these elements together? What follows is a sample agreement that covers most of the agreement elements discussed in this chapter. The sample is an affiliate agreement for a company I owned called One Minute Shopper. Use this agreement ONLY as a guide. Keep in mind that the needs of your program agreement may be different, so make sure you contact legal counsel when writing your own program agreement.

One MinuteShopper.com

Affiliate Agreement

This Agreement contains the complete terms and conditions that apply to your participation in the One Minute Shopper.com Affiliate Partner Program (the "Program"). As used in this Agreement, "we," "our," and "us" refer to One Minute Shopper.com, Inc., and "you" and "your" refer to the applicant. "Site" means a World Wide Web site, and the "MinuteStore" refers to our E Commerce icon and transaction tool that is to be displayed on your site in accordance with this Agreement in order to afford visitors to your site the opportunity to purchase products offered by us and to join the "MinuteShoppers Club" described below.

1. Enrollment in the Program

To begin the enrollment process, you will submit a complete Program application via our site. We will evaluate your application in good faith and will notify you of its acceptance or rejection. We may reject your application if we determine (in our sole discretion) that your site is unsuitable for the Program for any reason. Unsuitable sites include (but are not limited to) those that: Contain content that is unlawful, threatening, defamatory, obscene or otherwise objectionable; Promote sexually explicit materials; Promote violence; Promote discrimination based on race, sex, religion, nationality, disability, sexual orientation, or age; Promote illegal activities; Violate or infringe upon intellectual property rights. If we reject your application, you are welcome to reapply to the Program at any time. If we accept your application, we reserve the right to terminate this Agreement if we ever determine (in our sole discretion) that your site is unsuitable for the Program for any reason.

2. The MinuteStore

Once we notify you that we have accepted your site into the Program, we will authorize you to copy the

What's an Affiliate Information Page?

An affiliate information page is a page (or pages) on your Web site that explains clearly and concisely what your affiliate program is all about.

code for the MinuteStore from a password protected site (www.reporting.net) maintained for us by Be Free, Inc. ("Be Free") and display the MinuteStore on your site. We encourage you to place the MinuteStore, which you may use only on the terms and conditions of this Agreement, as prominently as possible on the most heavily trafficked pages of your site and to follow our instructions regarding the operation of the MinuteStore. From time to time, we will offer different products for sale through the MinuteStore and also may modify the logos and other information presented in, and the overall appearance of the MinuteStore. All such changes and modifications will occur automatically, without any prior notice to you. You will not be required to change any code, as we change our products automatically.

3. MinuteShoppers Club

We will encourage customers who visit the MinuteStore on your site to join our MinuteShoppers Club and take advantage of product presales and other promotions that we intend to offer exclusively to MinuteShoppers Club members. Members who join the MinuteShoppers Club from the MinuteStore on your site may view the product offers that we will make available from time to time to MinuteShoppers Club members. The MinuteShoppers Club members will view co-branded pages that we will maintain on our site. As a condition to our obligations under this paragraph, however, we expect you to provide to us, or to allow us to download from your site, the trademarks and logos that we may need to co-brand the Web pages contemplated by this paragraph. By entering into this Agreement, you grant to us a nonexclusive license to use those trademarks and logos, and any accompanying graphic images and text, solely for purposes of creating and maintaining co-branded Web pages for the MinuteShoppers Club.

4. Order Processing

We will process product orders placed by customers who purchase products or join the MinuteShoppers Club using the MinuteStore on your site. We reserve the right to reject orders that do not comply with any and all our requirements that we periodically may establish. We will be responsible for all aspects of order processing and fulfillment. Among other things, we will prepare order forms, process payments, cancellations, returns, and handle customer service.

5. Sales Tracking

We will rely on Be Free Inc. (Be Free) to track sales made to customers who purchase products or join the MinuteShoppers Club using the MinuteStore on your site. Be Free will make available to you the sales activity, as well as reports regarding end-user impressions and click-throughs, at its www.reporting.net site. You and we each agree to rely on, and not to challenge or dispute, the sales tracking and other information that Be Free compiles in connection with the Program, which will bind both you and us for all purposes under this Agreement.

6. Payment

You will earn a 10% commission on all products shipped to customers who purchase products from the MinuteStore on your site. You will also receive a 10% commission on purchases made by MinuteShopper Club Members who have joined the MinuteShopper Club through our MinuteStore on your site. If your sales exceed $3,500 for any month, you will receive 12% commissions on all products shipped for that month. If your sales exceed $7,000 for any month, you will receive 15% commissions on all products shipped for that month. All sales exclude any taxes or shipping costs that we may charge. We will pay all commissions that accrue on a monthly basis, within thirty days after each month end. If the commissions that accrue in any month total less than $10, we will hold the commissions and pay them to you thirty days after the end of the first month in which aggregate accrued but unpaid commissions total $10 or more. If a customer returns or receives a refund or credit for a product that generated a commission under this paragraph, we will deduct that commission from your next monthly payment or payments. If no further payments are due under this Agreement, we reserve the right to send you a bill for any commissions associated with returned products. As with sales tracking information, we have engaged Be Free to calculate the commissions that you will receive under the Program, and Be Free's commission calculations will bind both you and us for all purposes under this Agreement.

7. Policies and Pricing

All customers who buy products through the Program or join the MinuteShoppers Club are customers of One Minute Shopper.com. Accordingly, all One Minute Shopper.com rules, policies, and operating procedures concerning customer orders, customer service, pricing and product sales will apply to those customers. We may change our policies and operating procedures at any time, in our sole discretion. Product prices and availability may vary from time to time. Because price changes may affect products that you already have listed on your site, you may not include price information in your product descriptions. We will use commercially reasonable efforts to present accurate information, but we cannot guarantee the availability or price of any particular product.

8. Limited License

We grant you a nonexclusive, revocable right to use the MinuteStore and any other images and text that we may provide to you solely for the purpose of identifying your site as a Program participant and to assist in generating product sales through the Program. You may not modify the MinuteStore or any other graphic images or text that we may provide you in any way. We reserve all our rights in the MinuteStore, all such graphic images, text, our trade names and trademarks and all other intellectual property rights. You agree to follow our instructions respecting the use of your trademarks, and those instructions may change from time to time. We may revoke your license at any time by giving you written notice.

9. Responsibility for Your Site

You will have sole responsibility for the development, operation and maintenance of your site and for all materials that appear on your site. For example, you will be solely responsible for:

The technical operation of your site and all related equipment. The accuracy and appropriateness of materials posted on your site (including, among other things, all product-related materials). Ensuring that materials posted on your site do not violate or infringe upon the rights of any third party (including, for example, copyrights, trademarks, privacy or other personal or proprietary rights). Ensuring that materials posted on your site are not obscene, defamatory, libelous or otherwise illegal. We disclaim all liability for all matters relating to the development, operation, maintenance, and contents of your site.

10. Indemnification

You will indemnify, defend and hold us harmless against any and all claims, lawsuits, damages, and expenses (including, without limitation, attorneys' fees) that we may or that anyone may assert as a result of (1) our use of any trademarks, logos, graphic images, text or other materials that you may provide to us or allow us to use under paragraph 3; or (2) anything occurring on your site or arising from the development, operation or maintenance of your site.

11. Term of the Agreement

The term of this Agreement will begin upon our acceptance of your Program application and will end when terminated by either party. Either you or we may terminate this Agreement at any time and for any reason by giving the other party written notice of termination, which may be via email but must be responded to with a reply, stating receipt, within 48 hours. Upon the termination of this Agreement for any reason, you will immediately cease using, and remove from your site, all links to our commerce server, all One Minute Shopper.com trademarks, trade dress and logos and all other materials that we may have provided to you or allowed you to use in connection with the Program, and we will immediately cease using, and remove from our site, all trademarks, logos, graphic images, text or other materials that you may provide to us or allow us to use under paragraph 3. You are eligible to earn only those commissions that may accrue under paragraph 5 during the term of this agreement, and commissions earned through the date of termination will remain payable only if the customer does not cancel the order, return the products purchased or receive a refund or credit. We may withhold your final payment for a reasonable time to ensure payment of the correct commission amount.

12. Modification

We may modify any of the terms and conditions contained in this Agreement, at any time and at our sole discretion, by posting a change notice or a new agreement on our site. ALL SUCH MODIFICATIONS WILL TAKE EFFECT AT THE TIME WE SPECIFY OR, IF WE SPECIFY NO SUCH TIME, IMMEDIATELY UPON THEIR POSTING ON OUR SITE. IF ANY MODIFICATION IS UNACCEPTABLE TO YOU, YOUR ONLY RECOURSE IS TO TERMINATE THIS AGREEMENT. YOUR CONTINUED PARTICIPATION IN THE PROGRAM FOLLOWING OUR POSTING OF A CHANGE NOTICE OR NEW AGREEMENT ON OUR SITE WILL EVIDENCE YOUR BINDING ACCEPTANCE OF THE CHANGE.

13. Relationship of Parties

You and we are independent contractors, and nothing in this Agreement will create any partnership, joint venture, agency, franchise, sales representative, or employment relationship between the parties. You will have no authority to make or accept any offers or representations on our behalf. You will not make any statement, whether on your site or otherwise, that reasonably would contradict anything in this Section.

14. Disclaimers

WE MAKE NO EXPRESS OR IMPLIED WARRANTIES OR REPRESENTATIONS WITH RESPECT TO THE PROGRAM OR ANY PRODUCTS SOLD THROUGH THE PROGRAM (INCLUDING, WITHOUT LIMITATION, WARRANTIES OF MERCHANTABILITY, FITNESS FOR A PARTICULAR PURPOSE OR NO INFRINGEMENT, OR ANY IMPLIED WARRANTIES ARISING FROM A COURSE OF PERFORMANCE, DEALING OR TRADE USAGE). IN ADDITION, WE MAKE NO REPRESENTATION THAT THE OPERATION OF OUR SITE OR OUR COMMERCE SERVER WILL BE

UNINTERRUPTED OR ERROR-FREE, AND WE WILL NOT BE LIABLE FOR THE CONSEQUENCES OF ANY INTERRUPTIONS OR ERRORS.

15. Limitation of Liability

WE WILL NOT BE LIABLE FOR INDIRECT, SPECIAL, OR CONSEQUENTIAL DAMAGES (OR ANY LOSS OF REVENUE, PROFITS OR DATA) ARISING IN CONNECTION WITH THIS AGREEMENT OR THE PROGRAM, EVEN IF WE HAVE BEEN ADVISED OF THE POSSIBILITY OF SUCH DAMAGES. FURTHER, OUR TOTAL LIABILITY ARISING WITH RESPECT TO THIS AGREEMENT AND THE PROGRAM WILL NOT EXCEED THE TOTAL REFERRAL FEES PAID OR PAYABLE TO YOU UNDER THIS AGREEMENT.

16. Independent Investigation

YOU ACKNOWLEDGE THAT YOU HAVE READ THIS AGREEMENT AND AGREE TO ALL ITS TERMS AND CONDITIONS. YOU UNDERSTAND THAT WE MAY AT ANY TIME (DIRECTLY OR INDIRECTLY) SOLICIT CUSTOMER REFERRALS ON TERMS THAT MAY DIFFER FROM THOSE CONTAINED IN THIS AGREEMENT OR OPERATE WEB SITES THAT ARE SIMILAR TO OR COMPETE WITH YOUR WEB SITE. YOU HAVE INDEPENDENTLY EVALUATED THE DESIRABILITY OF PARTICIPATING IN THE PROGRAM AND ARE NOT RELYING ON ANY REPRESENTATION, GUARANTEE, OR STATEMENT NOT SET FORTH IN THIS AGREEMENT.

17. Miscellaneous

This Agreement will be governed by the laws of the United States and the state of Arizona, without reference to rules governing choice of laws. Any action relating to this Agreement must be brought in the federal or state courts located in Phoenix, Arizona, and you irrevocably consent to the jurisdiction of those courts and waive any claim that those courts constitute an inappropriate venue or inconvenient forum. You may not assign this Agreement, by operation of law or otherwise, without our prior written consent. Subject to that restriction, this Agreement will bind, insure to the benefit of and be enforceable against the parties and their respective successors and assigns. Our failure to enforce your strict performance of any provision of this Agreement will not constitute a waiver of our right to subsequently enforce such provision or any other provision of this Agreement.

Step Six—Tracking Your Affiliate Program

Chapter Summary

An important component of any affiliate program is the ability to provide objective, reliable, and credible reports on a daily basis for both you and your affiliates. Without a proper tracking and reporting system in place, it is close to impossible to comprehend the performance of your affiliate network and the effectiveness of your offers.

As for your affiliates, they need to have a way to see how much they have earned in your programs, and you need a way to calculate their earnings to pay them. Any good affiliate will demand to see reports of his or her performance on a daily basis, so your reporting system must provide this capability. You can either build a tracking and reporting system in-house using your resources or outsource it to third-party affiliate solution providers. The Big Four solution providers (Commission Junction, Dynamic Trade, BeFree, and Linkshare) can help recruit affiliates, set-up and manage your tracking and reporting program—and in some cases—pay your affiliates the money they've earned. Finally, the numbers generated by the tracking and reporting program you use can help you manage and improve your program over time.

very affiliate program, no matter the size or type, needs the ability to track and report activity across the network. You as a merchant need to know what traffic and/or sales are sent to you from your affiliates and, in turn, you need to report this activity back to them (see Figure 9.1).

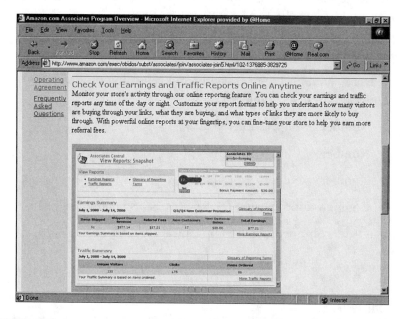

Figure 9.1
Here is an example of an online affiliate tracking report from Amazon's associates program.

If you can not provide affiliates with objective, reliable, and credible reports on a daily basis, good affiliates will neither sign up for your program nor stay in a program that gives the slightest hint of impropriety. It's also very important to know affiliate by affiliate which ones are performing well and why. It's crucial to decide upon a tracking and reporting system that meets both your and your affiliates' needs.

There are many ways to track your program and provide reports for your affiliates. Either do it in-house using your own tracking software or use a third-party affiliate program solution provider. Whichever you choose, the method should contain a minimum set of tracking and reporting elements.

The Elements of Tracking and Reporting

The purpose of a tracking and reporting program is to first give you a picture of how your affiliate network—and any particular affiliate in your network—is performing. Second, it should give you the necessary information to compensate each affiliate for traffic and sales generated by her. And third, it should provide an easy and timely process for your affiliates to obtain reports on their individual performance.

The basic elements of any tracking and reporting program consist of the following (see Table 9.1):

- Number of Impressions
- Number of Click-Throughs
- Number of Sales or Sales Leads
- Compensation Earned for Sales or Sales Leads
- Orders Shipped (where appropriate)
- Total Compensation to be Paid

Table 9.1

Sample Reports For the Week of July 17					
Impressions	Click-Throughs	Sales	Compensation Earned	Orders Shipped	Total Earned
1000	126	6	$293	5	$222

All these elements must be tracked by or for you and posted on the Web for your affiliates to see in an easy to reach location. Let's look at them one at a time.

Number of Impressions

This is one of the most important bits of information you can capture. It gives you a clear picture of how many times potential customers view your product or service offer. This component of your tracking program will tell you how many times your banner, graphic, or text link is seen by a visitor to an affiliate's site. That is to say, how many times an affiliate's visitor has seen your offer. The number of impressions of your offer from an affiliate site forms the basis of how well your program is performing. Even though you cannot accurately determine the amount of traffic an affiliate site attracts, by tracking impressions on the individual-affiliate and network levels, you can determine a number of things.

First, you can look at an affiliate's application to your program and see what total traffic numbers he claimed his site generates. Keeping in mind that the numbers could be exaggerated, compare those numbers to the number of impressions that are being reported for that affiliate. See if there is a wide discrepancy between his traffic and your impressions.

Second, if there is a wide discrepancy, then perhaps the affiliate is not placing your program links on many of the pages of his site or not on the pages most frequented by his visitors. If so, it would warrant a visit to the site to see where your links are placed. You can remind the affiliate that it's in his best interest and will generate more potential revenue if he would place your program links on the high-traffic Web pages of his site.

Third, if the affiliate is providing all the impressions he can but they are still very low, does mean that the affiliate should be dropped from the program? Not necessarily. The number of impressions is important, but what's more important are the click-throughs that follow.

Number of Click-Throughs

If the importance of generating impressions for your offer rests on the shoulders of your affiliates, the number of click-throughs rest with you both. A click-through is the number of visitors to an affiliate's site that actually click on your program link. There are a number of important variables here that will determine whether a site visitor will click on your offer. The first one, of course, is the offer itself. Is it strong enough to make a site visitor click on it to either find out more about the offer or make a purchase?

Your creative must be good enough to motivate a visitor to take action. As noted before, an affiliate can help by providing a personal recommendation for your offer using his or her credibility that visitors might trust, but as a merchant, the click-through responsibility rests squarely on your shoulders.

Do

DO compare an affiliate's traffic claims to the number of impressions you are receiving for your links. If there is a wide discrepancy between her traffic and your impressions, perhaps the affiliate is not placing your program links on many of the pages of her site or not on the pages most frequented by her visitors.

The click-through metric is important for another reason. You may have affiliate sites with a very low number of impressions, but their click-through rate may be as high or higher than those affiliates whose sites generate a larger number of impressions. What's important in the affiliate game is not so much the number of impressions a site delivers, but the number of sales, leads, or actions it produces.

Number of Sales, Leads, or Actions

This is where the rubber hits the road. The whole objective of your affiliate program is to provide a cost-effective way to generate sales, produce leads, or have a consumer perform some kind of action, such as filling out a form, joining a club, or entering a contest where you can capture marketing information in the process. Capturing and recording the number of orders and their dollar amount, or the number of clicks-throughs or actions taken, is vitally important for both you and your affiliates. If you want to see how well your program is performing, and if you want to have accurate information to compensate your affiliate, you must capture and record this information. Your affiliates, of course, will be equally interested in seeing this data on a daily basis.

Compensation Earned

Do

DO make sure that your affiliates understand that the compensation earned is not always the compensation paid out due to sales taxes, duties, shipping, and handling—even credit card fraud and bad debt—which is deducted from their commission checks.

The metric of most interest to your affiliates is the amount of compensation earned from the actions taken by visitors to their site. Your tracking and recording program must provide affiliates with the amount of money they have earned on a daily basis through your affiliate program for sales made, clicks recorded, and forms filled out by their site visitors. The reports should be timely and made easily available to affiliates.

Keep in mind that this metric shows the amount earned—not necessarily the amount that will be paid. For example, an order can be taken and a commission earned on the sale but that compensation amount might not be the amount finally paid to the affiliate. The amount earned could be less after all deductions are made, such as amounts collected for sales taxes, duties, shipping, and handling.

Orders Shipped and Actual Compensation

If your affiliates are earning commissions on products, they must understand that they are paid only on orders that are actually shipped. This metric should be included in your reporting program for affiliates to see.

After all orders have been shipped, click-throughs recorded, and any and all actions required taken by an affiliate site visitor, the actual amount of compensation paid should be made available to the affiliate for review. This amount would be exclusive of amounts collected for sales taxes, duties, shipping, and handling—even credit card fraud and bad debt—and will reflect the actual amount paid to the affiliate.

Timeliness of Reports

Affiliates are an impatient bunch. They've been known to check their activity and sales reports on an hourly basis. Your report postings do not have to be that frequent. Updating affiliate reports once very 24 hours is adequate. But the more ways for them to request reports the better. Affiliates should be able to view their activity and sales reports by day, week, month, and quarter. They should also be able to view individual sales and total sales for each of these periods.

You should make a separate, password-protected Web site available to them to view the different reports. If you are running your own report tracking and reporting program, you pretty much do all the previous. But if you use a third-party affiliate solution provider, make sure that it provides both the elements of the tracking and reporting program discussed and a timely way for affiliates to view their report.

Do It Yourself Versus Third-Party Provider

Apart from the details involved to start an affiliate program, you have one big decision to make—create the program in-house or outsource it to a third-party solution provider. Unless you are a large merchant with an IT department with lots of free time to build and manage a program on your own, like Amazon and the One and Only Network, it might be more reasonable to outsource it to a solution provider, such as Be Free, Commission Junction, or LinkShare.

On the surface it might look more cost effective to do it yourself. After all, you have to pay startup fees and a portion of the commissions you pay to affiliates to the solution provider, but there are other cost considerations to keep in mind.

First, consider paying your affiliates. That monthly or quarterly check has to be computed, recorded, written, and sent out. If you have thousands and thousands of affiliates, writing out these checks—most for small amounts—can take up a considerable amount of time for your payables department, not to mention the time required for tracking and reporting all this to your affiliates.

Second, you will need to have some way to serve the banner and graphic links to your affiliate's sites. To do this, you'll need an ad server. Someone will have to answer technical questions as to how and where to place the HTML code that links back to your program from the affiliate's site. This is no small task. This kind of technical support—especially for the many small sites that are not technically savvy—can eat up a lot of your IT personnel's time.

Third, you will have to take care of all your affiliate recruitment. As we discussed in Step Three, the affiliate solution providers expose your program to large pools of affiliates (see Figure 9.2).

On the other hand, you can probably save money by operating a program yourself using the affiliate program software that is available to companies. In this way you can avoid monthly fees and/or additional commissions fees the solution providers charge. And, of course, you'll be able to design your program exactly the way you want it. So it's pretty obvious that you will need to do some calculations as to how such a decision, in-house or outsource, will effect the bottom line of your program.

Leaving the option of writing an affiliate tracking and reporting program from scratch (an option most companies would not have due to time and expense), there are several affiliate tracking and management software programs that are available for use. Affiliate Link software from AffiliateZone.com (www.affiliatezone.com/) is

Don't

DON'T rely simply on cookies to track your affiliate program. Using cookies as a way to track future sales of a customer referred by a merchant doesn't always work. People can delete them from their PC or just turn them off in their browser. Also cookies eventually expire.

a low-cost software program that allows companies to start and maintain their own affiliate program for goods or services. It provides everything from signing up as an affiliate to providing real-time reports to checking administrative statistics. You don't have to be a programmer to use its software. AffiliateZone.com will install these scripts on your server and give you simple directions on how to use the software. AffiliateZone.com will also mail commission checks for you if you choose that option.

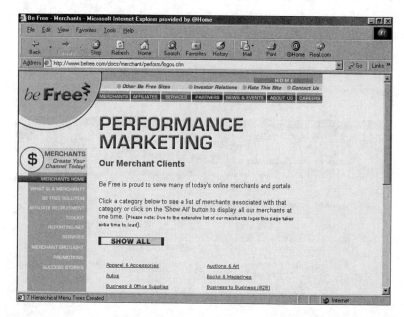

Figure 9.2
As a Be Free client, you affiliate program is listed on Be Free's site for all its affiliate clients to see.

AffiliateShop (www.affiliateshop.com), a service by Pendulab, offers a variety of features, including the affiliate application review, automated affiliate registration system, customizable individual payout rate for each affiliate, general announcement service to all your affiliates, anti-fraud mechanism, customizable look and feel of your affiliate registration form, two-tier tracking, and more.

AssocTRAC (http://www.assoctrac.com/) from the Internet Marketing Center features real-time tracking of stats, easy sign up of new affiliates, tracking through cookies and CGI Scripts, easy integration into your existing e-commerce systems, and an SQL relational database for quick accessing.

My Affiliate Program (www.myaffiliateprogram.com) from Kowabunga Technologies is Web based and their Affiliate Marketing Tracking, Automation, and Management application plugs-in to any Web site, giving you the ability to run your own affiliate program on your own terms, with your unique strategy.

Although these software programs cost some money, there is an affiliate management program that is totally free. FreeFiliate (www.freefiliate.com) is a FREE affiliate tracking service that is Web based—no downloading required—and is full featured, fully functional, and easy to use (see Figure 9.3). This service is supported by sponsor advertisements, and there is an option to pay a setup and monthly fee if you want to not have the advertising on your pages.

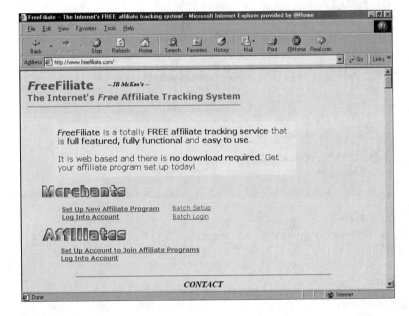

Figure 9.3
FreeFiliate is a totally free affiliate tracking service that is Web based.

But what about payments? If you're running your own program, how do you handle all those small payouts to your affiliates effectively?

Paying Affiliates Yourself

Writing hundreds or even thousands of checks a month payable to each affiliate is quite a time-consuming and costly task. But there is a way to do it quickly and inexpensively. A complementary service to your software program that many merchants are finding valuable is PayPal (www.paypal.com). Its Partner Program gives businesses a cost-effective way of handling the many smaller payments that tend to go along with affiliate reimbursement via electronic transfer.

Here's how it works. When you are ready to compensate your affiliates for a certain time period, you submit a list of e-mail addresses and payment amounts to PayPal. PayPal then automates a batch system to pay all your affiliates. Money is transferred from your bank account to each affiliate's "holding tank." The affiliate can then retrieve it by direct deposit or ask for a check to be mailed to her. You can even set a minimum amount to be paid. And here's the best part. The service is free to both you and your affiliates.

Another do-it-yourself payment solution is Infinia (www.infinia.com) (see Figure 9.4). Similar to PayPal, you can pay your affiliates electronically and often in amounts as small as $10.

Do

DO use the free P2P payment services such as PayPal if you plan to pay your affiliates yourself.

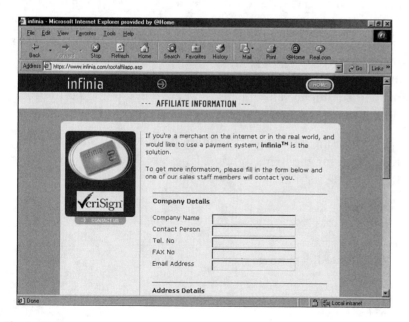

Figure 9.4
Infinia has a program where you can pay your own affiliates.

If all this sounds like too much work, or if you don't have the resources in-house to deal with a do-it-yourself approach to tracking, reporting, and management of your affiliate program, it's best to consider the services of the third-party affiliate solution providers.

Choosing a Third-Party Solution Provider

Though the do-it-yourself approach may seem more economically viable and can give you absolute control of your program, keep in mind that affiliate programs are becoming more and more sophisticated. Third-party solution providers are in the business of making money from affiliate programs, and they are motivated to stay on top of the affiliate marketing curve. This is very important to your program if you don't have the resources to commit a full-time staff to running your program.

There is another important consideration to choosing a third-party solution provider. Not only do third networks offer the management systems, services, and software necessary for navigating the details of an affiliate program, but they also serve as a channel for recruiting affiliates. The larger affiliate solution providers advertise heavily, trying to attract interested people to visit their site, learn about affiliate programs, and search for programs that will work for their site niche. This means you have a marketing partner that will help recruit targeted affiliates to your program.

When choosing a third-party solution provider, you should keep these following elements in mind. They are discussed in detail in the following sections:

- Cost
- Tracking
- Affiliate Recruiting
- Support
- Exclusivity

All these considerations and more should go into your decision of choosing a third-party affiliate solution provider. Use due diligence before hitching your affiliate program wagon to a solution provider's star. Things on the Internet just move too quickly to get oneself locked into an exclusive agreement.

Cost

Does the solution provider charge a set up fee? How much? Is there an annual renewal fee? Must you pay a percentage of the affiliate's earnings to the solution provider? How much? Are there monthly minimums that you should pay? How much and at what level do they kick in?

Does the solution provider write checks to your affiliates for you? If it does, what is the check-writing fee? What about affiliate recruiting fees, account rep fees, and banner serving fees? Do they exist? How much are they? Are all these costs à la carte or are they included in your monthly maintenance fees? Which type of fee program fits your business?

Tracking

How does the solution provider track and report stats to you and your affiliates? Some programs make you install sophisticated software on your PCs that requires days or even weeks of training to master. Do you have the time and personnel to dedicate to this task? Others require no software installation on your part. The tracking process is entirely Web based. Look at it as the difference between a licensing program and an ASP (Application Service Provider). Programs like these require only a few hours to get up and running.

Affiliate Recruiting

This can be a very important option to you when choosing among solution providers. How well they attract potential affiliates to their site and direct them to programs that fit their market niche can go a long way toward building your program quickly and effectively. On your travels around the Web and the trade magazines you read,

Do

DO use Commission Junction's direct deposit program. If you use Commission Junction as your affiliate solution provider, use its new direct deposit program to affiliates' bank accounts using the Federal Reserve Automated Clearing House (ACH) electronic transfer system. Using the system, you can directly pay all your U.S. and Canadian affiliates.

take note of the different banner ads placed by affiliate solution providers and see how well they are promoting affiliate programs to Web site owners.

Support

When you pick up the phone or send an e-mail you want real support at the other end of the line from you solution provider. Does she provide this? Is she prompt in her replies and does she answer your questions accurately? And what about your affiliates? How well does the solution provider support them? If she offers affiliate support, is she proactive in responding to your affiliates? If she is offering technical support or is writing your checks, can she be easily reached and does she respond promptly to requests?

Exclusivity

This one can be a show stopper. Does the solution provider require that you use ONLY her services and forbids you under contract to use any competing solution provider while you are with her? If so, this can dramatically reduce your visibility to potential affiliates. It can also hamper your attempts at joining other types of programs that, in themselves, are not solution providers but let you offer your products or services to their affiliates. Examples of these programs are ePod and vstore. As a merchant, signing an agreement with an exclusivity clause can be too much a price to pay if you intend to keep your affiliate program flexible and willing to take advantage of every new affiliate program improvement that comes along later.

Third-Party Solution Providers

Third-party affiliate solution providers come in two types. The easy to set-up and initial low-cost provider, and the more expensive and sophisticated higher-cost provider that supplies a range of services (see Table 9.2).

Do

DO be aware of any contractual clause that prevents you from using any other third-party solution provider while under contract with another. This could limit the growth of your program.

Don't

DON'T sign with a solution provider who excludes you from using the services of a competing solution provider. Look for an exclusivity clause in her contract with you.

Table 9.2

The Big Four Services Compared				
	Commission Junction	**Dynamic Trade**	**Be Free**	**LinkShare**
Set up	$1,295, plus $500 in escrow	$5000	$5000	$5000
Renewal Fee	$0	$0	$0	$1000
Commission	20%	Negotiated	2%–3%	2%–3%
Minimum Commission	$250	$0	$2000 month	$2000 month
Software Installation	NO	NO	YES	YES
Free Check Writing	YES	YES	NO	NO
Private Label Option	NO	NO	YES	YES
Time to Implement	1–2 days	2 weeks	2–4 weeks	2–3 days
Contract Length	12 months	12 months, can be cancelled with 30 day notice	12 months	12 months
Exclusivity Agreement	NO	NO	YES	YES

Be Free, Commission Junction, Dynamic Trade, and LinkShare are considered the Big Four of affiliate solution providers, although there are other smaller ones that you might choose depending on your affiliate program model.

Let's take a look at each of the Big Four and what they offer.

Be Free

Be Free (www.befree.com) (see Figure 9.5), the only publicly traded affiliate solution provider (Nasdaq: BFRE), boasts the category killers in its stable of companies, including America Online,

Barnes & Noble, and Gap, Inc. Be Free is expensive, but very good, and it offers a top-notch solution for sophisticated online retailers with lots of sales, as well as those who aspire to be the top players in their space.

Figure 9.5
Be Free boasts the big names in its stable of companies, including America Online, Barnes & Noble, and Gap, Inc.

Be Free has a sophisticated Affiliate Serving Technology called BFAST that can simultaneously monitor millions of hits on your banner links and tens of thousands of transactions generated from them. In addition, Be Free's banner linking technology, BFIT, targets, places, and tracks your banner links. From this, you can track the success of all your banner or text links to point of sale, which allows you to determine that a specific banner in a specific location led to the sale of a certain product.

You must install its software on your PCs and attend classes to learn to use the software properly. The trade-off here is that to have such a robust affiliate management software, it requires time to learn it. Set up costs $5,000, with transaction fees of 2%–3% of an affiliate's compensation, and a $2,000 a month minimum fee.

Be Free tracks pay-per-lead, pay-per-click, and pay-per-sale programs. It also offers automatic sign-up for your affiliates, and a choice of auto approval or manual approval if you want. Like the other affiliate solution providers, you can list your program on its site for its affiliates to review and join. Be Free announces new programs to its affiliate clients, which helps in your recruiting drive. It also has a system through which you can communicate with all your affiliates via e-mail.

All Be Free customers are assigned business consultants who will make recommendations based upon your business model and provide data points from other merchants' success, so you don't need to reinvent the wheel. Be Free can also assign an Affiliate Program Manager as an optional service at an additional cost.

Basic Be Free services for merchants include two programs for the price of one: affiliate and strategic partner programs, customized affiliate and partner Web site (`merchant.reporting.net`), unlimited business consulting from its affiliate consultants, unlimited technical support, unlimited support from a client development manager to build your program, unlimited access to the Be Free Customer Connection and affiliate knowledge base (where you can find any information you will need to manage a successful program), unlimited access to University Be Free (`www.betaught.com`), and recruiting of about 30 affiliates per day, every day. And Be Free provides a way to communicate with your partners via targeted messaging with 10,000 personalized e-mails per month at no additional cost. E-mails can be sent either as text or HTML.

Be Free offers a full suite of marketing services through the Be Free Marketing Platform at additional costs. These services include BSELECT Onsite (a real-time product or content recommendation service for site visitors), BINTOUCH (an e-mail customer referral service), check processing, the Advanced Marketing Pack (combining two of Be Free's most popular marketing tools—Dynamic Links and Auto-Merchandiser), affiliate support (Levels I & II), custom outreach, and affiliate program management.

In other words, Be Free supplies a very good, high-end system with the price to match. Be Free also requires that you sign an exclusivity agreement.

Do

DO choose an affiliate solution provider that offers more than just a tracking service. Look for a partner that will help develop your program.

Commission Junction

If there were a popularity contest in terms of number of merchants, Commission Junction (www.cj.com) (see Figure 9.6) would win. It is one of the leaders in the affiliate marketing industry and features more than 1,700 affiliate programs from a wide array of online merchants, including Fingerhut, The Sports Authority, and Tower Records.

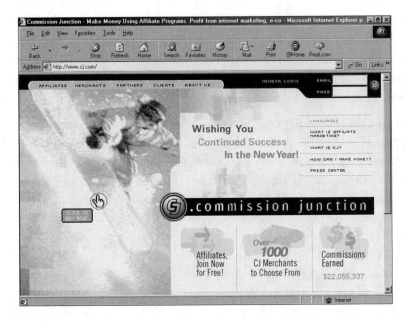

Figure 9.6
Commission Junction is one of the leaders in the affiliate marketing industry and features more than 1,700 affiliate programs.

Commission Junction (CJ) aggregates affiliates' commissions from all the merchants' programs that are a part of its program. Affiliates who earn over $25 in commissions from any of its merchants will be paid in one aggregate check every month. No specific account manger is assigned to the merchant, but the merchant is assigned to a client services group at no cost. Dedicated Account Representatives (DAR) are available for $2,500 per month with a one-year contract. There is a 90 day, "PowerLaunch" package available to new merchants for $2,000 per month for a term of three months.

Basic CJ services for merchants include Merchant Client Services Group, Web-based 24/7, real-time reporting and program-management interface, performance/term incentives and custom payout capabilities, aggregated affiliate payment, fraud detection and prevention, affiliate support, online knowledge base and FAQs, ad serving, auto-merchandizing and advanced link serving capabilities, product data feeds, and a two-tier recruitment bounty.

Its service is entirely Web-based. Because you don't have to buy or install any software on your PC, setting up CJ's program only takes a couple of hours. The set up fee is $795 with a renewal fee of $595 per year, and you have to pay 20% of the commission on each transaction you pay your affiliates. So if you pay affiliates $1 for a sales lead, you must pay CJ 20 cents. You also have to keep a minimum escrow account of $250, from which CJ pays your affiliates.

CJ's program, called EnContext, allows affiliates to create links to individual products on merchant sites. With this virtual store affiliates can select individual products from various merchants to create a customized store on their own site, earning commissions on all those sales.

CJ is committed to customer service and continual service enhancements and does not require clients to sign an exclusivity agreement.

Dynamic Trade

Dynamic Trade (www.dynamictrade.com) (see Figure 9.7) touts client merchants such as Eddie Bauer, Neiman Marcus, and Spiegel. Unlike the more well-known services like Be Free, Commission Junction, and LinkShare, Dynamic Trade stresses its ability to recruit quality performing partners that are revenue motivated and relevant, rather than the quantity approach of some other affiliate solution providers.

Dynamic Trade charges $5,000 in set-up fees. After the set-up fee, clients only pay for each sale or lead generated. That cost is negotiated with each client before the offer is made online. There are no monthly minimums for merchants and Dynamic Trade pays partners when they reach a $50 threshold. Every merchant is assigned an account manager who manages a small number of clients and stays in touch with them continually—this is included in the service to each merchant.

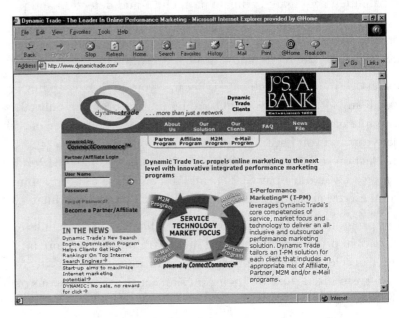

Figure 9.7
Dynamic Trade stresses its ability to recruit quality performing partners that are revenue motivated and relevant.

Dynamic Trade's tracking technology allows for even the most complex kind of partnerships. It develops individual personalized marketing strategies for each of its merchant clients by signing up powerful affiliates and integrating the pay-for-performance model into every aspect of its marketing strategy.

Dynamic Trade provides comprehensive, easy-to-use, Web-based reporting. No software installation is required. All reports can be downloaded and are completely customizable for merchants and affiliates. Merchants can track performance on an individual affiliate and promotion basis 24 hours a day, 7 days a week.

For additional costs, Dynamic Trade provides search engine optimization and e-mail programs that are purely pay-for-performance, as well as the ability for merchants to directly download individual product information to partner sites with its DDI 2.0 software.

Do

DO try to use a solution provider that does not require the installation of complex software to use its service.

Dynamic Trade does not require clients to sign an exclusivity agreement.

LinkShare

LinkShare (www.linkshare.com) (see Figure 9.8) claims to be the "first company to pioneer and launch an affiliate network," and its merchant list includes American Express, Dell, and Disney. Like Be Free, it offers a software system that you install on your PCs to manage your affiliate network. Installation time for the software on your systems is 2 to 4 weeks. It also offers a network of affiliate clients to merchants who want to recruit potential affiliates.

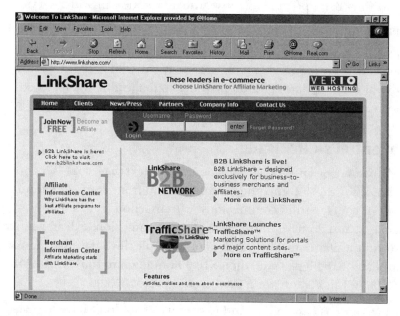

Figure 9.8
LinkShare claims to be the "first company to pioneer and launch an affiliate network."

Set up fees are $5,000 and transaction fees are 2%–3% of the earnings of your affiliates or a $2,000 a month minimum. There is also an annual $1,000 license renewal fee. Like the other solution providers, LinkShare does the tracking and reporting. Because LinkShare has attracted some big names, including Dell, you can benefit from the publicity it generates recruiting new affiliates. Its unique Linksynergy tracking software has some useful features, such as the Affiliate Content Spider that crawls sites for specific words or phrases you specify and the Grouping feature, allowing you to e-mail target specific affiliates.

Additional fees that include a $1.50 check-writing fee and a banner serving fee. LinkShare tracks pay-per-lead, pay-per-view, pay-per-click, and pay-per-sale programs.

Low-Cost Affiliate Solution Provider Services

If you're looking for some other options, bCentral's ClickTrade and ClickBank provide low-cost affiliate solution provider services.

Please note that the figures quoted in these following sections are examples, and some rates and fees are negotiable with some of the affiliate solution providers. Be sure to speak with a sales representative at each affiliate solution provider to determine the exact costs for your program.

bCentral's ClickTrade

Microsoft's bCentral's ClickTrade (www.clicktrade.com) is a good choice for those companies wanting no up-front costs. The trade-off, of course, is the commissions or transaction fees that they charge. You do have to pay 30% of the commission or lead you pay to your affiliates to ClickTrade. For example, if you are paying your affiliates $10.00 per sale, then $10.00 would go to the affiliate and $3.00 to ClickTrade, for a total cost to you of $13.00.

ClickTrade is easy to join and easy to use. You don't have to install any software, and ClickTrade handles all sales tracking and payments to affiliates. You will also gain broad exposure for your affiliate program by listing your program in its highly trafficked Revenue Avenue (www.revenueavenue.com) directory of affiliate programs.

ClickTrade will manage any cost-per-action, cost-per-lead, and commission-based programs (it does not manage pay-per-click programs) and pay affiliates with one aggregated check per month. An affiliate must earn at least $25 a month from all programs it is affiliated with to receive a check. This is important to affiliates because if your affiliate does not earn enough for you to pay them for that period but earns enough money from a combination of other ClickTrade merchants' affiliate programs, they still get a check for that month.

ClickBank

ClickBank is a combination e-commerce solution and affiliate solution provider for Web businesses that deliver unique products and services over the Internet itself (via Web pages, files, or e-mail). ClickBank has a one-time $49.95 activation fee, and a $1 + 7.5% fee per sale. There are no monthly fees, and it enables real-time sales of your digital goods or services, provides international fraud screening by ccScan, handles all customer billing and billing inquiries, connects you to its network of over 60,000 active affiliates, provides you and your affiliates with real-time sales reporting, and sends you and your affiliates a paycheck twice each month.

QuinStreet

Another option for merchants interested in launching an affiliate program is QuinStreet (www.quinstreet.com), "the specialty product network." QuinStreet is not just another affiliate network; rather it provides something new and different to the affiliate space, and its clients include Procter & Gamble, Apple, and Kraft. In a departure from the affiliate solution provider concept, QuinStreet is an end-to-end consumer marketing organization dedicated to bringing quality merchants and creative that works to its membership base.

QuinStreet acts on behalf of manufacturers to develop the links used on affiliate sites and often develops the selling sites too. Its team of consumer experts is dedicated to driving up response and conversion rates so that its members maximize their earnings. Partnering with QuinStreet requires no up-front costs and no infrastructure. Merchants in the QuinStreet network pay 8% to 25% commission, plus they receive ongoing revenue, which varies from merchant to merchant, for referrals and $1 to $75 for leads generated by their sites. Commissions are issued monthly with a threshold of $5.

For more information on the affiliate solution providers, go to www.affiliatemanager.net/asp.htm.

Making Sense of the Numbers

Whether you use a homegrown tracking and reporting system or the services of a third-party solution provider, making sense of the numbers will help you manage and develop your program to profitability. Making sense of the number of impressions, clicks, leads, and sales that appear on your daily reports not only tell you how well an individual affiliate is performing, but also how well your marketing initiatives are working. You've spent a lot of money designing your promotions and creating the creatives. The numbers generated by your tracking program can tell you a lot about how successful your marketing efforts have been—and can be—in the future.

So, where do you start?

First, set up a table that contains the necessary reporting statistics that you'll need to make sense of your numbers (see Table 9.3).

Table 9.3

Affiliate Network Analysis			
	Month 1	Month 2	Month 3
Total # Impressions	350,000	400,000	450,000
Total # Click-throughs	10,500	12,000	13,500
Conversion Rate	3%	3%	3%
Total # Transactions	105	180	270
Conversion Rate	1%	1.5%	2%

Once you've created your table, the first step is to look at the total number of impressions your banner or text links are generating across your affiliate network. Then look at the total number of clicks or click-throughs on your banner or text links. Using these two numbers, calculate the conversion rate of impressions to clicks. You may be generating a large number of impressions, and that impression rate may be growing month to month due to the addition of new affiliates or a better job of attracting visitors by some of your better affiliates. But what's important is the conversion rate of those visitor impressions to visitor action.

Do

DO study and analyze your click-through reports to see how successful your marketing efforts are and whether your creative is making customers click on your offer.

Don't

DON'T use the same creative—graphic or text—for more than a month or so. Keep your creative fresh and constantly changing. You expect to see content change on your affiliate sites and they expect to see your creative change as well.

If your impressions are going up but the number of click-throughs are stagnant or going down, these are red flags telling you either that your offers are not generating interest or perhaps your affiliates are no longer placing your offers on their high-traffic Web pages. Bad positioning on your existing affiliate sites is one reason for a dropping impression rate, but another one is new affiliates that do not generate enough traffic— this can lower your overall impression rate. So it's best to look at both existing affiliates and their prior impression rate. If they seem in line but your overall impression rate is dropping, its time to look at the new affiliates and what they are generating.

In other words, if you discover that the majority of your impressions are being served by the same group of affiliates, the falling click-through rates are more likely a function of the need for new creatives.

The next number to look at is the action taken after a visitor clicks on your offer. This action can result in a sale, a lead, or filling out a form or entering a contest.

Obviously you want to see these actions, or transactions, grow higher and higher each month. That's the purpose of your affiliate program. If people are interested enough in clicking on your offer but do not perform the transaction, it reflects on your ability to justify the offer and close the sale.

Another important use for your transaction rate is seeing which affiliates are performing best in your program. At first glance, your best affiliates would be thought of as those with the highest impressions and click-through rates. But that's not necessarily so. An affiliate could generate a low number of impressions AND a low number of click-throughs, but his conversion rate of impressions to transactions can be high. An affiliate may have lower traffic than other affiliates in your program, but that traffic may be highly targeted, resulting in higher transactions for you.

That's why studying the numbers generated from your reports is very important in managing a successful affiliate program.

Step Seven—Paying Your Affiliates

Chapter Summary

How you pay your affiliates and when you pay them are two important elements of an affiliate program. You'll find that affiliate payment plans can vary considerably, depending on your strategy to attract customers and the type of affiliate program you are running—pay-per-sale, pay-per-lead, pay-per-customer, pay-per-click-through, two-tier, or residual revenue program. When you pay your affiliates is also an important part of your payment plan. When to pay them takes into account how often you cut checks to affiliates, what the minimum check amount should be, any thresholds they must meet before being paid at all, and whether affiliates should be paid at higher levels as they generate higher sales.

You must be aware of the red flags that can signal affiliate program fraud. Although affiliate marketing fraud is not a big problem as of yet, it's only a matter of time before unscrupulous affiliates make use of software to garner fraudulent payments. By monitoring your program stats frequently and analyzing them closely, you should be able to protect yourself from affiliate fraud.

If it can be sold online, then there's probably an affiliate payment plan designed for it. Besides commodity products, there are seminars, credit cards, merchant accounts, marketing programs, advertising—even real estate—sold through affiliate programs today. And although there's very little that can't be sold or acquired through an affiliate program, there are some basic rules to keep in mind when designing an affiliate payment plan.

Compensation plans are as varied as affiliate programs themselves. They range from a 15% commission on some Amazon books, to 1% on Dell PCs. On the financial services side, LendingTree (www.lendingtree.com) offers up to $14 per qualified application and NextCard (www.nextcard.com) offers $20 per enrolled cardholder. Consumer retailers such as FogDog (www.fogdog.com) offer a fairly typical 5%.

So when marketing a product or service through an affiliate program, you must think about the type of affiliate payment model that best fits what you are selling. Every affiliate payment model does not work with every product or service. Some models work better than others do. For instance, does your product or service lend itself more to paying for each sale or does it have a long sales cycle more suited to paying affiliates for sales leads?

Payment Plans—How Much to Pay

You'll find that affiliate payment plans are all over the map because several forces are at work. For most companies, it's their gross profit margins that dictate the payouts to their affiliates. That's why commissions are relatively low on commodity items, such as books, CDs, videos, PCs, and consumer electronics. There's not much there to pay affiliates.

For companies that sell downloadable products, such as software and books, the margins are a lot higher. In these cases a merchant can pay a much higher pay out. Sometimes even this doesn't happen. Merchants tend to be stingy with their affiliates and forget that they are a true business partner and should be compensated at the level of their best portal partners. If you have the margin to pay affiliates higher—do it. Treat your affiliate partners the same way you would any strategic business partner. Check your competition. Know your own margins and customer values. Think about all the ways and combinations of ways to pay your affiliates, and offer a way for them to earn revenue from the lifetime value of the customers they send you.

Short changing such an important sales channel will only hurt you in the future.

Affiliate marketing doesn't always work for high-ticket items such as automobiles or homes because people don't buy enough of them to make the affiliate model work. A straight commission program selling homes or cars would earn payments that were few and far between for an affiliate partner. A better payment program would be a pay-per-lead plan, where a car dealer or real estate company would pay the affiliate for each qualified lead that he or she sends to the agent's site. A good example is Autoweb.com (www.autoweb.com) (see Figure 10.1). It pays affiliates for every customer they bring to Autoweb's Web site who lists a vehicle to sell or completes a purchase request for a new or pre-owned vehicle.

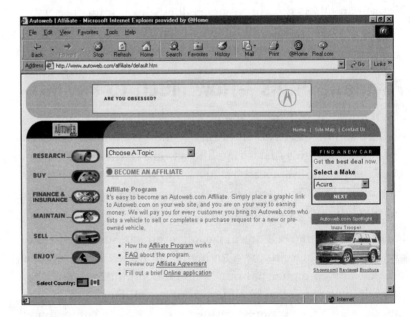

Figure 10.1
Autoweb will pay affiliates for every customer they bring who lists a vehicle to sell or completes a purchase request for a new or pre-owned vehicle at Autoweb.

If you want to pay only for sales that are made, then a pay-per-sale plan is best for your program. If you want to build a prospect list of potential customers or perhaps collect demographic information on consumers to use later on for marketing purposes, then a pay-per-lead plan would be the way to go. Or perhaps the type of business you have would benefit best from paying a one-time bounty on any customers referred to you by your affiliates. Then again, you might consider offering an affiliate program to Web site partners that gives them the opportunity to earn additional revenue from a two-tiered or residual-income program.

So choosing the right type of affiliate model is important to the success of your affiliate marketing program—and there are several to choose from:

- Pay-per-Sale Programs

- Customer Acquisition Programs

- Pay-per-Lead Programs

- Pay-per-Click Programs

- Two-Tier Programs

- Residual Earnings Programs

Affiliate marketing is very flexible and comes in all shapes and sizes. You will also find that the affiliate models are sometimes used in combination (see Table 10.1). When you're trying to decide what type of affiliate model to offer, it's good to look at what models are currently being used on the Net and how they're applied to selling actual products and services.

Table 10.1

Merchant Affiliate Programs and Their Affiliate Models						
Merchant	Per Sale	Per Customer	Per Lead	Per Click	Two-Tier	Residual Earnings
Amazon	YES					
ClubMom			YES			
EToys		YES				

Table 10.1 (continued)

Merchant	Per Sale	Per Customer	Per Lead	Per Click	Two-Tier	Residual Earnings
PayTrust			YES			
Flowers Fast	YES			YES		
TechnoSurf		YES			YES	
eSportStuff	YES				YES	
Virtualis	YES					YES

Let's take a closer look at some typical affiliate programs and what they offer their affiliates.

Pay-per-Sale—Commission Based/Revenue Sharing Programs

One of the oldest forms of affiliate marketing is the pay-per-sale plan. In this model, the affiliate is paid a predetermined percentage for each sale generated by his or her site visitors. Although this seems simple on the surface, not all commission-based programs are the same. The most common offer a flat commission rate on each sale no matter how much an affiliate sells. Other pay-per-sale models offer a sliding scale of commissions—the more an affiliate sells, the higher the commission rate. This gives the affiliate an incentive to more vigorously promote the merchant's product or service. Your commission rates can be higher for high-margin goods, such as books or software, that can be downloaded by or e-mailed to customers.

Forrester Research interviewed 50 retailers with online affiliate programs that were in place for at least three months. According to this report, most sites pay an average 9.2% commission rate to affiliates, but to recruit the best affiliate sites, some affiliate programs pay 20% or more.

Here are some examples of the pay-per-sale model.

The granddaddy of all pay-per-sale affiliate programs is Amazon.com (`www.amazon.com/exec/obidos/subst/associates/join/associates.html/`). Affiliates that join its program earn commissions of up to 15%. Amazon carries hundreds of thousands of book titles on almost every conceivable subject, paying 15% on over 400,000 select titles and 5% on more than 1.1 million additional book titles, CDs, and other products. Amazon does not require its affiliates to meet sales quotas to receive a commission. It pays quarterly commissions on every eligible sale regardless of how much the affiliate sells.

The Sports Authority sells equipment, footwear, and apparel for indoor and outdoor activities. Through its affiliate program (`www.thesportsauthority.com/affiliate/index.jsp`), Web sites receive all the tools they need to quickly and easily build their own online sporting goods store and start making money from their site. The program pays up to a 10% commission to the affiliate on each sale. The Sports Authority has partnered with Commission Junction—an affiliate solution provider—to provide affiliates with dependable third-party tracking, customized reporting, and monthly commission checks with a $25 minimum pay out per check.

Two other popular products that sell well on the Net are posters and prints. AllPosters.com (`www.allposters.com/affiliates/affiliatesstart.asp`) (see Figure 10.2) is a leading retailer of posters and prints, with over 50,000 items including an extensive selection from movies, music, sports, and fine art. It pays its affiliates a 15%–20% commission on each sale. Affiliates can choose from over 50,000 images to place on their site that link to Allposters.com. That's what's unique about Allposters' program. Instead of supplying a generalized banner link offering posters for sale, affiliates can actually place individual images of posters that can be purchased with a link directly to that offer.

Do

DO consider using a pay-per-sale model. This model is the most direct and most profitable example of a pay-for-performance affiliate marketing program.

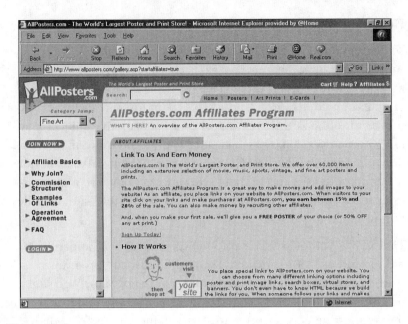

Figure 10.2

Allposters.com's affiliates program is unique. Affiliates can place individual images of posters that can be purchased with a link directly to that offer.

Standing products, such as books, CDs, toys, sports equipment, and posters, are not the only things that can be sold through an affiliate program. Take iPrint for example. iPrint (www.iprint.com) is an online printing company that does professional print jobs for its customers. It will take online orders for business cards, stationary, signs, and banners and ship them to the customer. Affiliates earn a 5% commission on every paid order placed and shipped through the link on their site. In addition, the affiliate also makes money on every reorder from its site.

More and more, the traditional click-and-bye affiliate model is being replaced with the click-and-buy one. Over the last few years, a new type of pay-per-sale affiliate program has emerged. This program does not sell products themselves, but sells the products of other online merchants. The program gives affiliates the ability to set up an actual store on their site and earn commissions on every product they sell. These programs have improved upon the traditional pay-per-sale affiliate model by allowing the affiliate to keep the visitors on their site while they shop and buy.

vstore (www.vstore.com) (see Figure 10.3) is one example. vstore's model allows the affiliate to keep the visitor on their site after a purchase is made. With vstore, affiliates can sell products from over 130 distributors. vstore offers affiliates a choice of themes and categories to feature in their store, such as a NASCAR, Elvis, or an Irish store. Current commissions range from 2%–25%, depending on the type of products the affiliate sells.

Figure 10.3
vstore's model allows the affiliate to keep the visitor on their site after a purchase is made.

Then there's Mercata (www.mercata.com/). Just about all pay-per-sale affiliate programs work on a fixed price model. Not so with Mercata. With its e-commerce system, the more people who buy a product the lower the price will go. It is offering to let Web sites to participate in this new way of selling on the net through its affiliate program. Affiliates earn a 5% commission on sales generated through a link from its Web site. Through Mercata, affiliates can sell personal electronics, home and kitchen, baby, lawn and garden, home office products, appliances, jewelry, tools, and other merchandise categories.

Finally, even intangibles can be sold through a pay-per-sale affiliate program. 180096hotel.com (www.180096hotel.com/html/hrnaffil-iatelee.html) is a large hotel-reservations network that sells 50% of all non-airline system hotel reservations over the Internet. It features hotels in 27 major destinations worldwide. Using its affiliate program, an affiliate can build her own hotel booking area on her site with its own look and feel. The affiliate is paid a 5% commission on all hotel rooms booked on her site. With the average sale of a premium hotel room going for $350, the average commission per sale earned by an affiliate is $17.50.

Customer Acquisition Programs—Bounty Programs

Different from the pay-per-sale programs are the customer acquisition programs or bounty programs. Whereas affiliates in the pay-per-sale programs get paid each time a customer buys from their site, the customer acquisition program only pays once—upon the acquisition of the customer. In other words, the affiliate site is paid a fee for each new customer referred to the merchant who sets up an account. The customer must be a new, unique visitor and must purchase at least one product or service. Normally, any sales made by the customer later do not earn a commission for the affiliate.

Many products and services lend themselves to this type of program, more so than the pay-per-sale model. Here are some good examples:

With eToys (www.etoys.com/html/affiliate_home.shtml), affiliates can offer toys from one of the biggest toy stores on the Net. eToys will pay an affiliate $10 for every new customer she sends to its site. The eToys Storefront is the recommended feature for affiliates. This Storefront has a number of different links to many areas within the eToys site as well as the eToys popular quick search.

1st American Card (www.1stamericancardservice.com/FindersFee.html) is a company that offers credit card accounts for merchants who want to accept credit cards on their site.

Affiliates who direct qualified merchants to 1st American Card earn from $25.00–$450.00 per approved merchant.

Do

DO consider paying a bounty for each customer instead of paying a commission on a sale to the affiliate if your sales cycle is long. Many products are not an impulse buy regardless of the sales pitch made by a good affiliate. Paying a bounty to the affiliate if the lead he sent previously buys is a fair way to compensate an affiliate for his work.

Teknosurf AdWave (`reports.advertising.com/webmaster/ signup.jsp`) offers Web site owners a way to generate revenues from their site with advertising. Affiliates can have sponsors, such as Hotmail, Amazon, Ebay, and Disney, sponsoring their site and paying the affiliate for every visitor they send to Teknosurf. It pays $5 for every Webmaster an affiliate refers who joins and $2 when he or she refer someone who joins.

InnovioOffice (`www.innovio.com/affiliate.html`), a small-business, e-commerce, Web-hosting, e-mail, and Internet access solution provider, pays affiliates a bounty of $50 when a prospective customer clicks the link on an affiliate's site, signs up for InnovioOffice, and maintains the account for 32 days. Affiliates can make up to an additional $40 depending on which InnovioOffice service the affiliate's referral chooses.

Internet.com Seminar Affiliate Program (`www.internet.com/ affiliates/`) organizes seminars with events taking place in New York, San Francisco, and London. Events serve fields, such as affiliate programs and solutions, search engine promotion and strategies, and computer technology. By promoting internet.com seminars on its Web site, an affiliate can earn $50 per registration. Other bounty programs that pay per sign-ups are JFAX.COM (`www.jfax.com/affiliate.html`), B3 Productions (`www.b3.com.au/affiliates.htm`), and Vault.com (`www.vault.com/vstore/pages/affiliate.cfm`).

JFAX.COM (`www.j2.com/about_j2/affiliates.asp`) offers its customers a complete, unified messaging service—voice mails and faxes in their e-mail in-box—while affiliates earn a 50 cent bounty for every free Fax sign-up, along with an additional $3.00 should the subscriber upgrade to its premium service. B3 Productions hosts feature-rich personal Web sites. Affiliates that promote its program can earn a $50 or $100 bounty for each friend or colleague it signs up for a Web site.

Vault.com (`vault.com/admin2/affiliate.jsp`) (see Figure 10.4) provides career management and advancement tools to a professional audience. Affiliates that add Vault.com links to their Web site, e-mail, newsletter, or classified ads can earn $2.00 every time a customer referred to them signs up as a member of Vault.

Do

DO consider a bounty or customer acquisition model if your product or service takes a long sales cycle. In this case, the affiliate site is paid a fee for each new customer referred to you who sets up an account

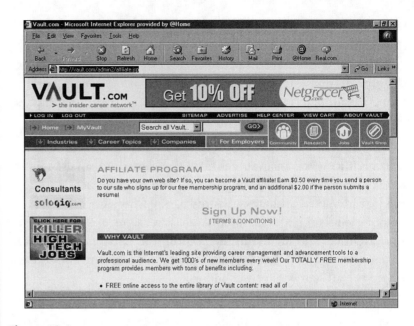

Figure 10.4
Affiliates earn $2.00 every time a customer referred to them signs up as a member of Vault.

Pay-per-Lead—Lead Generation Programs

Some products do not sell well directly on the Internet. In this case, affiliate selling can help you acquire a number of pre-qualified leads and prospects that you can follow-up with and close later on. This model also works well to register people for services online. In the world of business there are customers and there are prospective customers. These prospective customers are sometimes called leads, and every successful business must attract a continuous number of them. There are a number of affiliate programs that do just that.

The pay-per-lead payment plan does not necessarily require that a customer lead actually purchase something. This model could include collecting e-mail addresses or filling out application forms, such as creating mailing lists and membership applications. A merchant will pay an affiliate simply for the chance to follow-up on a lead that may become an active customer.

Here are some examples of pay-per-lead programs.

ClubMom (`http://www.clubmom.com/areas/corporate/affiliates.jhtml`) (see Figure 10.5), the first free membership organization created exclusively to reward and celebrate Moms every day, pays $1 ($1.25 after 50 referrals) for each mom that registers for a free membership. Because the ClubMom site (`www.clubmom.com`) features original content, the articles, checklists, and other proprietary matter make great, high-conversion affiliate links.

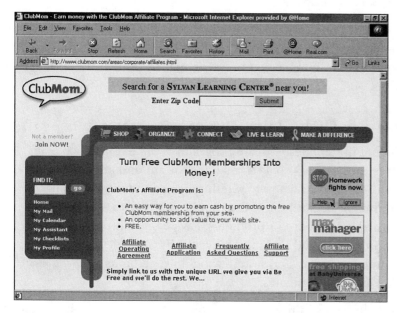

Figure 10.5
ClubMom pays $1 ($1.25 after 50 referrals) for each mom who registers for a free membership.

Collegiate Funding Services (`www.cfsloans.com/`), a leading provider of repayment solutions to student loan borrowers, will pay affiliates $1.25 per lead.

PayTrust (`affiliate.paytrust.com/aff/aff_home.htm`), a payment solutions provider that allows subscribers to receive, pay, and organize all their bills online, will pay at least $20 for every customer an affiliate refers.

TigerQuote (www.tigerquote.com/) compares quotes from dozens of leading insurance providers—auto, home, life, and health—and helps its customers obtain the best possible plan and rate. It pays affiliates $2 per lead.

Another life insurance site with a pay-per-lead program is Termco.com (www.termco.com/), which sells term life insurance for consumers who want to compare term life rates online. Affiliates earn $5.00 per qualified lead for sending qualified insurance shoppers to the termco.com site.

Finally, there's YAC (www.yac.com/). It pays affiliates $1.00 for each new subscriber that registers for a free personal YAC Number. A YAC Number is a new way of managing the phone calls, voice messages, and faxes people receive every day—free.

Pay-per-Click—Click-Through Programs

One of the simplest affiliate programs is the pay-per-click plan. Here the affiliate is paid a small fee for any and all traffic generated from the affiliate site whether or not customers purchase a product or perform an action on the merchant's site. Although simple, it does have its problems. Pay-per-click programs are open to wholesale fraud and must be carefully tracked. There have been complaints of bait-and-switch tactics by merchants and wholesale click frauds by affiliates.

To help combat this problem, companies such as the ClickTrade Service (www.clicktrade.com), an affiliate network-reporting agency, have instituted a number of fraud protection measures to alleviate this problem. For example, among other measures, ClickTrade only records a lead or sale if it occurs on a Web page the advertiser has deemed as an allowed URL. It also states that affiliates will be credited (at most) only once every 24 hours for each unique surfer IP address. All the affiliate solution providers take measures to detect and prevent fraud. Still, because of their simplicity, pay-per click programs are very popular among merchants and affiliates alike. Here are some examples of the pay-per-click model:

NetSponsors.com (`www.netsponsors.com/right_frame.htm`) is an advertising network that pays 14 cents per click-through. It also pays $4 for every site an affiliate refers to its network.

About (`affiliates.about.com/index.htm`) (see Figure 10.6) pays $0.01 for each qualified click-through from an affiliate site to the content from more than 700 expert guides on About. The About program offers banners to its expert guides, as well as search banners for its entire site.

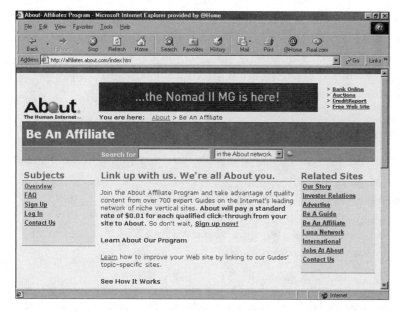

Figure 10.6
About pays $0.01 for each qualified click-through from an affiliate site to the content on About.

1 Nation Online (`www.1nol.com/webmasters/index.asp`) offers free Internet service just about anywhere in the United States. It will pay affiliates $.05 per click-through.

Affiliates that place EONS' Network banners (`eons.com/linkto_eons.htm`) on their site earn $0.15 per unique click-through. EONS is a network of Web resources, including Web site creation tools, promotion tools, e-mail, and many other personal and Web-site resources.

Don't

DON'T immediately jump to the conclusion of fraud. Before approaching an affiliate about fraud, remember that some ISPs, including AOL, recycle IP addresses. This can spoof the appearance of fraudulent activity.

BabyZone.com (www.babyzone.com/affiliate/), a company created and developed by parents, for parents, provides its site visitors with information, resources, and support on a wide range of parenting topics. It pays affiliates who link to its site $.05 per click-through. Flowers Fast (www.FlowersFast.com/getpaid.htm), an online flower shop, pays $.05 per click-through and a 10% commission if someone buys from its site.

Affiliates that join Private For Sale.com's program (www.PrivateForSale.com/aff.html) can offer home searches directly from its site. It offers the Official Multiple Listing Service for the private home seller. Home sellers post listing online and upload photos. Affiliates receive $.01 per click-through and 10% per sale. It is a good program for Web sites that are in any way affiliated with real estate or home design and furnishings.

Two-Tier Programs

Another payment plan that has become very popular over the last few years is the two-tier model. These programs offer a referral fee when affiliates sign up other affiliates under them. A good example again is Teknosurf AdWave. It pays affiliates $5 for every Webmaster an affiliate refers who joins and $2 when they in turn refer someone else who joins.

Here are some examples:

Outsource 2000 (www.outsource2000.org/), a source for certified, home-based career resources, will pay 20% commission on first level and 10% on second level. Commissions come from memberships, products, and services.

HootingOwl.com (www.hootingowl.com/), a search engine that allows Web site owners to pay a small fee so their Web site appears as one of the top listings for a search word or phrase, pays a two-tier commission of 20% on the first tier and 10% on the second tier. Its affiliate program also pays lifetime commissions.

SendMoreInfo (www.sendmoreinfo.com/Page02.cfm) (see Figure 10.7—a program for individuals—pays its members for every e-mail message they and their second-level affiliates receive. The first-tier affiliate gets $.05 for every e-mail they receive, plus they get $.02 for every e-mail their referral receives or sends. Each member receives a personal Web site to send their friends and prospects to in order to sign up for the program.

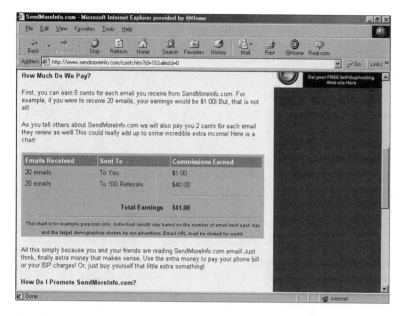

Figure 10.7
SendMoreInfo affiliates get paid for every e-mail message they receive. And if one affiliate member tells others about SendMoreInfo.com, she will also get paid 2 cents for each e-mail she reviews as well.

With eSportStuff (www.esportstuff.com/affiliates.htm) first-tier affiliates earn a 10% commission every time someone referred by them purchases from eSportStuff. When an affiliate refers other affiliates he receives a 5% commission from his referrals. eSportStuff sells and auctions sports gear, trading cards, sports collectibles, and everything sports.

Residual Earnings Programs

Affiliate program commissions are not about how much anymore, but how long. So more and more affiliates are interested in getting paid for the lifetime value of the customers they send to you—one that provides residual earnings over the life of the customer. After all, the affiliate has worked hard to promote a program and deliver a paying customer to the merchant. For all her hard work, the affiliate would like to earn continued revenue from site visitors that have become steady customers of a merchant.

Here are some examples of residual earnings programs:

The AWeber (www.aweber.com/) Follow-Up Autoresponder tool earns affiliates a 20% recurring commission on each monthly service charge plus 10% from its second-tier affiliates.

DebtGuru.com (www.debtguru.com/affiliate_how.shtml), a debt-reduction program, pays affiliates $4 for first tier and $1 for second tier. Affiliates also earn $1 residual commission each month when a client makes his or her payment through the affiliate's first-tier link and $.25 for payments made through the affiliates second-tier links.

DomainsMatter.com (www.domainsmatter.com/earnings.html), a fully automated domain name registration site, offers affiliates a 20% commission plus 5% in residual earnings.

eBookstand.com (www.ebookstand.com/affiliate.html) (see Figure 10.8) pays affiliates 10% on the sales of its e-books plus, for every author the affiliate refers and who submits work, the affiliate earns $25 plus a residual 5% on all the sales of that author.

Do

DO offer to pay your affiliates for all future sales to a customer the affiliate sends to you using a residual earnings program.

Figure 10.8
An affiliate of eBookstand.com earns 10% on the sales of its e-books plus $25 for every author the affiliate refers who submits work to e-books.

Infogenerator Systems (`www.infogeneratorpro.com`), a developer of automated e-mail marketing technology, pays out 30% commission on each sale made for the lifetime value of the customer. Finally, Virtualis (`www.virtualisys.com/vr/radams45/vrp.html`), a Web-hosting service, offers a recurring 10%–30% commission on monthly fees.

Capital One (`www.capitalone.com`) recognizes the entire customer value at day one, paying a one-time up-front payout of $25 of the lifetime value of the customer to the affiliate.

The OneandOnly.com Associate Network (`www.oneandonlynet-work.com`), the most widely-used matchmaking and romance site on the Internet, pays 15%–40% for every subscription. OneandOnly.com issues commission checks monthly with no minimum.

As you can see, a company can create an affiliate program for just about any product or service sold on the Net. All it takes is a little forethought and planning to choose the right affiliate payment plan to make your program a success.

Payment Plans

When to pay affiliates is just as important as how much to pay them. When to pay them takes into account how often you cut checks to affiliates, what the minimum check amount should be, any thresholds they must meet before being paid at all, and whether affiliates should be paid at higher levels as they generate higher sales.

Payment Frequency

The vast majority of affiliate programs pay affiliates either once a quarter or once a month and require a delay in generating the first commission check. Affiliates prefer to be paid once a month, and most affiliate payment plans are definitely moving in that direction. Yours should too. Initial delays in payment are important for two reasons. One, a 30- or 60-day delay in writing the first check gives you an idea of what kind of affiliate partner you have and how well he or she will contribute to your program. Two, a 30- to 60-day delay in paying affiliates gives you a chance to process any

Do

DO pay affiliates within a reasonable time. They should be paid no later than 30–60 days after they have earned their commission.

immediate returns or solve customer service problems that would affect the amount of sales that the affiliate has generated over that period of time.

It also provides you with a pool of commissions due the affiliate that you can tap later if refunds to customers are required down the road. The withholding of earnings works primarily for pay-per-sale and customer bounty programs and should not be used for pay-per-click or pay-per-lead.

Minimum Payments

You must decide how small a check you will cut affiliates when their check is due. Whether you pay monthly, quarterly and with a delay in payment, do you really want to cut a check for a few dollars or even a few pennies? Of course not. So you have to decide the minimum check amount you will cut for each affiliate. The minimum average most programs pay ranges from $10–$50 dollars per check. You would want to put in place a policy where sales for a given pay period that do not meet the minimum to process a check will be carried over to the next pay period, and see whether the combined amount meets the minimum to process a check. It's conceivable that a small affiliate with few sales, click-throughs, or leads might not see a check for months.

The minimum check amount policy will not make the small or under-performing affiliate happy, but it is necessary for you to keep program expenses down and at the same time, perhaps give an incentive to the under-performing affiliate to try harder. Worst case, if the under-performing affiliate cannot reach the minimum after several months of activity and you have worked with the affiliate to help her promote your program, then that affiliate should be cut from your program.

Payment Threshold

The next consideration for when to pay is more of a "whether" to pay. In the beginning some affiliate programs made it a requirement that no payment will be made at all unless the affiliate achieved a certain number of sales or dollar amount. These programs used thresholds to determine whether an affiliate should be paid at all for the payment period. This type of payment plan is not recommended, and those merchants who have tried either lost affiliates after they switched to threshold policy or have had a difficult time recruiting affiliates. The rule is, if an affiliate makes a sale or his visitor performs the required action, he should be paid for it, and paid under the payment frequency and minimum check policy set by you.

Rewarding High Producers

Your payouts can be higher to those affiliates who sell more than others can. You might want to consider paying your highest-producing affiliates a larger commission. Either a larger commission percentage or a bonus based on the number of sales or dollar amount for any given period of time. Not only does this reward affiliates who are helping you the most, but it is a fine incentive for affiliates to try harder. Another thought to attract these quality affiliates is to pay a high first purchase commission on the first-purchase a customer makes as an incentive to affiliates to attract new customers.

The capacity for an affiliate to earn large commissions is also going to play a role in attracting the top affiliates. The United States Affiliate Manager Coalition maintains a list (www.usamc.org/highest.htm) of the highest monthly payouts to individual affiliates. The top ten reported commission checks cut through December 2000 were:

$86,137.84—CyberRebate.com

$75,203.75—ClubMom, Inc.

$50,000.00—Ancestry.com

$37,291.50—Eversave.com

$26,000.00—MyFree.com

$23,000.00—The One and Only Network

$15,000.00—giggo.com

$12,500.00—Half.com Inc.

$12,000.00—GiftCertificates.com

$11,461.00—Greenfield Online

Do

DO consider using payment thresholds to pay high-producing affiliates more than others after they reach certain levels. This rewards your top performers and gives an incentive to your other affiliates.

Dealing with Program Fraud

Affiliate marketing can help put additional dollars into your bank account that you would not normally have—and do it without any up-front costs. But affiliate marketing has a dirty little secret—the potential for fraud.

We all know that what we see happening on the Net is not always as it seems. Individuals with programming abilities beyond the average merchant's have figured out ways to scam others out of their hard-earned cash. Although affiliate marketing fraud is not a big problem as of yet (very few cases outside of the adult entertainment pay-per-click programs have been reported), it's only a matter of time before some unscrupulous affiliates might make use of software to garner more per-click payments. There are software programs out on the Net that are able to automatically activate a link even when no real person clicked on that link.

What's your defense against program fraud? A well-managed affiliate program, and that means checking your program stats frequently—daily if possible—and analyzing them closely. Here are some of the warning signs:

Any brand-new affiliate that signs up for your program and within a week or so racks up more impressions and clicks than even your super affiliates is a red flag. When you see this, check out his or her site immediately. Look at all the referring URLs. Referral URLs that don't match the site's profile are a sure warning sign, and the same goes for referral URLs that generate a 404 error. A fraudulent affiliate might not be so greedy at the outset. He may hide his trumped up traffic by showing days of low activity and then days of very high activity. Monitoring your stats closely may show a pattern here that would raise your suspicions.

Another technique to use is a friendly conversation. If you suspect an affiliate of fraudulent behavior, try to get as much information about him as you can in a friendly, non-confrontational way. Ask him about his or her site. How it's doing. What kind of traffic he is getting and from where. Who is his target audience and if you can be of any help increasing his earnings with you. If you don't get a response after a reasonable period of time, this can be a red flag too.

Do

DO be careful of pay-per-click compensation models. They are most vulnerable to affiliate fraud.

Finally, if you are using a third-party solution provider, you may be able to get help from her. Some have programs in place that can track fraudulent affiliates and will tell you that such-and-such affiliate is deemed a fraudulent risk. On the other hand, if you suspect an affiliate of fraud, inform your solution provider and ask whether she has seen any suspicious activity across her entire network. Because she tracks all affiliates in her program across all merchant programs, she might be able to see patterns that show fraudulent affiliate behavior.

Before approaching an affiliate about fraud, remember that some ISPs, including AOL, recycle IP addresses. This can spoof the appearance of fraudulent activity.

By monitoring your program stats frequently and analyzing them closely, you should be able to protect yourself from affiliate fraud.

PART III

Managing Your Affiliate Program

Managing Your Program

Chapter Summary

Once your affiliate program is up and running, the work really begins. A large network of affiliates, great creative offers, and a good affiliate compensation program is only the start of a successful affiliate program. Running an effective program is more than a part-time endeavor. You must be prepared to support your program and your affiliates with a full-time staff focused totally on managing your affiliate program.

Who in your organization will manage your affiliate program and keep your affiliates loyal? These challenges must be met and overcome for your affiliate program to deliver on its promise. Whether you outsource the solution to these challenges or meet them in-house, the most important investment you can make in your affiliate program is that of staffing an adequate affiliate team. Managing a successful affiliate program takes work and is a process that continues long after your new program is launched.

Now that you have your program set up with hundreds of affiliates in your network and making initial sales and acquiring customer leads, you may think your job is done. Far from it. In fact, it's just beginning. If you think running an affiliate program once its set up is a part-time endeavor—just checking stats once in a while and sending out checks periodically—think again.

Even if you are using a third-party affiliate solution provider to do most of the heavy lifting of your affiliate program, you still have loads of work to do to make you program a success. How well you manage your program after it's launched and how you support your affiliates will make or break most any affiliate program. In fact, poor program management and the lack of support to affiliates is where most programs fail.

There are important tasks to consider to make your program a roaring success, like who in your organization will manage your affiliate program, how you will keep in constant communications with your affiliates, and in what ways you can keep your program fresh and your affiliates loyal. All these factors, plus supporting your affiliates with marketing assistance (this is covered in Chapter 12, "Communicating with Your Affiliates") will determine just how well your affiliate program will perform for you.

Personnel Requirements

The most important investment you can make in your affiliate program is that of staffing an adequate affiliate team. Most programs build their program, then add the responsibility of Affiliate Manager to an existing employee along with that employee's existing duties at the company. This is a mistake. You'll need a full-time team to manage your affiliate program.

You need to make sure you have the right number of staff members. According to the "Merchant Report 2001" from Affiliate Metrix, 45% of merchants have two full-time employees or more managing their respective affiliate programs.

Do

DO join the United States Affiliate Manager Coalition at www.usamc.org where you can pick the brains of fellow affiliate managers, learn what ideas have worked, and what is a huge time waster. Network, ask questions, pick up tips, and improve the caliber of your affiliate program.

Finding the Right Team Members

The team would have the responsibility of targeting, identifying, and recruiting potential affiliate partners and designing win-win programs for them. They should also be responsible for managing existing affiliates by communicating personally with your top performers, communicating via e-mail and telephone frequently with your other affiliates, and creating ongoing promotions for all affiliates and rewarding highly successful ones.

They should also be prepared to offer any technical assistance necessary without having to bother your existing IT staff. Your affiliate staff should be the ones designing the promotional banner links, writing contextual links, creating coupons, gift certificates, tracking stats, promotions, and special offer pages, and fulfilling many other merchandising needs for an active affiliate program. The team is also responsible for developing best practices and education materials for the affiliates.

Finally, whoever they are, your staff members should be easily accessible via e-mail and phone.

When building your team, your affiliate manager is key. Choosing the right kind of manager will set the tone for your entire program. Don't expect to find someone with years of experience in affiliate management. The industry is too new for that. Also, don't look for someone from the corporate world or a recent b-school graduate. What's important here is experience with Internet marketing and some experience with affiliate programs, or the ability to recruit and manage business partners.

Do

DO look for an affiliate manager who has good people skills. He will be dealing closely and on a personal basis with your affiliates.

Look for someone who is high on people skills and can adapt to change quickly. You're looking for out-of-the-box thinkers who can see relationships that others don't see. This is particularly important when choosing affiliate candidates. Knowing the Web well and having good browsing experience are prime skills necessary for targeting, identifying, and recruiting good affiliates.

Look for people who have experience buying online. They may not have e-commerce experience on the business side, but they should at least know what it means to be a customer on the consumer side.

A person who has joined an affiliate program or two is another good candidate. She would be exposed to the mechanics of affiliate programs and would know from day one what works for affiliate and what does not. In fact, it's a good idea to have both your affiliate manager, when hired, and her staff actually join some affiliate programs themselves. Have them set up a Web site on one of the free domain servers and experience first-hand those programs that closely match yours. Then, to help educate your other company employees about affiliate marking, have them set up their own sites and join those programs. This way you'll be establishing more awareness and support for your program.

Above all, you're looking for a person with vision. One who will set the direction of your program and be its evangelist to the rest of your company. His or her focus should be the customer first—that is, your affiliates—and he should have very good communication skills. The affiliate manager will be responsible for showing your face to your affiliate partners, and what they see and hear from the affiliate manager will drastically affect the success of your program.

Compensation

And what should you pay your affiliate manager? Compensation is all over the map. The United States Affiliate Manager Coalition recently surveyed affiliate marketing professionals regarding their annual incomes, and based on 43 respondents, the survey showed that 7% of affiliate marketers are making less than $40K per year; 44% earn $40K to $59K per year; 30% earn $60K to $79K per year; and 19% earn $80K or more annually.

With a lot of work and some luck, you might be able to find team members who will work for less than the average just to gain the experience. These are students or other young people looking to gain Internet marketing experience as unpaid interns. You can look for these people at Internship Programs.com (www.internshipprograms.com) or call your local universities.

Ultimately, the best affiliate manager for you is not necessarily the one with the Harvard MBA, but rather the person who has his or her own site and knows how to make money with affiliate marketing.

Although it is recommended that you at least have an affiliate manager to oversee your program, it is preferable to have an affiliate team. The affiliate manager will excel if she is able to focus on managing the program, budgeting and coordinating with the finance people, and building support within the company. There should also be an affiliate outreach person on the affiliate team who proactively scours the Internet to recruit targeted sites.

It's a tremendous help to have a dedicated affiliate tech on the team. This person coordinates back-end implementation and functionality of the program (especially necessary for an in-house program), troubleshoots any breakdown in tracking, and pulls reporting data for the affiliate manager. Last, an affiliate analyst is a key position to focus on some of the items that are often neglected by affiliate managers, such as managing relationships with top affiliates, analyzing the performance and trends of affiliates, and developing promotions and offers for the affiliates.

Outsourcing

Affiliate marketing is growing, and it's growing fast. According to popular quotes, some sites are making 40% of their revenue from affiliate sales. And if that number is overstated, and a more realistic figure is a 10%–15% increase in revenue, who wouldn't like to have 15% more sales right now? So time is of the essence. The time to start is now.

One way to build your management team and your program quickly, or to jump-start a stalled program, is to outsource it to a knowledgeable consultant or organization that specializes in managing affiliate programs. Some of the better-known affiliate program consultants were named in Chapter 4, "Step One—Planning Your Affiliate Program." Some others are listed here.

ADNet International (www.adnetinternational.com) (see Figure 11.1) launches and develops performance marketing for companies of all sizes, monetizing traffic through tested, proven Internet strategies that generate profits. Its team members include Patrick Anderson and Declan Dunn. ADNet provides automated storefronts, systems, and training to improve conversion and sales by creating immediate, responsive relationships with visitors, building

Do

DO participate in the CashCorner discussion board. It's an interactive message board that connects you with affiliates and merchants so you can learn directly from others already in the field. It's at www.cashpile.com/CashCorner/conferences/.

viral marketing lists of consumers and businesses, tracking knowledge of customers' buying behaviors, and automating businesses to generate residual income with little extra effort.

Figure 11.1
ADNet International launches and develops performance marketing programs for companies of all sizes.

ADNet helps funded companies, such as Internet Wire (www.internetwire.com) and WebPartner (www.webpartner.com), grow their business through strategic action plans, pay-per-performance marketing, and innovative methods of converting Internet traffic to sales. Some of the privately financed properties in development are Active Marketplace (www.activemarketplace.com) and AssociateZone.com (www.associatezone.com).

As mentioned in Chapter 4, two other consultants with an intimate knowledge of affiliate programs are Keith Kochberg and Linda Woods. Keith Kochberg runs a small marketing consulting firm called imarketing ltd. (www.imarketingltd.com), and Linda Woods offers a variety of affiliate marketing services as the Affiliate Goddess (www.affiliategoddess.com).

There are many companies on the Net that can help. One such company is Affiliate People (www.affiliatepeople.com). It can provide you with a turnkey solution for the daily management and marketing of your affiliate program. You are given a dedicated affiliate program manager who spends 40 hours per month marketing and supporting your program. With E-Base Interactive (www.ebaseinc.com), you can outsource your junior-level and senior-level affiliate manager duties. It provides affiliate management, recruitment, and support, and helps you communicate with your affiliates.

EcomWorks (www.ecomworks.com) is similar to E-Base Interactive and Affiliate People, but it also manages your affiliates by applying retail merchandising techniques as well as attracting new customers to your site, building brand identity, and generating sales.

Rob Flynn, a former client program manager at Be Free, started FlightPath Marketing (www.flightpathllc.com) (see Figure 11.2). The services available from FlightPath include day-to-day management, affiliate recruitment, compensation analysis, affiliate base analysis, affiliate communications, and performance analysis.

Do

DO investigate using an affiliate consultant to bring your program up to speed quickly and efficiently.

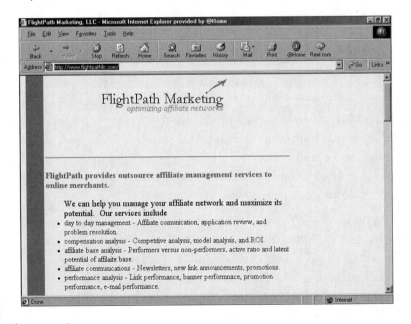

Figure 11.2
FlightPath will provide your program with everything from affiliate recruitment to day-to-day management of your affiliate program.

Mass-Transit Interactive offers clients a wide selection of affiliate marketing services, including the establishment of a client's network, recruiting and management of both base affiliates and super affiliates, structuring and managing different promotions to affiliates, reporting and analysis, and providing innovative tools to optimize network performance.

Another company that manages affiliate programs is TargetMarket Interactive (www.tmi-la.com). Its staff has knowledge and expertise in managing programs through Be Free, Commission Junction, and LinkShare. TargetMarket Interactive develops affiliate program strategy and implementation, including the defining of program objectives, managing and assisting in the launch of the program, and the development of an in-house affiliate marketing staff for its clients.

Other affiliate management companies include Affiliate Performance (www.affiliateperformance.com), Carat Interactive (www.carat-na.com), i-traffic (www.i-traffic.com), LinkProfits (www.linkprofits.com), SK Consulting (www.skconsulting.com), and Vizium (www.vizium.com). The services of these companies don't come cheap (see Table 11.1).

Table 11.1
Sample Affiliate Management Companies and Rates

Affiliate People http://www.affiliatepeople.com/	$2,495 per month
Alliance Builder http://www.alliancebuilder.com/	Begins at $2,000 per month
E-Base Interactive http://www.ebaseinc.com/	$50,000 to $65,000 per year for full-time management, or $50 to $60 per hour for part-time management

Table 11.1   (continued)

Sample Affiliate Management Companies and Rates

Greater Than One http://www.greaterthanone.com/	$5,000 to $15,000 for strategy, creative and Web development, technical integration, testing, and launch; $2,000 to $10,000 per month after launch depending on client needs.
Vizium http://www.vizium.com/	$30,000 to $45,000 for First Stage and then $7,000 to $10,000 per month.

Not to be left out of the affiliate marketing revolution is the United Kingdom (UK). As affiliate marketing has gained popularity in the UK, companies have emerged to help UK online merchants manage their affiliate programs. Like their U.S. cousins, DVisions Limited (www.dvisions.co.uk) and simplesiteUK (www.simplesiteuk.com) will establish an affiliate network for a merchant, recommend a solution provider, make commission structure recommendations, and perform contract negotiation and implementation. They will also recruit and manage affiliates, create and structure promotions to affiliates, and create banner links.

Ukaffiliates.com (www.ukaffiliates.com) is a full service, UK affiliate marketing solution, and it handles all the administration of running an affiliate program using bespoke tracking software. Its services include the promotion and marketing of client affiliate programs to its network of affiliates, monthly reports with analysis of sales, and the management of commission payments.

One of the premier consultants in the UK, is Neil Durrant (www.affiliatemarketing.co.uk/consulting.htm). He not only runs a very good affiliate directory site in the UK but also consults with merchants on their affiliate program and can work with their management team.

Do

DO consider using an affiliate solution consultant outside the U.S. if you plan to offer your affiliate program internationally.

Any way you want to approach it, there is an affiliate management solution to meet any size program. Since new resources become available all the time, be sure to look at the latest affiliate consultants, listed at www.affiliatemanager.net/consultants.htm, and companies available for affiliate program outsourcing at www.affiliatemanager.net/outsource.htm.

Keeping Your Program Fresh

One of the key challenges of an affiliate program is keeping it fresh and keeping it pertinent. If your stats tell you that your affiliate program is not measuring up like it used to, or if you feel you should be getting a better response from the offers placed on your affiliate partner site, then your creative and marketing copy may be getting old and tired or you may not be getting the most out of the traffic generated by your affiliate partners.

Ask yourself these questions: Are you using the same old creative you've used for the last few months? Do your offers reflect the needs of your potential customers? Do they reflect the season and are changed every few weeks to capitalize on seasonal events? And here's a very important thought: Have you reaped the benefits of the traffic generated from your affiliate site whether or not they have bought something from you? If you are not doing all these things, you are not keeping your offer fresh to customers and building loyalty with your affiliates.

It's not how many affiliates you have, it's how productive they are. Making them more productive is the prime objective of your affiliate management team.

Test and Test Again

Your affiliate management team should have these two basic rules hung over their computer:

- Track Everything
- Try Everything

We've already talked about how there is gold in your affiliate tracking reports. Careful and detailed inspections of those reports gives you a window into the performance of your program in general and specific affiliate and affiliate types in particular. But once you know what's happening in your affiliate network, how do you make changes to increase its effectiveness?

One way is to continuously test new creatives. The way to determine the best creative for a particular product or site is relentless experimentation and testing. You should be doing the following on a regular basis:

- If your affiliate links, such as banner ads, button promos, and text links, have not been updated in the past few weeks, change them. Affiliate links need to be regularly changed, analyzed, and refined. Just about any promotion's effectiveness will get old and decline over a period of time.

- Test your types of links. Which works better on specific types of Web sites: banners, buttons, text, text with banners, or text positioning? Perhaps your offers work better on sidebars with promotional copy and not across the page. Test one featured product instead of a general promotion for the products or services you sell. Results will differ wildly depending upon your affiliate partner sites.

- Test and refresh promotions. Schedule and test different promotions for different affiliates and categories, and evaluate which are the most successful.

- Test specific offers. Some offers work better on some sites than others even if the audience is nearly the same. If you sell PCs, you may find that computers sold on education sites differ from those sold on business sites. Create computer configurations that focus on that audience.

- Along similar lines, test your pricing models. Change your price on certain sites and see whether sales increase. Perhaps you can use the same price but change the sales terms and see whether that changes the response to your offer.

- In addition to testing the tools of the affiliate program, test the results you are able to reap when paying extra attention to some of your up-and-comer affiliates.

Do

DO test your program creative and marketing materials frequently. Also check your affiliate reports in detail, looking for patterns and trends in sales and responses.

Finally, start small. When you do a test, it's just that, a test. Don't run any test network wide. Run any test on a small handful of sites or on a small number of category sites. Try the test for a short time, such as a week or so. Use your reporting stats to judge whether it's worth doing on your entire network. If so, roll it out to all your affiliates where appropriate.

Personalization

Affiliate marketing is young, and there will soon be a number of technology tools that can increase the performance of affiliate programs over the coming months and years. One technology that shows promise is personalization. Personalization tools will someday automatically select affiliate links and target promotions based on the content that the customer is viewing, the customer's identity, and the customer's preferences. Yo! (www.yo.com) (see Figure 11.3) is an example.

Yo! uses collaborative filtering technology to recommend the right product to the right person at the right time. By just adding a few lines of HTML code to your site, Yo! learns from each interaction on your site and the others in its network to continuously improve the accuracy of your product recommendations. This can help improve the targeting of your offer and increase your conversion rate of hits to sales.

BSELECT (www.befree.com/docs/merchant/person/index.htm) is a personalization technology available from Be Free. Completely hosted and supported by Be Free, BSELECT is quick and easy to implement. BSELECT learns with each customer interaction, capturing click-stream information to make personalized recommendations in real time. It's a useful tool to enrich your customers' online experience and turn them into loyal customers, and it's completely anonymous.

BSELECT relies on customers' actual Web site behavior, such as the things they access, choose, reject, and buy. It uses the patterns that emerge from those thousands (or millions) of visits to figure out what people are looking for, then instantly displays the most appropriate links as recommendations. The merchant is able to choose from banners, buttons, pop-ups, or text with this technology. The personalization technology of BSELECT is different from collaborative filtering or rules-based systems, because BSELECT does not require the maintenance of data. It learns from each interaction in real-time, correcting itself when it is wrong and reinforcing itself when correct with Adaptive Relationship Modeling (ARM).

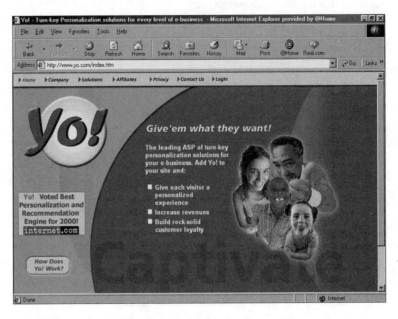

Figure 11.3
Yo! Gives each visitor to your site a personalized experience.

Do

DO check out BSELECT from Be Free, which can make personalized product recommendations in real time to site visitors.

Promotions and Special Events

One of the best ways to keep your program fresh is to align your promotions with seasonal and special events. By interspersing promotions that match well-known seasonal events with your special and general promotions, you make your program look new and timely and keep your affiliates happy by refreshing your content on their sites.

Start with the basic seasonal holidays. In the United States, plan promotions where appropriate around Christmas, New Years, Thanksgiving, Halloween, Labor Day, the Fourth of July, and Memorial Day. Include special events, such as Father's Day, Mother's Day, and St. Valentine's Day. Then there are the seasonal periods, like summers and vacations, weddings, and the spring, and standing events, such as anniversaries, birthdays, and baby and wedding showers.

Be creative and think of how you can use events and certain times of the year to sell your products and services. How about using the anniversary date of the Michalangelo virus when it arrives each year to promote your virus-protection or back-up products and services? Computer products can be promoted specifically during back-to-school days in addition to the holiday gift-giving season. Tax season around March and April is a prime time to sell accounting and tax-preparation products and services.

Have your creative department make specific banners and other graphic links that reflect the season. A consumer's eye will be better drawn to ads that promote St. Valentine's Day cards for sale than a general link that says "Buy your greeting cards here" or to an offer for a PC configured specifically for the back-to-school set instead of just a common add for a Pentium III. If you look at just the preceding examples and use a little creativity about your products or service, you'll see that there is the potential for changing your offer and creative nearly every few weeks (see Table 11.2).

Table 11.2

Potential Seasonal and Special-Event Calendar	
Month	**Possible Event Promotion**
January	New Year's Clearance Sales
February	St. Valentine's Day, Winter Sports
March	Presidents' Day
April	Taxes
May	Labor Day
June	Weddings
July	Fourth of July
August	Summer Vacations
September	Back to School, Memorial Day
October	Halloween, Fall Sales
November	Thanksgiving
December	Christmas, Kwanza, Hanukah

In addition to creating frequent promotions for the affiliates to use to market your site, it's important to develop internal promotions for your affiliates to reward performance and loyalty.

One promotion that has received great results with ClubMom affiliates is a monthly drawing for a site makeover (performed by the affiliate team). This promotion was started as a test to encourage affiliates to improve their sites in order to improve their commissions. It all started with a targeted e-mail to 300 affiliates that had links up but were yielding very little performance. The following e-mail had a response rate of more than 50% and, since the initial e-mail, 45% of the affiliates have received commission checks—none of these affiliates had previously received a commission check.

> *Hi <<FIRST NAME>>*
>
> *I was taking a look at your site and I think it has the potential to earn a lot more commission from ClubMom. Last month, you sent <<# OF CLICK IN PREVIOUS MONTH>> clicks to ClubMom for a total of $<<AMOUNT EARNED IN PREVIOUS MONTH>> in commissions.*
>
> *I would like to invite you to submit your site for consideration for the ClubMom Site Makeover. This is an exclusive, new opportunity where I will personally work with one affiliate per month and provide assistance in marketing and design, including search engine optimization, homepage re-design, and site promotion.*
>
> *If you are interested, reply to my e-mail by midnight on this coming Sunday (Sept. 10). I will contact the chosen affiliate by Wednesday, Sept. 13. Let me know if you have any questions.*

GiftCertificates.com (www.giftcertificates.com) ran a contest for affiliates where it asked the affiliates to make a suggestion about its program and ways to improve it. According to Ryan Phelan, affiliate manager at GiftCertificates.com, the one-time promotion went off well, and it was a great way to have all its affiliates become consultants for it. In this contest, the top five suggestions received a $25 SuperCertificate.

Another successful promotion was run by enews.com (www.enews.com) where it sent a free enews.com keychain to affiliates for answering a survey on its HTML/non-HTML newsletter. Of its

75,000 affiliates, a few hundred responded to the survey, and it was considered a success because the prizes were low-cost and it made the affiliates feel heard, plus it helped shape the newsletter in a way the affiliates wanted it.

Build an E-mail Marketing List

If you check with some of your best affiliates, you'll probably find that they have built an opt-in e-mail list that they use to sell the products and services of the affiliate programs they participate in. You should take a leaf out of their book and do the same.

E-mail marketing is one of the best marketing tools on the Net today—when done right. Getting the visitors to your affiliate sites to opt-in to a mailing list and obtaining their e-mail address with some demographic information and what their interests may be can be a powerful tool in your marketing efforts. One strategy is to present the opportunity to join the mailing list as an exclusive shoppers' club. The club would promise to give members a first look at any new products, or special sales offered only to them. The club can also act as a vehicle to target offers to specific members thus personalizing your offer.

You may even add additional value to the e-mails you send out by including an eZine in the club benefits. The eZine could contain informative and entertaining material on your product or service and how it can be of use to recipients. An eZine adds value to your marketing message and can help increase revenue. To have your eZine rise above the normal marketing e-mail, you need to make sure it includes good content. Although an eZine is a promotional vehicle for your product or service, to get it read you need to include useful information that your target audience can use and appreciate.

Pick a topic or an issue that matches your product offering. For example, if your company sells outdoor apparel, information about the features and specifications of the apparel may not be very interesting. But telling your audience where to use that apparel is another matter. Your periodic eZine containing your marketing message about a particular hunting jacket could be well received if you also write about hunting lodges or hunting trips where the consumer can wear it.

Don't

DON'T make your email to affiliates strictly a promotion vehicle for your company and its products. Give affiliates tips and advice on how to succeed in the affiliate game, like how to make their site more attractive to visitors and how to build a newsletter list.

So how do you build such a list?

Get your affiliates to build it for you. You already rely on your affiliates to draw traffic to your site, so why not ask them to help you find subscribers? After all, their visitors are already viewing your offer whether or not they click it and come to the site. Why not give their site visitors a chance to not only buy your merchandise but also sign up for your shoppers' club and subscribe to your eZine? And if you are able to tag the subscriber or the member with the name of the affiliate site they came from and market to them in their name, you are well on your way to creating a strong and loyal relationship with your affiliates.

Imagine if you told your affiliates that you'll be collecting names and e-mail addresses of their visitors. Suppose you tell them that you'll use these email addresses to actively market to their opt-in subscribers in the affiliates' name. Inform your affiliates that in the future all sales generated from these efforts will be added to the affiliates' earnings. Do you think that they'd be happy knowing that you're sending personalized messages to each prospect they send you and earning a commission if the prospect buys?

There are a number of ways to collect names and e-mail addresses of prospects to market to later on. First, place not one, but two links on your graphic banners. One part of your banner would display the latest promotional offer you have at the time and link to that page on your site. The other part of the graphic—or a separate graphic entirely that's not even connected with an offer—would link to your shoppers' club and/or eZine sign-up page. Another way is to offer a contest, free sample, or gift to entice a customer to join or subscribe.

Setting up an opt-in e-mail list takes some understanding of how a listserv works. You need your IT people to program the process of sign-up, confirmation, and the sending of your promotional newsletter or eZine.

An alternative to creating this program in-house is to purchase one off the shelf. Mail Master Pro (`www.bizpromo.com/mmp.html`) is a CGI script that you host on your server to build, maintain, and send out your newsletter or eZine. With Mail Master Pro you can send out a personalized text-based newsletter (and even create it in

HTML format if you want). Another product is Postmaster General (www.postmastergeneral.com). It's a Web-based e-mail management-and-delivery service that will automatically subscribe and unsubscribe people from your e-mail list in addition to sending out your newsletter.

Sandy BayNetworks (www.sandybay.com) offers a suite of integrated e-marketing solutions in its E-Marketing Service Partner (ESP) strategy to maximize the ability of merchants to acquire, retain, and create loyal affiliates. The suite includes a Membership Engine (opt-in e-mail/site registration), E-mail Engine (including list management), and a Newsletter Engine.

Marketing through e-mail on a periodic basis is a great way to keep your offers and your business in front of your customers and prospects—and a method that keeps your program timely and fresh.

Get the FAQ

One component of your program that can be a great efficiency tool is the Frequently Asked Questions (FAQ) file for your affiliate program (see Figure 11.5). Your FAQ should be comprehensive, with an overview of your program, information on commission payments, basic instructions on setting up links and maintaining the affiliate account, marketing and promotion policies, and any other relevant questions that affiliates often ask directly of the affiliate manager. Because most affiliates will not bother to visit the FAQ on your site, make it a practice to e-mail it to affiliates multiple times each year. This will help provide a more informed pool of affiliates, and it will cut down on affiliate inquiries.

Because staffing a program is a perennial issue, an affiliate manager needs as much help as possible to analyze performance and consult affiliates. Although all affiliate managers covet more data and resources, these are luxuries for too many. However, WebPartner (www.webpartner.com) offers a very helpful product called Affiliate Advantage that helps translate all the data you receive on your affiliate sites into business intelligence that you can leverage to increase revenue.

Do

DO create an FAQ of your affiliate program. The FAQ should include all possible questions that an affiliate may ask and should be posted ion your Web site.

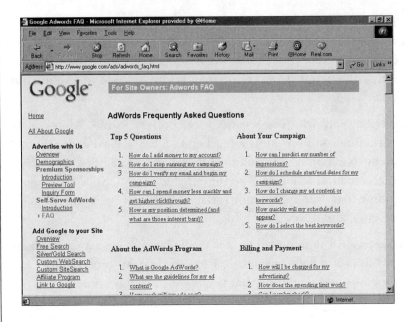

Figure 11.4
Google has a good example of an FAQ for their affiliates.

Some of the ways that Affiliate Advantage can help an affiliate manager to measure and improve the effectiveness of her affiliate program are to show how affiliates are merchandising your site, provide insights into the quality of customer experience at their affiliate sites, measure and rank affiliate performance to better assess ROI, and identify a set of best practices in performance and merchandising that can be deployed across their affiliate network.

Communicating with Your Affiliates

Chapter Summary

Ongoing communications with affiliates is vital to the success of your program. You should provide a number of different ways for affiliates to communicate with you, you with them, and with one another. Your affiliate program should include a newsletter sent at least monthly to all your affiliates informing them of changes in your program, new offers and marketing tips, and other motivational and inspirational advice to help them sell your offers better.

In addition to the newsletter communications, it is important to send targeted communications to affiliates. Tutorials are an important communication tool to provide your affiliates with the know-how to succeed in affiliate marketing. You should also include communications and feedback mechanisms on your site that help build a sense of community and a team feeling among your affiliates. Examples of these are affiliate discussion boards and forums, e-mail discussion lists, Webrings, and live chat sessions with your affiliate management team and among affiliates themselves. Finally, surveys and an affiliate advisory board will often provide constructive feedback that will help you improve your program.

Affiliates are your business partners and they don't expect to have a relationship with a faceless program. So communicating with your affiliates on a regular basis, asking for and sharing their feedback with other affiliates, and developing a community that gives your affiliates a forum to exchange ideas is critical in gaining and maintaining affiliate loyalty—and staying ahead of your competition. Here's why. Affiliates tell you what works for them in other programs by asking you for the same things. Establishing open communications with your affiliates not only helps them, but can improve your program and make it more competitive as well.

It is essential that the lines of communication are moving two ways. Although you must keep in constant contact with your affiliates, it is also vital that you enable them to be in contact with you. Many affiliate programs post a generic e-mail address for the affiliates to contact, and then respond slowly or not at all. You should be treating each affiliate as an important partner, so give them the e-mail for somebody on the affiliate team and respond within 24 hours. Also, make a phone number available, and if you really want to service your affiliates at a high level, provide ICQ/IM addresses, so affiliates can contact the affiliate team for one-on-one interaction in real-time.

Don't be afraid to revert to the stone ages and use snail mail once in a while to send post cards, t-shirts, or promotional trinkets to your affiliates.

Building a communications channel with your affiliates includes the following communication elements:

- Affiliate Newsletters

- Targeted E-mail

- Tutorials

- Discussion Boards or Forums

- E-mail Discussion Lists

- Webrings

- Live Chat Sessions

- Other Feedback Mechanisms

Do

DO become a four-tool player in affiliate communications by publicizing your e-mail, phone, ICQ/IM, and snail mail.

It is important to keep in mind that one of the key elements of affiliate loyalty is communications. Affiliate communications is a pro-active endeavor. It's absolutely up to you to initiate communications and respond to all affiliate inquiries for help and information within 24 hours. Put it this way: if you're not listening to your affiliates, your competitors will.

Affiliate Newsletters

You should be sending out periodic newsletter to all your affiliates—no less than once a month—that include important news, selling tips, success stories of other affiliates, and your latest product or service promotions. Its purpose should be to motivate and encourage your affiliates.

If you do not currently publish a newsletter, or you feel that yours could use some fine-tuning, try including the following parts in your affiliate newsletter:

- Earnings of your top 10 affiliates

- Code for automatic rotation links

- Names of the affiliates of the month

- Affiliate, marketing, and search engine tips

- A co-marketing plug

Start out each of your newsletters listing the commission amounts for the top 10 earners in the past month. Do not name names or shows URLs, just the amounts earned for the last month. Let's face it, making money is the reason your affiliates joined your program, and they would like some idea of their earnings potential. By listing the commission amounts for the top 10 earners in the past month, your affiliates can see what they can potentially earn, compare what they've earned, and see the potential of your program.

The next element of your newsletter should include your linking codes. This might sound silly because the code is available to all your affiliates when they log in to their account on your Web site or that of your affiliate solution provider. But you'd be surprised how many affiliates sign up for your program and never place your links on their site. There are a number of reasons for this (covered in Chapter 7, "Step Four—Choosing the Right Affiliates"), but one of the biggest is that they never bother to get the code. By including your code in every newsletter you place it right in their inbox.

Including success stories in your newsletter helps other affiliates not only see what can be earned in your program, but how to do it. This approach not only rewards one of your affiliates with a slap on the back and a "good job" but also provides you with a chance to showcase a site that is doing things right. The affiliate of the month award gives your other affiliates a look at what works in your program and a chance to emulate those best practices. Do not use your best performing sites as examples—just your good performing sites. This way you're not broadcasting to your competitors who your best sites are so they can poach them.

Following the affiliate of the month award are the tips. Here you want to include marketing tips that can help your affiliates not only sell your offers better, but promote and improve their sites to increase their traffic, which increases the visibility of your offers and your sales.

Finally, wrap up your newsletter with a co-marketing plug. Swap spots in your newsletter with companies that have affiliate programs selling products that compliment but do not compete with your own. By promoting complimentary programs, you help your affiliates make additional money, and your program in turn gets promoted by your co-marketing partner for that month in their affiliate newsletter.

Here's a sample affiliate newsletter from ClubMom that puts it all together.

```
=============================================

Welcome to the ClubMom Affiliate Newsletter

=============================================

We are looking forward to writing lots of commission

checks in 2001!

This month:

1. Top Ten Affiliates (December 2000)
```

Do

DO include affiliate success stories in your newsletter. This shows affiliates that sites can make money from your program and motivates them to try harder.

2. What's New with the Program?

3. Affiliate of the Month: Contest Hound

4. New article & checklist for your site

5. Affiliate Tip: More on affiliate mini-sites

6. Marketing Tip: Buy search engine traffic

7. Take a look at QuinStreet

8. Affiliate Contest: $100 for your opinion

9. Attn. Super Affiliates: AffiliateFORCE 2001

10. Affiliate Photo Gallery: Pictures of you

****

1. Top Ten Affiliates (December 2000)

****

How much money can you earn with the ClubMom

Affiliate Program? Below are the amounts

earned by the Top Ten Affiliates last month.

1) $12,976.25

2) $7,238.00

3) $5,920.00

4) $5,650.50

5) $3,848.75

6) $1,943.75

7) $1,897.50

8) $1,670.00

9) $1,530.00

10) $1,155.00

****

2. What's New with the Program?

****

Link to the new ClubMom Moms on Wheels section.
ClubMom has teamed up with General Motors to create
the ultimate car driving, riding and buying guide
for moms.

Below is your affiliate code for a 120x60 button
to link to Moms on Wheels (this has been our best
performing affiliate link for the past 7 days).

```
<IMG
SRC="http://service.bfast.com/bfast/serve?bfmid=26370742&sit
eid=<<SITEID>>&bfpage=moms_on_wheels" BORDER="0" WIDTH="1"
HEIGHT="1" NOSAVE ><A
HREF="http://service.bfast.com/bfast/click?bfmid=26370742&si
teid=<<SITEID>>&bfpage=moms_on_wheels" TARGET="_top"><IMG
SRC="http://www.clubmom.com/images/affiliate/testdrive1_120x
90_unl.gif" BORDER="0" WIDTH="120" HEIGHT="90" ALT="Click
here for your free ClubMom membership"></A>
```

Note: Get it! 2 Trivia Challenge ends on Jan 31

Chat with the ClubMom Affiliate Team and other
affiliates. We have a chat every two weeks. Next
chat is on January 16, 2001 at 9 PM (ET). Go to
http://www.clubmom.com/areas/connect/chat_index.jhtml

Coming soon... we will be offering a freebie
magazine offer (full subscriptions with no
strings attached).

****

3. Affiliate of the Month: Contest Hound

****

Congratulations to ClubMom's Affiliate of the
Month, Bob Gunther of Contest Hound. Contest
Hound brings you the latest online contests &

sweepstakes. Plus instant win lotteries, trivia, freebies, crosswords, humor and online games. Sign up for the free newsletter, every issue packed with valuable contests, trivia games and more. All that is needed is a blank email to contesthound-subscribe@topica.com. Bob is a stay-at-home father to a 15 month old daughter named Neva.

****

4. New article & checklist for your site

****

The current featured article is "Sanity Tips for Eating Out With the Kids," and we've added a new link section: checklists (the most popular area on ClubMom). The January 2001 checklist is "Childproofing Your Home." Pick up the code for this article at http://clubmom.reporting.net.

****

5. Affiliate Tip: More on affiliate mini-sites

****

Last month we mentioned affiliate mini-sites, and got a huge response and lots of questions. Basically, mini-sites are a single Web page that is designed to attract a targeted audience through the search engines, and then send them through an affiliate link to earn commissions. Due to popular demand, we've created some ClubMom affiliate mini-sites (one focuses on ClubMom as

a whole, another is geared towards baby sites).
You can find the mini-site code by logging in
to http://clubmom.reporting.net, and selecting
"Mini-site HTML" in the "creating links" section.
We encourage you to make some changes to the HTML
code provided to personalize it - this will make
the file more unique and increase your chance of
ranking well in the search engines.

Submit your new mini-site (as well as your entire
site to these main search engines):

AltaVista: http://www.altavista.com/cgi-
bin/query?pg=addurl#form

Direct Hit: http://www.directhit.com/util/addurl.html

Excite: http://www.excite.com/info/add_url_form

Fast Search: http://www.alltheWeb.com/add_url.php3

Go/Infoseek: http://addurl.go.com/dynamic/freeNewUrl

HotBot: http://hotbot.lycos.com/addurl.asp

Lycos: http://home.lycos.com/addasite.html

NBCi: http://home.nbci.com/LMOID/resource/0,566,-
1077,00.html

Nothern Light:
http://www.northernlight.com/docs/regurl_help.html

****

6. Marketing Tip: Buy search engine traffic

****

One of the keys to making money with affiliate
programs is driving targeted traffic to your site,
though that can be a pretty tough task. But there
are more than fifty sites that want to help you

drive cheap, targeted traffic (not only to your
site, but directly through your affiliate links).
Pay per click search engines enable you to drive
traffic for pennies. The most popular/expensive
is GoTo.com, but there is a great directory to
help you find the best search engines for you at
http://www.payperclicksearchengines.com/
If you buy words to link directly through ClubMom
affiliate links, please be sure to send the copy
to scollins@clubmom-inc.com before submitting it
to the search engines, or just ask and we'll write
up the copy for you.

****

7. Take a look at QuinStreet

****

As you know, Affiliate Programs are facing new
challenges everyday. A recent development that
you really can't miss comes from a company called
QuinStreet. They really seem to understand what
I have been writing in my articles and where the
industry is headed.

They represent over 25 great merchants, including
Hooked On Phonics, Kiss my Face, Balducci's and
Fitness Quest. They have onsite merchandising
experts and the latest in technology and creative
services.

Go to http://quinst.com/c.jsp?area=bonrukyubeishinasuyoda
to enroll or call Rick Natsch at 650/595-6203.

```
************************************************
```

8. Affiliate Contest - $100 for your opinion

```
************************************************
```

ClubMom is giving away $100 to an affiliate every
month in the Model Affiliate Awards Contest!
To enter the contest, all you have to do is write
an answer (between 200-500 words) to the month's
question and e-mail it to Marla at
mbaskerville@clubmom-inc.com.
January 2001 question is: What helpful advice
would you tell someone interested in joining
affiliate programs that you wish you had known?

```
************************************************
```

9. Attn. Super Affiliates: AffiliateFORCE 2001

```
************************************************
```

The AffiliateFORCE 2001 Internet Affiliate
Marketing Summit will be held April 20-23 in
Miami Beach, FL. I went last year (and I'll be
going again this year), because it's a great mix
of affiliates, merchants, business owners,
affiliate managers, consultants and Webmasters
from around the world.
For more information, go to
http://www.affiliateforce2001.com/

```
************************************************
```

10. Affiliate Photo Gallery: Pictures of you

```
************************************************
```

```
We are creating an Affiliate Photo Gallery, where

we will feature our very own ClubMom Affiliates

and the names of their Website(s). If you would

like to participate, send your picture and Web site

info to Marla at mbaskerville@clubmom.com.

You can take a peek at the photo gallery at

http://www.rewards-for-moms.com/affiliates/

****************************************************

As always, we'd love to hear from you! Drop us a

line and let us know if you have any suggestions.

Regards,

Shawn Collins

Affiliate Manager

ClubMom, Inc.

200 Madison Avenue, 6th Floor

New York, New York 10016

tel 646.435.6513

fax 646.435.6600

http://www.clubmom.com
```

You might want to include a question in each newsletter giving affiliates an opportunity to have their say about your program and posting their reply on your affiliate discussion where other affiliates can respond and comment.

All in all, an affiliate newsletter is an essential communications component and is the cornerstone of any affiliate management program.

Targeted E-mail

In addition to the affiliate newsletter, targeted e-mail is an excellent tool to increase your percentage of active affiliates, and may assist and improve some of your lower-level affiliates.

Don't

DON'T fall into the trap of thinking you know what's best for your program. Ask your affiliates what they want and need from your program in particular and affiliate programs in general. You may receive some valuable information to improve your program.

The unfortunate truth is that the majority of your affiliates will never bother to put up links. So make it easier. Send out an e-mail to the inactive affiliates with code for one of your links. Tell them you are available to help and include your contact information. Odds are that if an affiliate has not put up your link within a week of joining your program, then that link is never going up on their site.

How do you know which affiliates are inactive? Check your reports. If they are not serving up any impressions or clicks, they're not going to be able to generate any commissionable activity. Be Free offers an Inactive Affiliates report that makes it easy to identify which affiliates have not recorded any impressions. This report is based on whether an affiliate has served up any impressions, so it's not foolproof, because some affiliates remove the 1×1 pixel (which tracks the impressions) from their affiliate code.

Also, targeted e-mail is ideal for identifying underperformers and offering advice on how they could improve their results with your program. Segment out those affiliates that have a lower click-through rate than the average affiliate. Provided that you have a quality creative that is rotated every four weeks, you can expect to see a click-through rate of about 3% or so.

According to Nielsen Netratings, banner ads had a click-through ratio of .36% in March 2000. But click-through rates for the Commission Junction network are between 3% and 4%. Comb through your affiliate stats and when you find affiliates with a high rate of impressions with a low rate of clicks, you've got to check out their sites and help them.

Bear in mind that most affiliates are not marketing experts, and the reason many affiliate sites do not perform well is because of ad placement. Just look at the affiliate sites and locate your links. Odds are that the low performers do not have your ads "above the fold." Let them know this and their/your numbers will improve.

As mentioned in Chapter 11, "Managing Your Program," one targeted e-mail to ClubMom affiliates had a response rate of more than 50%, and since the initial e-mail, 45% of the affiliates have received commission checks—none of these affiliates had previously received a commission check.

This e-mail was targeted to sites that had affiliate links on their sites, but were not generating any results. The premise of the e-mail was that anybody who responded would be eligible for a free site makeover from the ClubMom affiliate team.

An important principle of the success of a targeted e-mail is to write a compelling subject line. Affiliates already receive too many e-mails, and it's a struggle to even get e-mail opened by your affiliates. Be sure to mention the name of your company and ask a question that you think the affiliate would be likely to answer yes. The subject line for the makeover e-mail was, "Would you like a site makeover from ClubMom?"

Tutorials

Don't take basic marketing tenets for granted when managing your affiliate program. There are a lot of folks out there who can use help. They are anxious to improve their sites and earn more commissions, but they simply don't know where to find the information. You can improve the quality of your affiliates, and therefore the performance of your program by educating your affiliates.

Provide tutorials on relevant subjects to your affiliates and you will have increased loyalty, as well as a better critical mass of affiliates. Some topics that would be helpful to your affiliates are how to rotate banner ads, buy your own domain, and create an HTML newsletter. There are tutorials and other educational materials available for free distribution at www.affiliatemanager.net/education.htm.

Of course, good placement in the search engines is a hot topic among affiliates. There is a free e-book called *Search Engine School* from the United States Affiliate Manager Coalition (www.usamc.org) that you can share with your affiliates. This e-book is a collection of tutorials that focus on optimizing a site for the search engines, and it can be downloaded at www.usamc.org/sesebook.htm (see Figure 12.1).

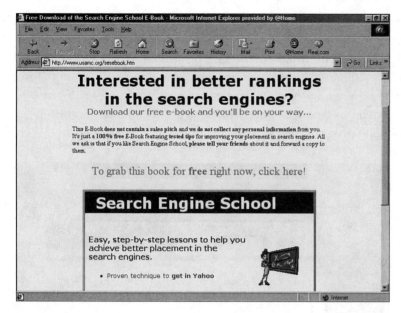

Figure 12.1
Search Engine School is a collection of tutorials that focus on optimizing a site for search engines.

Discussion Boards or Forums

Everyone has an opinion, and you can use this bit of human nature to improve and enhance your affiliate program. Set up a discussion board or forum for your affiliates on your site where they can discuss issues relating to affiliate programs in general, yours in particular, and ways for them to improve their site and increase the traffic that flows to it. By moderating and participating in these posted discussions, you can learn more about what affiliates want, the problems they might be having with your program, and even recommendations from them on how to improve it. These posted discussions can even act as content for your affiliate newsletter.

Creating a space on your site is only one way to invite and enter into a discussion with affiliates. By volunteering your program to be evaluated by your affiliates, with AffiliateVoice (www. affiliatevoice.com) you can gauge how well your affiliate program is doing from your affiliates' standpoint (see Figure 12.2.). AffiliateVoice is an independent rating system that enables affiliates

Do

DO Build Your Community with No Programming. "Build Your Own Community" offers software that lets you build guest books, discussion forums, polls, and many more great interactive features, including start pages for visitors that direct them to your site. Find "Build Your Own Community" at www. buildacommunity.com.

to voice their opinions about the programs they participate in. This independent rating system enables merchants to better understand how well their affiliate marketing programs are operating and provides affiliates with valuable information about a program before they sign up. Through a satisfaction survey, affiliates can give anonymous feedback and provide you with valuable insight for affiliate program development.

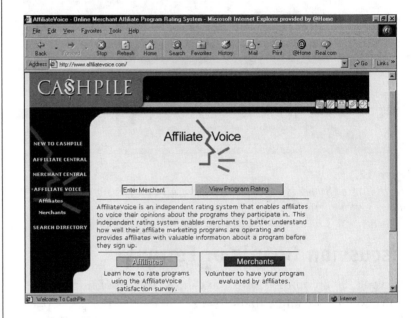

Figure 12.2
AffiliateVoice is an independent rating system that enables affiliates to voice their opinions about the programs they participate in.

In addition to the fact that AffiliateVoice allows affiliates to candidly provide feedback on your program, it also provides an opportunity for you to gain more exposure for your affiliate program. A favorable rating can attract countless new affiliates willing to market your product or service, because the programs that earn "Top-Rated" Program status are featured on CashPile.com and in the CashPile Newsletter.

Webrings

Many affiliates are new to Web design, marketing, and virtually every facet of succeeding in affiliate marketing. Webrings provide affiliates with multiple benefits. Not only will a Webring drive additional traffic to affiliate sites, but it will also provide a sort of search engine of affiliates in your program where affiliates can glance at a variety of sites in your program and see how they are promoting you.

Yahoo! WebRing (`webring.yahoo.com`) is a free service where you can create a Webring for your affiliate program in a matter of minutes. One example is the ClubMom affiliate Webring (`nav.webring.yahoo.com/hub?ring=clubmomaff`) (see Figure 12.3). There are also many Webrings dedicated to affiliate marketing in general, such as the Affiliate Program Webring (`nav.Webring.yahoo.com/hub?ring=affiliates`), which is run by Fox Tucker (`www.foxtucker.com`), an affiliate marketing consultant in the United Kingdom.

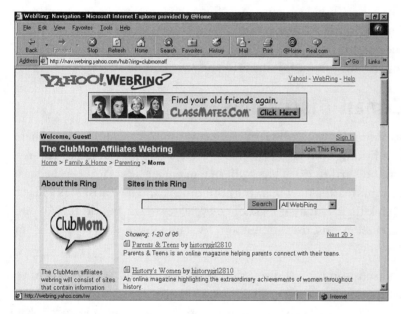

Figure 12.3
ClubMom has an affiliate Webring.

Chat Sessions

Another good feedback mechanism to use with affiliates is to host live chat sessions on your site. You can invite your affiliates through an e-mail or in your affiliate newsletter to visit you during the chat session at a designated time to discuss a particular topic or hold a general bull session. You can discuss a particular topic, such as how to increase sales, or ask advice about the best way to run your next promotion. Or you can ask for a topic from your affiliates themselves by including a request in your newsletter.

But be prepared to respond to negative feedback when it comes up. Run a lively, give-and-take chat session and respond to criticism by stating you will take those comments under consideration. Don't dismiss them out right. Remember that you are getting real-time information about your program from your business partners. Treat it that way. It's inevitable that a chat will hit a quiet point, so be sure to have some canned questions to spur discussions.

Establish a regular schedule for your chats and determine this schedule by asking your affiliates what works for them. For instance, ClubMom runs an affiliate chat two times per month— one at noon and another at 9 p.m.—to facilitate the varying schedules of affiliates. Try running your chats for a period of one hour, and archive them for any affiliates that could not participate.

Do

DO man your chat rooms. Nothing kills a chat room tool like people dropping by and asking, "Is anybody there?" and having no response. That is why a chat moderator should always be present when you have your chat room open.

E-mail Discussion Lists

Running a site can be very time consuming and, for your affiliates, just finding time to stop by your Web site to join in a discussion can be hard to do. That's where e-mail can help. You can be sure that no matter how busy they are during the day, affiliates will check their e-mail at least once every few days. In addition, e-mail discussion lists are the best and least-expensive ways to build community.

A discussion list is a discussion board via e-mail. Subscribers to your discussion list receive e-mails on a regular basis, containing comments that are "echoed" to every other subscriber on the list. Every subscriber on the list receives every post to the list. All posts to the list are done via an e-mail message sent to the list.

Creating an e-mail discussion list and offering to your affiliates is an easy way for them to respond to comments made by fellow affiliates without having to go to a Web site and navigate around the discussion board or forum postings. Like the discussion boards, affiliates can discuss what banner links work best for them, answer questions from other affiliates about both the program and issues relevant to running a Web site, and share marketing tips and success stories. You can also use the list to make new announcements or for early notification of sales that could not wait for the next issue of your affiliate newsletter.

Discussion lists are easy to set up if you use the services of companies like Yahoo! Groups (groups.yahoo.com). This free resource is easy to use and doesn't require the efforts of your IT department.

Affiliate Feedback

Affiliates have a lot to say, and their feedback can be a very positive force in the shaping of your program. It's all a matter of asking affiliates what they want and giving it to them. Along those lines, you also should be open to asking your affiliates what they do not want and be willing to change your program to reflect the wants of your affiliates—being responsive and acting on the needs of affiliates is the ultimate way to increase loyalty.

When the members of the ClubMom affiliate e-mail discussion list were asked what they didn't like about affiliate marketing, they were very eager to share their opinions (see Table 12.1).

Table 12.1

What Affiliates Do Not Want
Requiring use of the 1×1 pixel
Late commission checks and payment thresholds
Lack of response from the affiliate team
Limited creative
Reducing commission rates
Lag time in approving affiliates
Switching affiliate solution providers
Wrongful accusations of fraud
Lack of promotions or offers

What's a Pixel

Short for *Picture Element,* a pixel is a single point in a graphic image.

One of the biggest complaints was the requirement that affiliates include the 1×1 pixel in their affiliate code. The 1×1 pixel is a tiny, clear graphic that is placed within links from many affiliate solution providers as a method to track the performance of various link types. However, affiliates can't use the 1×1 pixel in text newsletters, or scripts and software that rotate banners.

Most affiliate programs issue commission checks after affiliates reach a threshold of $25 or $50. Affiliates would rather receive a check every month, no matter the amount. But they are not nearly as concerned with the thresholds as they are with programs that do not abide by their own agreements and neglect to pay affiliates within the agreed upon time periods.

Perhaps the biggest complaint from affiliates is that they can never seem to get a response from affiliate managers when they send e-mail. On the topic of poor communication, affiliates are displeased with the deficit in updates regarding new promotions, sweepstakes, sales, and offers. And affiliates would like some praise every once in a while, just like any diligent employee in your company. Show a little appreciation or acknowledgement for performance now and then.

Whereas some affiliate programs may have been created for the express purpose of free branding, those affiliate managers that operate a fair program would be well served to offer a variety of tested, quality creatives. Affiliates complain that too many programs offer up slow-loading graphics, large image sizes, a lack of choice in size and style of creative, no text links or content, and the absence of direct product links. As we mentioned in Chapter 5, "Step Two—Choosing Your Program Model," a good affiliate program should offer tested text links, banner ads, text/banner ads, storefronts/mini-sites, and content.

If your boss told you that you were doing a good job, but you would be getting a pay cut, how would you like it? Affiliates have a very ardent dislike for a program that reduces their commissions. It's understandable that you want to own your category and lure in the best affiliates with high commissions, but if your budget cannot sustain these commissions, you're doing more harm than good for your program by starting high and then lowering your rates. However, it is an acceptable practice to publicize a temporary increase in commissions provided that you fully disclose that it is temporary. There are two distinct camps in affiliate marketing, those who insist that you must manually approve every affiliate, and those who automatically approve all who apply. While each strategy has its pros and cons, the only factor that concerns affiliates is the fact that programs with manual approval take too long to review sites.

Chapter 9, "Step Six—Tracking Your Affiliate Program," discussed tracking your affiliate program. The decision of whether to run every component of your program in-house or to utilize an affiliate solution provider is one of the most important questions facing an affiliate manager. A key aspect of this decision is not necessarily whether your choice is best for you right now, but rather, which solution is going to be scalable and flexible for you down the road. It's essential to conduct due diligence when you are determining how you will track your program. If you decide to change the way you track your program after you have already become established, you are going to rankle and lose a large portion of your affiliates.

One of the issues surrounding management is fraud and how to eliminate it. You must strike a balance between being vigilant overzealous. Good affiliates that are wrongly accused of fraud will not likely stick around with your affiliate program, so do your homework before making accusations. The use of Internet boosters, like Netsetter (www.netsetter.com), and the fact that AOL (www.aol.com) and WebTV (www.Webtv.com) users are represented by a finite bank of IP addresses, can simulate fraud to some fraud-detection techniques.

Finally, a big complaint from affiliates is that they feel like they are working for nothing, because many programs do not provide tools for them to succeed. One of the basic success tools to help affiliates facilitate clicks and conversions is to provide them with offers and contests. Not only will your current affiliates achieve more success if their links are more compelling, but you will attract additional successful affiliates if you offer freebies and operate sweepstakes.

Other Feedback Mechanisms

Besides the feedback and communications vehicles of a newsletter, discussion boards, and a chat and e-mail discussion list, you can create a more selective program that could tap the advice and experience of certain affiliates.

One way is to build an affiliate advisory board made up of some of your best affiliate partners. Use them to test new affiliate program features, contests, new commission rates, or anything else you'd like to have their opinion on before you decide to incorporate it into your program. Another idea is to conduct a concise, comprehensive survey representing a broad array of your affiliates—new ones, old ones, successful and struggling ones. Ask them their opinion of your program—their strengths and weaknesses. This information will give you insight into how to better serve your affiliates. When you survey your affiliates, provide an incentive for them to complete the survey for you. While it is in their best interest to provide feedback to you, their time is valuable, and a token of your appreciation will definitely increase the response rate.

Finally, try thanking your best affiliates for the sales they earn for you. Send e-mails to your top affiliates and thank them for their support by offering them the opportunity to pick out anything on your site as a gift. It's a nice gesture of appreciation that would be very appreciated.

Supporting Your Affiliates

Chapter Summary

Affiliate support doesn't end with the signing of the agreement and placing links on an affiliate's site, nor does servicing your affiliate's program marketing needs and educating him or her on your products, services, and program. Treating your affiliates like true business partners means not only helping them make your program a success but also helping their Web sites succeed as well.

Building a long-term, interactive relationship with your affiliates with their success in mind is critical in building a successful affiliate program. That means helping your affiliates not only reach your sales goals but also achieve their full potential. You have to work with your affiliates not just to grow your sales but to also grow their sites by teaching them how to market successfully on the Net, not just market your program successfully.

Encourage your affiliates to know your product so they can seriously recommend it to their site visitors. In addition, provide affiliate support pages on your site that

- Help them create a successful Web site
- Point them to resources on the Net that help them improve their site design and content
- Help position and market their site
- Build a newsletter mailing list
- Well-position their site in the search engines

Using the resources of the Net is a great way to offer marketing and promotional help to your affiliates. Finally, encourage affiliates to build an opt-in e-mail list that they can use to periodically stay in contact with their site visitors who subscribe and to constantly promote your product or service offer.

Just as it takes work to successfully run your affiliate program, it also takes work for your affiliates to earn decent revenue from it. Simply creating a Web site, putting up your offer links, and waiting for the commissions to roll in is not enough to earn money for them and increase sales for you. Keep in mind that the bulk of Web sites that join your affiliate program have little know-how about how to market their site on the Net.

Affiliates need to work hard at developing and promoting their sites and convince people to visit them. And you can help. After all, the more successful your affiliates are at generating traffic to their sites, the more impressions your offer will make and the more click-throughs and sales you will receive. Putting it simply, the more successful your affiliates sites are, the more successful your affiliate program will be.

This doesn't mean you have to go into the e-commerce consulting business to help your affiliates become a success. Far from it. But there are some things you can do to help your affiliates optimize their sites and merchandise your offers that will increase their commissions and your revenue. Affiliates are your business partners and are a direct arm of your sales department. And just as a new employee has to be brought up to speed, your affiliates cannot be expected to perform at their highest level without training and guidance. This can take the form of both offline and online guidance—offline with direct one-to-one contact and online with access to resources on your site.

The formula for a successful affiliate program is simple. Increase the number of potential customers who view your offer on your affiliate sites, increase the number of sales they produce, and increase the number of times they return to buy again. To do that you need to service your affiliates properly, support and train them to sell your offer, and help build a list of prospects and customers to encourage new and repeat sales.

Servicing Your Affiliates

It's obvious that affiliates are the cornerstone of a merchant's affiliate program. But it's a wonder that so few programs actually service their affiliates and treat them like true business partners. The relationship between you and your affiliates is an interactive one that builds and supports a mutual dependence. If your affiliates are not happy or are not provided the necessary marketing tools, training, and support, they will either under perform or, if they're good, leave for a more lucrative and supportive program somewhere else.

It's not the number of affiliates that matters, but the quality of the relationship you have with them. Creating that relationship with personal service is the key to building a successful and profitable affiliate network. That means helping your affiliates not only reach your sales goals but also achieve their full potential.

A good example of someone who supports affiliate marketing efforts is Declan Dunn. He sees his affiliates as true business partners. Working closely with them, he offers to pay half of the advertising costs that they spend to promote his books. If these affiliates are willing to go the extra mile and promote his product, he's going to make sure he helps. It's a win-win situation for both Dunn and his affiliates. He gets more exposure across the Net for his new book and his affiliates make more sales.

Do

DO consider offering to pay some of the advertising expenses that your affiliates might incur promoting your products and services.

You may think that paying your affiliates' advertising costs is going too far in supporting your affiliates. But if you see affiliates as your partners in business and not as a source for cheap advertising, this makes sense. The bottom line is this: To be a real success in affiliate marketing you have to look beyond what is considered affiliate marketing today. Just offering a set of links, some promotional copy, a tracking and report mechanism, and a marketing tip or two is not enough to set you apart from your competitors' programs and to keep your affiliates loyal.

You have to work with your affiliates not just to grow your sales but to also grow their sites by teaching them how to market successfully on the Net. They must do more than just market your program successfully. All this may seem like extra work and expense, but it'll pay off in the long run. Look at it as a marketing expense. Take some of the marketing money that you would use for acquiring more affiliates who might or might not perform, and use it to supply training materials and advice to your current affiliates. Increase their success on the Net and they will increase yours.

Categorize and Customize Your Support

Most affiliate programs see their affiliates as one big undifferentiated group of Web sites, but that's not true. Each Web site is different and will have a different approach to promoting your offers. One general banner or text link will not work for every affiliate. Creating a separate marketing and merchandising program for each affiliate obviously isn't possible. But if you look at your network hard enough and analyze the different sites that it contains, you may be able to find similarities among them from which you can create different affiliate groupings and offer different linking methods.

First, have someone on your affiliate management staff do nothing but visit your affiliate sites with two objectives in mind:

- Have him create a set of criteria to use to group your affiliates into a few site categories.

- Once these groupings are determined, decide the best strategies to help affiliates achieve their sales goals for your program.

Once these strategies have been determined for an affiliate site, you might give your team a bonus for every site that improves sales by applying a group strategy.

What could these different marketing strategies look like? Besides banner and text links, there are other ways for individual affiliates to promote your offers. Some might work for all your affiliate groupings, whereas only one or two will work with others.

- If an affiliate needs content for her site, newsletter, or eZine, write articles about your product or service subject area. These should be informative and entertaining for the reader and provide links to your products or service, a survey or contest, or a link back to your site to capture a sales lead or make a sale.

- Supply different size ad copy—with links—for those affiliates that want to advertise in eZines or have a newsletter of their own they send out to their site subscribers. Make sure to include a few witty lines of copy with links that they can place in the e-mail signature line to help generate click-throughs from the recipients.

- Some affiliates might want to have more than a simple banner link, or text link or button on their Web pages. Some might want to place images of your products that link directly to those products on your site for purchase. In this way, they could select images of products specific to the content of their site. By communicating with your affiliates, you might find other marketing strategies that they could use that fit within the way they market their site.

Review each affiliate group and match them up with your linking and marketing methods. And most important of all, encourage them to know your product or service.

Encourage Affiliates to Know Your Product

Just because affiliates choose to join your program and sell your product or service, that doesn't mean they know a whole lot about what you sell. You need to take the time to teach them the basics of your merchandise. That includes knowing the demographic mix of their sites—who comes to their sites and why—and then targeting that mix with your offers. But suppose you have affiliates that seem to join programs that have no relationship to the content of their sites or join every new one that comes down the information highway? What to do with them?

The easy way is to just drop them from your program. But how do you know that some those affiliates might not turn out to be some of your best? If you are willing to make an extra effort with your program, you may very well mold some of those into the 5% of affiliates that provide 95% percent of your program revenue. All they may need is a little guidance on how to position your offer within the context of their sites. It may only take some effective target marketing to help them position their sites to visitors better— along with better placement of your offer on their sites. Taking time to work with sites that respond to your offers of assistance may turn these sites into your better performers.

The quickest and most important way to teach affiliates about the value of your offer and how to merchandise it is to have them use your product or service. If you're selling a single product or an individual service, have then purchase it and use it—better yet, give it to them if you can—with the expectation that they will do the following:

- Have them use the product and see it as their own. By getting a hands-on experience with your offering they can better understand what it is and how it works so they can better position it within the context or their Web sites.

- Expect them to give your product or service their personal recommendation to the visitors of their sites. After all, if they've used your product or service—and you assume they are satisfied with it—their trust and credibility with their visitors will transfer to your offering, making an easier sale. By putting their stamp of approval on your offer, your and their sales will increase. Their personal recommendation should include some important details, such as what they like about your product or service, what it will do for their site visitors, and why they should buy it. Getting their visitors to part with their hard-earned money is a lot easier if the affiliates, personally have used your product or service and can recommend it.

Do

DO encourage your affiliates to use your product or service. Then ask them to advocate its use to their site visitors on their Web sites and e-mail communications.

Provide an Affiliate Support Site

The net is an almost infinite storehouse of information. So why not provide links to this information for your affiliates to use to improve their site design and content, help position and market their sites, build a newsletter mailing list, and well-position their sites in search engine results? Using the resources of the Net is a great way to offer marketing and promotional help to your affiliates. This is especially important if you have limited time and resources.

Provide Access to Internet Resources

Your first step is to create a place on your Web site for your affiliates that provides a list of Net resources to help them make their sites (and selling your program) a success (see Figure 13.1). The very first thing you need to have on your affiliate support pages is an extensive FAQ (Frequently Asked Questions). Because affiliate programs generate so much interest and countless questions, it is important to create and continually update your FAQ section. Take some time to think through all the common questions that your affiliates have or may ask. Post them with your answers on your affiliate support pages. This will save you countless time answering the same questions via e-mails and phone calls that you have answered time and time again.

Provide Information About Free Advertising

On your affiliate support pages, be sure to list sites where affiliates can get free advertising, create free polls, add free discussion boards and chats, offer free e-mail, obtain free content, and join programs that will help them become better marketers. You can provide links to sites offering free search engine submission services, banner exchanges, e-mail list builders, and many other free services on the Net. For more affiliate support resources, visit www.affiliatemanager.net/support.htm.

Do

DO offer your affiliates, both on your site and in your newsletters, links to resources on the Web that will help them improve the use of their site, bring repeat visitors back to their site, and show them how to promote their site.

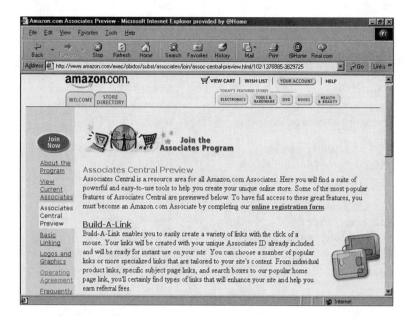

Figure 13.1
Amazon has a place on their site called "Associates Central"—a helpful resource for its affiliates.

Here are just a few examples of the resources you can provide on your affiliate support pages (see Table 13.1). These are courtesy of Cashpile.com.

Table 13.1

Online Affiliate Support Resources	
Web Site	**Description**
Search Engine Directories http://www.cashpile.com/ mission.merchants/CP/tools/ search_engines.cfmsub	List of search engines for Web sites.
Search Engine Positioning http://www.cashpile.com/ merchants/cp/tools/ positioning.cfm	Tools to help a site achieve higher rankings.
Managing Web Presence http://www.cashpile.com/ merchants/cp/tools/ presence.cfm	Optimize a site's design and performance.

Table 13.1   (continued)

Online Affiliate Support Resources

Web Site	Description
Banner Ads http://www.cashpile.com/ merchants/cp/tools/banner.cfm	Create and exchange banner ads to generate traffic to a site.
Opt-in E-mail http://www.cashpile.com/ merchants/cp/tools/email.cfm	Deliver specialized messages to a target audience—opt-in subscribers only.
Auto-responders http://www.cashpile.com/ merchants/cp/tools/ responders.cfm	Save time by automatically sending a reply to the e-mail address that sent an the original message.
Newsletters http://www.cashpile.com/ merchants/cp/tools/ newsletter.cfm	Keep in touch with customers on a regular basis.
Online Classifieds http://www.cashpile.com/ merchants/cp/tools/ classified.cfm	Post an ad for a minimal fee or submit a small ad at no cost.
Web Stats http://www.cashpile.com/ affiliates/CP/tools/ Webstats.cfm	Tools to help gauge the effectiveness of advertising and marketing efforts.
Free E-Mail http://www.cashpile.com/ affiliates/CP/tools/ free_email.cfm	Free Web based e-mail sources.

Learning how to submit your Web site and get good placement in the search engines is important for your affiliate sites in generating traffic—traffic you need to see your offers. Keywords Wizard (www.keywordwizard.com/word.html) is a free search engine keyword tool that lets Web sites analyze the best keywords to use when listing their sites in the search engines. AffiliateToolKit (www.affiliatetoolkit.com) is a free meta-page creation tool, whereas search engine optimization services and tools can be found at Top Web Promo (www.prosperity-now4u.com/).

A good source for free advertising is reciprocal linking or trading links with other sites. You can link to a good list of such Web sites at AdAbility (www.adbility.com/show.asp?). In fact AdAbility (see Figure 13.2) is one of many Web sites that provide marketing sources and site tools—many of them free—to affiliate sites to help boost traffic and promote their sites. Another such site is CashPile.com (www.cashpile.com). CashPile provides both you and your affiliates with free marketing tips, tools, and original content.

Do

DO encourage affiliates to buy the marketing and sales books offered on the Net to help them improve their marketing and sales skills and learn how to make affiliate selling a success for them. A good source of such books for affiliates is at www.usamc.org/bookstore.htm.

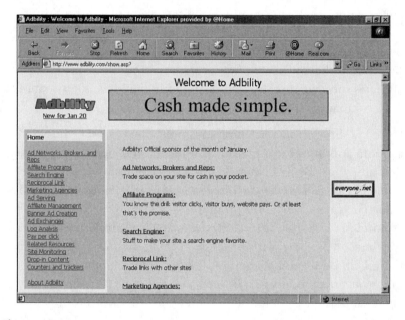

Figure 13.2
AdAbility is one of many Web sites that provide site tools—many of them free—to help affiliate sites.

Another helpful resource for your affiliate support pages is to list a handful of good e-mail newsletters that let your affiliates place an ad for $15 to $40. Point them to E-zineZ.com (www.E-zineZ.com), BestEzines.com (www.BestEzines.com), and LifeStylesPub.com (www.LifeStylesPub.com). Then write several ads your affiliates can use. Put them on your Web site and have them available via autoresponder.

Online resources like these will help your affiliates improve their sites and their marketing knowledge, at the same time showing your affiliates that you really see them as business partners. It sends the message loud and clear that your success depends on their success.

Better yet, why not make a little money joining their affiliate programs while helping your affiliates?

Books and Other Training Systems

When setting up your affiliate support area, include links to affiliate programs that you've joined that feature books and training systems geared toward helping affiliates succeed. Remember, just because you're a merchant doesn't mean you can't be an affiliate. By offering these affiliate training materials, you'll be helping your affiliates succeed and also adding an additional revenue stream to your company.

Here are three affiliate training programs that you as a company can join and offer to your affiliates while earning a commission at the same time. Declan Dunn sells a very good training system for affiliates called *Winning the Affiliate Game* (www.activemarketplace. com). Two other books and programs that can assist your affiliates are *Make Your Site Sell* (affiliate.sitesell.com) by Ken Evoy and *Nothing But 'Net* (www.1-internet-marketing.com/nbn/) by Michael Campbell. Both can help your affiliates optimize their sites and help convert shoppers into buyers. Visit www.affiliatemanager. net/reading.htm for a list of recommended reading for affiliate managers and affiliates.

Some other helpful programs for your affiliates are those that help them track each of the programs they have joined. Affiliate Manager (www.Webbizbrokers.com/free/pam.htm) is a free database program designed specifically for tracking affiliate information. Data stored includes company, category, payment schedule, payee information, contact information, and Web site details. An affiliate can store the required HTML code needed for his or her affiliate programs, track payments, and keep notes.

Do

DO consider joining affiliate programs that help train your affiliates to be more successful as an affiliate—while making a commission at the same time.

Another tracking program for affiliates is Affiliate Assistant (www.affiliateassistant.com) (see Figure 13.3). It offers you an opportunity to not only help your affiliates improve their efficiency, but also to make money by signing up as an affiliate. When they buy the program, you get a commission.

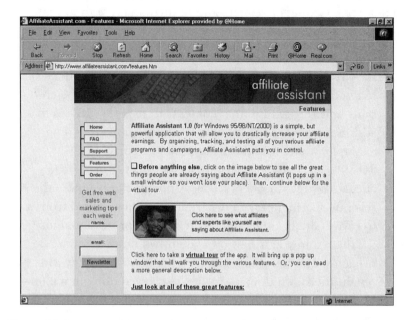

Figure 13.3
Affiliate Assistant helps those Web sites participating in an affiliate program to increase their commissions using the Affiliate Assistant software. In addition, you can make money as an affiliate selling the program to your affiliate partners.

The newest entry in the arena of tracking programs for affiliates is AffTrack Affiliate Tracking Systems (www.afftrack.com). AffTrack has developed a proprietary technology that allows the super affiliate to automatically track participation in multiple affiliate programs for accounting and analysis purposes. This includes Be Free, CJ, LinkShare, and programs outside of these networks. In addition to that, AffTrack has the ability to gather and aggregate any transaction data that merchants provide and integrate that with Web-based reporting systems, e-mails, and FTP files.

The Eight Things Every Affiliate Should Do

No matter what kind of program you have, there are certain things every affiliate should do that will increase his or her chances of selling your product or service, and in turn, make your affiliate program more of a success.

1. **Get a Domain Name**: Ideally, each of your affiliates should have its own domain name. This always gives a site better visibility with the search engines and directories and the credibility and recognition that comes with its own URL (Web address) instead of an extension of someone else's. For example, what looks more credible to a consumer— `http://geocites.yahoo.com/custom_shirts/` or `http://www.customshirts.com`? Affiliates can promote the revenue-sharing affiliate programs they have joined from a free Web site but they will create a more professional image for them and you if they own their own domain name. Be proactive and tell your affiliates where and how they can obtain their own domain name. Their own domain name— if memorable—would receive more repeat traffic and make the search engines easier to find them because many of them search the URL for keywords, too.

2. **Pick a Web Site Theme**: Web sites join an affiliate program to make money. They make money from the traffic they attract to their site. So a theme for their site should be chosen that would attract a fair amount of visitors to their site. The consensus of opinion in the affiliate marketing game is that a site will need at least 500 targeted visitors a day if it wants to make a reasonable income from the affiliate programs it has joined. The word *targeted* is the operational definition.

3. **Target Their Market**: Trying to sell to everyone is selling to no one. If an affiliate is serious about making money with affiliate programs, he must find a market niche and target it. He must know his visitors or the market he seeks to attract. To this end, he needs to choose affiliate programs whose products or services match the audience that he attracts to his

site. This is not as difficult as it seems. For example, if an affiliate's site attracts those interested in business, any kind of product or service that businesses would use would apply. Programs that offer office supplies, computer products, marketing, and financial and accounting services, are all potential offers that an affiliate can place on his site. The affiliate's task is to create content that attracts those interested in business issues and subject matter of business on a regular basis. Work with your affiliates and help them focus on their targeted audience with resources that point to free content. Help them create program links that promote individual products and services that fit well within the context of their sites.

4. **Focus, Focus, Focus:** Many affiliates make the mistake of joining dozens of programs at a time with little regard for their audience or whether they compliment one another. They figure the more programs they join, the more money they can make. Unfortunately, the opposite is true. All too frequently you will see sites that just have a splash page consisting of little more than banner links from dozens of affiliate programs. Tell your affiliates that sites like these do not succeed in earning money for their owners. Not only will they not attract traffic, but the affiliates will have little chance of converting the little traffic they do generate into actual sales, click-throughs, or return traffic. Impress on them the importance of joining only a few complimentary affiliate programs and concentrate on providing attractive content that will generate traffic and sales for them and you.

5. **Keep the Site Simple:** One of the best ways to drive visitors away from a site once they come to it is to load it up with heavy graphics, animations, sound, plug-ins, and other technological bells and whistles that slow the downloading of the site. If generating revenue is the prime purpose of their site, then site content that loads fast and offers true value without gimmicks will capture the attention of the site visitor and increase the click-through traffic. Another point to remind your affiliates of is your banner and text-link placement. Putting these at the top of their pages will result in more hits and click-throughs. Always emphasize the KISS method: Keep It Simple, Stupid!

Do

DO encourage your affiliates to focus on merchant affiliate programs that complement each other. Discourage your affiliates from selling products that do not complement the content of their site.

6. **Market Their Site:** It goes without saying that the "build it and they will come" strategy of Web marketing does not work. You must impress upon your affiliates the need to market their site. This includes registering with search engines and directories, learning how to get better placement in those engines and directories, advertising in eZines and newsletters, and participating in newsgroups and discussion lists. Links to all these resources should be on your affiliate support pages. In addition, you should recommend that they start their own newsletter or eZine, and promote their site in the signature file of every e-mail they send out.

7. **Keep It Fresh:** Impress upon your affiliates the need to constantly revise their sites and site content. They are selling your product or service, not just posting an ad on their sites for your company. That means they have to sell your offer and place it within the context of their sites. And this context—or content—must be refreshed frequently to continue to attract repeat visitors. This is important because most products are not purchased the first time a consumer sees an offer. It may take several impressions before they make a buying decision. One of the best ways to attract repeat visits is to build an opt-in e-mail list.

8. **Build an Opt-In E-mail List:** An opt-in e-mail list is probably one of the most powerful Internet marketing tools around. Using this list to contact site visitors who have opted to receive it gives your affiliate a chance to offer your products or service again and again. This can entice visitors to return to make a purchase or perform an action that will generate revenue for you and your affiliate. Affiliates can use this opportunity to promote the benefits of your product or service. It will also help their subscribers, at the same time helping the affiliate.

Encourage your affiliates to deal with the information they collect in an ethical manner. Discourage spam, which not only hurts your affiliate's reputation and forces subscribers to opt-out of future mailings, but also hurts the reputation of your company, which the affiliate represents.

Do

DO remind affiliates that spamming is forbidden. You may need to clarify what spamming is to new affiliates. Most affiliate spammers do so unintentionally because they are new and simply don't know better.

A well-managed and well-administered e-mailing program builds a close relationship between your affiliate and her subscribers—a relationship that increases her earnings and your sales. Anything that can hurt that relationship should be discouraged. Affiliates should also make it very clear how the information collected from their newsletter or eZine subscribers is to be used. A privacy statement should accompany every sign-up page on your affiliate sites stating that the e-mail addresses and other personal information will not be given, traded, or sold to a third party. Offering an affiliate support page on your site that helps affiliates reach their earnings goals will also help your affiliate program reach its sales goals.

Of course, to offer proper support to your affiliates, your affiliate team must be up to date on the latest news, tips, and techniques in affiliate marketing. According to a report from Affiliate Metrix (www.affiliatemetrix.com), the majority of affiliate marketing professionals are reading columns on the industry, such as ClickZ (www.clickz.com) (see Figure 13.4) and SAM Magazine (www.sammag.com).

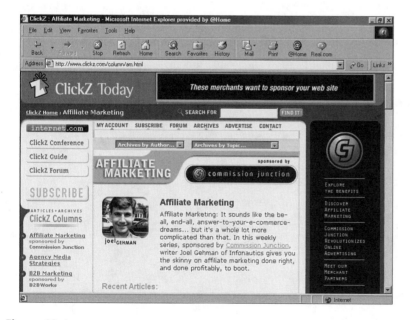

Figure 13.4
ClickZ contains an archive of numerous articles on affiliate marketing that are invaluable to a merchant.

In affiliate marketing, knowledge is most assuredly power.

Now it's time to get started. If you follow the instructions laid out in the previous chapters and use the resources in the appendices that follow, you will go a long way toward making your affiliate marketing program a success for your company.

The 10 Deadly Sins of Affiliate Marketing

There are a number of mistakes to avoid when establishing your affiliate program, but ten of them are especially egregious. These are the deadly sins of affiliate marketing. Making any one of these can seriously harm the effectiveness of your program. Making any combination of them will likely lead to a program that is dead on arrival.

1. **No affiliate manager**

   Many companies launch an affiliate program with the anticipation that it requires some heavy lifting early on, but then runs itself thereafter. The truth is that having a person dedicated to the day-to-day operations of the affiliate program is a necessity. And this person should be easy to reach with customer service questions. If there is no name attached to the program, as well as some level of customer service, your program is doomed from the start. Your affiliate manager should be highly visible and accessible, and when the affiliates do reach the affiliate manager, they had better get a quick response. It's not acceptable to have a single employee dedicate part of his or her time to the management of a program. CRM (Customer Relationship Management) is essential, and the affiliate programs that realize this are the perennial top performers.

2. No answers to frequently asked questions

Even though you have a FAQ (frequently asked questions) for your site, that's not enough if you are going to operate an affiliate program. Your main FAQ may cover your company and site thoroughly, but there are a wide variety of questions that are specific to your affiliate program: Does it cost anything to join? How can I sign up? How do I create a link to your site? When will I get paid?

If you don't know what people are going to ask, try a handful of friends and employees to navigate through your program and write down two or three questions. Answer these questions and you've got a FAQ. As your program grows, you will receive questions from your prospective affiliates—whenever you answer a new question, be sure that the question and answer are added to the FAQ. And make it a practice to send the FAQ (highlighting any updates) to your affiliates once or twice each year. Answer those questions before affiliates have a chance to ask them—now that's efficiency!

3. No privacy statement

Do affiliates join your mailing list when they sign up for your program? Do you intend to sell or share your database of affiliates with other companies? If so, it is recommended that you share this information with your affiliates. If you decide not to divulge this information, you could seriously harm your credibility. If you do not currently have a privacy policy, you can refer to the privacy policies of some other companies to get an idea about the general components, but you should have a lawyer draft your actual privacy policy to ensure that it is done legally and correctly.

4. No Agreement

How often will you be paying your affiliates? Can non-U.S. residents participate in your program? How much will you pay? Is there any reason why your affiliates would forfeit their commission? Although these documents may seem like unnecessary bureaucracy, they are absolutely essential. Spell out your terms in your affiliate agreement and not only will you gain more credibility, but you will also avoid potential legal disputes. The affiliate agreement is the document that dictates affiliate rights and protections, and it must be posted prominently on your site for all prospective and current affiliates to read.

5. No investment in the affiliates

Don't set up an associate program unless you are willing to share a reasonable percentage of profits with your associates. Low commissions can be a huge stumbling block for your program, but how much is enough? This is a tricky question with many variables. Will you be paying a flat fee on each transaction, a percentage of the sale, or for each click?

In some categories with low margins and high prices, it is reasonable to pay out a low percentage. But in many segments, it is unacceptable to offer less than 5% of the gross sale. Flat fees and pay-per-click models are totally dependent on the product and cost. To determine the best commission for your program, research your competitors and try to give a little more than they are giving to the affiliates. Of course, the bottom line is a key factor, and you're not going to give up your entire margin for the sake of the affiliate program, but if you are offering a paltry commission, you will not have any affiliates.

6. No marketing support

Amazingly, many affiliate programs have little or no marketing support. This is counterintuitive considering it is in the merchant's interest to help the affiliate succeed. Make sure you offer your affiliates training, not only in how to sell your product or service but also in how to make their Web site a success. Show your affiliates how to drive more traffic and convert at a higher rate. Also, don't forget to educate your affiliates on the basics of marketing, because they are not basics for many of them. Update your marketing materials regularly to reflect new tips and techniques. Keep your offers creative and your copy fresh and timely—stale affiliate tools beget a stale affiliate program.

7. No community support

It is in your interest to foster support for your affiliates, yet many affiliate programs offer no community support. There are a number of easy-to-implement community features that can instantly make your program more robust, friendly, and useful. Set up an e-mail discussion list for the exchange of ideas and peer consultation. Provide a Webring to members of your affiliate program so they can drive traffic to one another's sites and learn from the marketing techniques applied at other affiliate sites.

Host a chat for your affiliates once or twice a month—this provides them with the chance to have real-time interaction with you and their peers, which is a great opportunity for you to utilize them as a focus group for upcoming plans. Community is important to an affiliate program, as it generates loyalty among the affiliates and provides the affiliate manager with an avenue to provide meaningful, personalized interaction with the affiliates.

8. No way to find your affiliate program

Believe it or not, there are quite a few companies that operate affiliate programs, and they do not link to the program from their home page, or any other page for that matter. People must be able to find your program if you want them to join you in marketing your product or service. Although the affiliate program directories will generate some traffic, you cannot expect to operate a successful program if you rely solely on this method.

Not only should you display a prominent link on your home page, but it is also a good idea to incorporate a blurb in your e-mail signature about your affiliate program. If you have a newsletter, plug the program. When you send out an invoice, plug the program as well. And don't forget the footer! It has become a common convention to link to your affiliate program information page from the footer on all pages of your site. It all comes back to the KISS method—keep it simple, stupid! If you build it and hide it, they will not come.

9. No statistical reporting

Do your affiliates have a means to track their statistics online? As a result of the robust statistical reporting from the affiliate solution providers, affiliates not only want online statistics, they demand them. They are going to expect this feature and if you do not provide it, your competitor probably does. Don't risk losing affiliates. If you utilize a third-party affiliate solution or an off-the-shelf affiliate software, the online reporting should be a given. At a minimum, you should provide your affiliates with a breakdown of the pay periods, sales, returns, and total balance—preferably in real time.

10. No online application

Just as with the online reporting, you should also be provided an online application if you are using a third-party affiliate solution or affiliate software. If you choose to create your online application in-house, note that some potential affiliates will be sensitive about the transmission of their personal information. Bear this in mind, because if you do not have a secure server for transmission of their personal information, you could be turning away a lot of potential salespeople. Your affiliate program must reach a minimum level of sophistication, and if it fails to do so, you are going to turn away a lot of prospective affiliates. Asking for a potential affiliate to send an e-mail as her affiliate application is not considered an online application and is strictly verboten.

Affiliate Marketing Master Plan

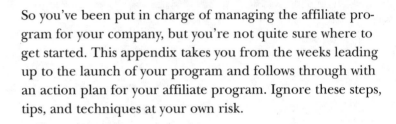

So you've been put in charge of managing the affiliate program for your company, but you're not quite sure where to get started. This appendix takes you from the weeks leading up to the launch of your program and follows through with an action plan for your affiliate program. Ignore these steps, tips, and techniques at your own risk.

Previous Weeks

The steps that lead up to the launch of your affiliate program will play a big part in whether you hit the ground running or start to second guess this whole affiliate-marketing thing. You know that old saying that hindsight is 20-20? Well, this is your chance to do everything correctly the first time around.

The first item is to determine the staffing of the affiliate team. It cannot be emphasized enough—you must have at least one person dedicated to the management of the program, and preferably more than one.

The affiliate team is sort of a figurative term. In addition to the requisite marketing people on the team, you must also go to great lengths to curry favor with a tech and finance person in your company—they will be invaluable to your success and growth. Take them to lunch and extol the virtues of affiliate marketing and how it will be a key to your company's success. You really need that internal support to prosper.

After the affiliate manager and the rest of the affiliate team have been identified, they should head the search committee for an affiliate solution. Crunch all the numbers, and figure out how much you will be able to budget for your program. Then, research the options: building a solution internally, purchasing an off-the-shelf affiliate software, or working with an affiliate solution provider.

The choice of your affiliate solution is one to be decided with gravity, so do not jump into a contract without checking out all the options, speaking with references, and assessing the technical requirements of your company.

After you have decided on the affiliate solution, you have to determine all the basics of your program and then implement it into your site. In addition to determining the payment model (pay-per-sale, customer, lead, or click, as well as two-tier and residual earnings), you have to decide on the payment frequency (monthly is suggested) and payment threshold (try $25 or less).

Also, implementation of the new affiliate program will require that you have an affiliate agreement and privacy statement (created by a lawyer), a FAQ, and some banners and text links to offer when the program rolls out.

When everything seems to be in place, the affiliate team should exhaustively test all the components of the affiliate program to be sure that every aspect is functioning correctly.

- Determine the staffing for the affiliate team

- Build internal support

- Check to see that your affiliate solutions are implemented properly

- Implement the new affiliate program

- Quality assurance and testing

Week 1

Congratulations—this is the first week that your program is live. You are going to want to generate some immediate attention, so issue a press release. If you are working with an affiliate solution provider, ask them if they will be creating a press release or announcement. Even if they do not write one, they often have boilerplate copy you can use. Also, you will want to submit your program to the affiliate program directories.

It's essential that members of your affiliate team are well versed on the industry and any developments that occur. There are a handful of discussion lists and newsletters that are required reading: Associate-it (www.associate-it.com), AssociatePrograms.com (www.associateprograms.com), CashPile (www.cashpile.com), ClickZ (www.clickz.com), Refer-it (www.refer-it.com), ReveNews (www.revenews.com), and USAMC (www.usamc.org).

Right from the start, you will be receiving a steady stream of questions from affiliates and prospective affiliates. Handle these queries quickly and you will gain the confidence of your affiliates. As you receive questions, log them to get a sense of which questions are coming from affiliates. This can be useful in the design and operation of your affiliate program. If possible, get members of the affiliate team to rotate the responsibility of checking the affiliate e-mail on weekends. The little investment in time goes a long way with the affiliates in loyalty and dedication to your program.

Because your affiliates will expect you to be experts on your own program, it's essential for your affiliate team to be affiliates for your program. Market your program with your own site, and you will be much better equipped to tell your affiliates how to do it. If you cannot pass your own payment threshold and tally some commission checks of your own on a regular basis, how are you going to tell your affiliates how to do it?

It is also important to continuously lurk and participate in the major affiliate marketing discussion boards. The affiliate team should make it a regular habit to take part in the boards at AssociatePrograms.com (webwizards.net/AssociatePrograms/discus), iBoost (www.webdesignforums.com), CashPile (www.

`cashpile.com/cashcorner/conferences`), and ReveNews (`www.revenews.com/opinion/discuss.cgi`).

The first week is also the time that you should keep a close eye on your competition. Be sure that the affiliate team joins the programs of competitor sites. If multiple people belong to each competitor program, you are more likely to catch their various targeted e-mails and pick up practices you can apply to your own program. Compare every facet of their programs to yours and closely monitor what is said about them on the message boards.

Be sure to initiate and maintain a recruitment effort for the top sites. Keep track of those sites that join and those that do not join, so you can touch base with them again in a couple of months.

- Send out press releases

- Submit your program to affiliate directories

- Subscribe to discussion lists and newsletters

- Answer affiliate queries within 24 hours, and keep a log of the questions asked

- Have members of your affiliate team join other merchant affiliate programs, create their own personal sites, and then place the affiliate programs they've joined on their sites.

- Participate in discussion boards

- Monitor the competition

- Identify and track prospective affiliates

Week 2

The first week is just a warm up. You're just getting started now, and the results will be coming in intermittently, but with increasing frequency. It's an exciting time.

At this point, the affiliate team ought to start looking at which of your banners, buttons, and text links are performing. The same goes for the competition. If they are getting better clicks and conversions than you, figure out why and adapt your program. It is also important to continually participate in the discussion boards. Affiliates may start posting questions about your program, so be there to answer them before an uninformed person posts incorrect or inflammatory information about your program.

Your recruitment effort should grow as time goes by. Continue to keep track of those sites that join and those that do not join, so you can touch base with them again in a couple of months.

After week two, you've been bringing in new affiliates for a week, which means you've also been bringing in plenty of inactive affiliates that have not posted your links and may very well not post them without a reminder. This week, you should begin a weekly ritual of touching base with sites that have joined in the past week and not added your links to their site. Ask them if they need your help or have a question, and include their affiliate code in the e-mail.

It's also not too early (it never is) to begin your affiliate education effort. Begin a series of short tutorials for your affiliates that cover essential topics, such as how to submit their site to search engines, register a domain, and rotate banners on their site.

Now that your program has been up for a week or so, touch base with the affiliate managers of some sites that target similar customers and chat about working together in various capacities to promote one another's programs.

And for all those questions from affiliates, take a look at the most frequently asked questions and add them to your FAQ.

- Have the affiliate team test and track performance of their own and other programs on their personal sites
- Participate in discussion boards
- Monitor the competition
- Identify and track prospective affiliates
- Target e-mail to inactive affiliates
- Compose tutorial
- Establish co-marketing relationships
- Review log of questions asked by affiliates and add any new questions and answers to your FAQ

Week 3

By week three, the affiliate team will be falling into some essential routines and the affiliate program will be gaining momentum.

Just as with the previous week, the affiliate team sites should be reviewed to determine any trends for the performance of your program. Similarly, continue participating in the discussion boards and monitoring the competition. Also, as you search for more affiliates, keep an eye on those who have not joined and check back with their sites to see if they have joined the competition.

Also, be sure to stay on top of those inactive affiliates, and track the response rates from your contacts with the inactives: How many end up putting your links on their sites? Play around with the e-mail you send out to see whether some letters get a better response.

Think about some of the hurdles that the affiliate team has experienced in creating their sites and use this as fodder for a new affiliate tutorial.

And now that your program is running, try reaching out to some other affiliate managers in your area to get together to exchange war stories and tips. The United States Affiliate Manager Coalition (www.usamc.org) provides contact information for groups in New York City, Philadelphia, San Francisco, Seattle, and Washington, DC.

Those questions are increasing from the affiliates, and many are the same. Don't forget to add them to your FAQ.

- Have the affiliate team test and track performance of their own and other programs on their personal sites

- Participate in discussion boards

- Monitor the competition

- Identify and track prospective affiliates

- Target e-mail to inactive affiliates

- Compose tutorial

- Network with other affiliate managers
- Review log of questions asked by affiliates and add any new questions and answers to your FAQ

Week 4

You're rounding out the first month of your program, and things are really kicking in to gear. While you continue with the routines of previous weeks, it's also time to incorporate some more "best practices" to your program.

In addition to your previously outlined duties, now is a good time to begin building a community for your affiliates. eGroups (www.egroups.com) provides a free service for you to set up a quick and easy community for your affiliates. Create a group there and you can begin an e-mail discussion list for you to communicate with affiliates, and to foster peer communication among your affiliates. Also, start up a regular chat for your affiliates. If your site does not have chat software, CashPile does (www.cashpile.com).

Also, because you're coming to the end of your first month, it's time for your first monthly newsletter. Some suggested components are earnings for the top 10 affiliates, code for automatic rotation links, an affiliate of the month announcement, tips (affiliate, marketing, and search engine), and a co-marketing plug.

At this point, you will also want to switch out your original banners and text links—stale creatives equals lousy results. You should take a look at which links performed best and apply those lessons to your future creatives.

It's also a good time to enhance the linking options of your affiliates. Since contextual links perform better than a 468×60 banner plopped atop a page with no content, it will be to the benefit of the affiliates and your program if you provide new content (including appropriate affiliate links) each month for them to plug into their sites.

- Have the affiliate team test and track performance of their own and other programs on their personal sites
- Participate in discussion boards

- Monitor the competition

- Identify and track prospective affiliates

- Target e-mail to inactive affiliates

- Compose tutorial

- Network with other affiliate managers

- Establish a community for your affiliates

- Publish a monthly newsletter

- Switch out your banners and text links

- Test techniques and analyze

- Create content for your affiliate sites

- Review log of questions asked by affiliates and add any new questions and answers to your FAQ

Week 5

The first month in your affiliate program is history now. Your company will start to appreciate some tangible results, and affiliate marketing will be well on its way to revolutionizing the way you do business.

Again, continue with your routines. The number of inactive affiliates should be slowing down at this point, and the number of new questions they ask will be limited. Be sure to keep your ear to the ground about what your affiliates are saying in the discussion boards, and think about tweaking your program if you're not happy with the performance. One school of thought is that you should give three months for your affiliate program to get legs, but that is old school. You're working on Internet time, and three months without results is not acceptable.

This will be the first time that you pay your affiliates, provided that you are paying monthly. Remember the close relationship that you established with one of the finance people in your company? It's time to renew it, because you're going to need to spend some money to pay those affiliates who have been getting results for you.

- Have the affiliate team test and track performance of their own and other programs on their personal sites

- Participate in discussion boards

- Monitor the competition

- Identify and track prospective affiliates

- Target e-mail to inactive affiliates

- Compose tutorial

- Network with other affiliate managers

- Participate in your affiliate community

- Review log of questions asked by affiliates and add any new questions and answers to your FAQ

- Cut commission checks

Week 6

By the time you've reached week six, your affiliate program should be indexed in all the directories and any kinks that emerged should be ironed out. Keep up with the routines and analyze your stats to date. You should see some trends that will help with your long-term budgeting.

- Have the affiliate team test and track performance of their own and other programs on their personal sites

- Participate in discussion boards

- Monitor the competition

- Identify and track prospective affiliates

- Target e-mail to inactive affiliates

- Compose tutorial

- Network with other affiliate managers

- Participate in your affiliate community

- Review log of questions asked by affiliates and add any new questions and answers to your FAQ

Following Weeks

As your program becomes more grounded, you should continue with all your previously initiated routines, as well as bringing new innovations and ideas to your program.

It is essential to maintain a constant flow of two-way communication with your affiliates. At a minimum, you will be sending a monthly newsletter. This should be complimented by targeted e-mails to work with the super affiliates as well as the under-performing affiliates.

To keep your program fresh and your affiliate productive, try to switch out your creatives every month. This does not mean you have to have brand new creatives from month to month, but maybe four months of fresh creatives that are rotated.

At this point, you've been paying affiliates and providing excellent support, so it's a good time to begin collecting affiliate testimonials. If you are paying for the referral of new affiliates, the testimonials can make great banner copy. Testimonials also serve well to market your program on the affiliate program information page on your site.

There are a number of affiliate marketing conferences throughout the year, including AffiliateFORCE (www.affiliateforce.com), Affiliate Solutions (seminars.internet.com), and IIR Online Allies (www.iir-ny.com). Make it a priority to attend one or two of these events (at least) each year for excellent networking opportunities, education, and the latest information on the industry.

Whether or not you have been pleased with the performance of your program to date, it's time to step it up a notch. Now that your program is up and running, it's time to get together with other departments in your company to set up some compelling offers to tie into your affiliate program. Although you may be marketing a great product or service, it's going to move even better if it's tied to a sweepstakes, freebie, or coupon.

On that note, it's also a good time to work on internal promotions for your affiliates. Another strong component of your affiliate community is the practice of rewarding the affiliates that perform well. Offer incentives to reach milestones, as well as promotions that are equally likely to reward any and all the affiliates, such as a weekly give-away of gift certificates, services, or other desirable commodities.

And to minimize repetitive questions, make it a practice to e-mail your FAQ to affiliates twice a year. This has long been a common practice on Usenet, and it is a very useful method for keeping your affiliates up to date and educated about your program.

- Have the affiliate team test and track performance of their own and other programs on their personal sites

- Participate in discussion boards

- Monitor the competition

- Identify and track prospective affiliates

- Target e-mail to inactive affiliates

- Compose tutorial

- Network with other affiliate managers

- Publish a monthly newsletter

- Participate in your affiliate community

- Switch out your banners and text links

- Test techniques and analyze

- Create content

- Collect affiliate testimonials

- Attend conferences

- Develop affiliate promotions

- Review log of questions asked by affiliates and add any new questions and answers to your FAQ

- E-mail FAQ a minimum of twice yearly to affiliates

Affiliate Directories

Here's a list of affiliate directories where you can submit your affiliate program. Some of these directories will send you many sign ups a day, but most will provide minimal results. However, it can't hurt to be listed in every directory. It can be time consuming to submit your affiliate program to all of the directories, so it is suggested that you consider one of the affiliate directory submission services, such as Affiliate Announce (affiliatetoolkit.com/affiliate-announce/). The nominal cost of $80 is well worth the time saved. Those directories marked with an * are a must for you to submit your program.

* 2-Tier Affiliate Program Directory

www.2-tier.com

4AffiliatePrograms.com

www.4affiliateprograms.com

4 Your Site.com

www.4yoursite.com

ActiveIncome.com

www.activeincome.com

Affiliate Advisor

www.AffiliateAdvisor.com

Affiliates Directory

www.affiliatesdirectory.com

Affiliate Forum

www.affiliateforum.com

AffiliateFind.com

www.affiliatefind.com

Affiliate Guide

www.affiliateguide.com

Affiliate Junction

www.theaffiliatejunction.com

Affiliate Match

www.affiliatematch.com

Affiliate Options Directory

www.affiliateoptions.com

Affiliate Programs Central

www.affiliateprogramscentral.com

Affiliate Programs Directory

www.Affiliate-Programs-Directory.com

Affiliate Promoter

www.affiliatepromoter.com

AffiliationPro

www.affiliationpro.com

Affiliate Trade Links Network

www.atlnetwork.com

Affiliate World

www.affiliateworld.com

Affiliates4U

www.affiliates4u.co.uk

Associate Cash.com

www.associatecash.com

* Associate-It

www.associate-it.com

* Associate Programs.com

www.associateprograms.com

Associate Search

www.associatesearch.com

BecomeAnAffiliate.com

www.becomeanaffiliate.com

Cash Cows

www.cash-cows.com

* CashPile.com

www.cashpile.com

Clicks2Lead

www.Click2Lead.com

Click Associates

www.clickassociates.com/indexfinger

ClickQuick

www.clickquick.com

ClickQuest

www.ClickQuest.com

Clicks Link

www.clickslink.com

Creative Opportunity.com

www.creativeopportunity.com

EasyCashMaker.com

www.easycashmaker.com

Free Affiliate Programs.com

www.freeaffiliateprograms.com

Gr1innovations.com

www.gr1innovations.com

Hits4me.com

www.hits4me.com/income.asp

i-Revenue

www.i-revenue.net

LinksThatPay.com

www.linksthatpay.com

loadedaffiliate.com

www.loadedaffiliate.com

Make Money Now

www.makemoneynow.com

Masterclick

masterclick.8m.com

OpportunitySeekers

www.opportunityseekers.com

Profits-To-Go

www.profitstogo.com

PWDNet Online UK

www.pwdnet.co.uk

Qango Revenue Street

www.qango.com/rs/

Referral Madness

www.referralmadness.com

* Refer-It

www.referit.com

ReveNews.com

www.revenews.com

Revenue Makers

www.revenuemakers.com/Directory

simplesiteUK

www.simplesite.co.uk

SiteCash.com

www.sitecash.com

Start Earning

www.startearning.com

Top 10 Affiliates

www.top10affiliates.com

Two Tier program

www.twotierprograms.com

Webmaster-Opportunities-Affiliate-Programs-Make-Money

www.webmaster-opportunities-affiliate-programs-make-money.com

Webmaster Programs

www.webmaster-programs.com

Webmasters Help Center

www.webmastershelpcenter.net/directory

WebWorker

www.referralincome.com/index/fr.affiliates.linksctl.html

Above the Fold   Part of a Web page that is visible after the page has loaded; normally it is the top part of a Web page. This term is derived from the newspaper industry, referring to the portion of the front page that is visible with the paper folded.

Affiliate   A Web site owner that earns a commission for referring clicks, leads, or sales to a merchant.

Affiliate Agreement   Terms between a merchant and an affiliate that govern the relationship.

Affiliate Information Page   A page (or pages) on your Web site that explains clearly and concisely what your affiliate program is all about.

Affiliate Link   A piece of code residing in a graphic image or piece of text placed on an affiliate's Web page that notifies the merchant that an affiliate should be credited for the customer or visitor sent to its Web site.

Affiliate Manager   The manager of an affiliate program who is responsible for creating a newsletter, establishing incentive programs,

forecasting and budgeting, overseeing front-end marketing of the program, and monitoring the industry for news and trends.

Affiliate Program (also an Associate, Partner, Referral, or Revenue Sharing Program)   A merchant pays a commission to an affiliate for generating clicks, leads, or sales from a graphic or text link located on the affiliate's site.

Affiliate Program Directory   A directory of affiliate programs, featuring information such as the commission rate, number of affiliates, and affiliate solution provider. Associate-It, AssociatePrograms.com, and Refer-it are among the largest Affiliate Program Directories.

Affiliate Solution Provider   A company that provides the network, software, and services needed to create and track an affiliate program.

Associate   A synonym for affiliate.

Auto-Approve   An affiliate application approval process where all applicants are automatically approved for an affiliate program.

Auto-Responder An e-mail feature that automatically sends an e-mail message to anyone who sends it a message.

Banner Ad An electronic billboard or ad in the form of a graphic image; these come in many sizes and reside on a Web site's Web page. Banner ad space is sold to advertisers to earn revenue for the Web site.

Charge Back An incomplete sales transaction (merchandise is purchased and then returned) that results in an affiliate commission deduction.

Click & Bye Refers to the process of an affiliate losing the visitor to the merchant's site once they click on a merchant's banner or text link. What you should strive for is "Click & Buy," where customers stay on the affiliate's site—or seem to—and buy the product or service.

Click-Through The action when a user clicks on a link.

Click-Through Ratio (CTR) The percentage of visitors who click-through on a link to visit the merchant's Web site.

Co-Branding A situation where affiliates are able to include their own logo and branding on the pages to which they send visitors through affiliate links.

Collaborative Commerce Networks
Networks of merchants and Web sites that work hand in hand as true business partners. Merchants treat their affiliates as sales and distribution channels worthy of any and all support that manufacturers would give to their resellers.

Commission The income an affiliate receives for generating a sale, lead, or click-through to a merchant's Web site. Sometimes called a referral fee, a finder's fee, or a bounty.

Cookies The small files stored on the visitor's computer that record information that is of interest to the merchant site. With affiliate programs, cookies have two primary functions: to keep track of what a customer purchases, and to track which affiliate was responsible for generating the sale (and is due a commission). Be especially wary of programs that only use cookies because they have many inherent limitations: the user can turn them off, they expire after a certain date or time, and they can be deleted off the visitor's computer.

Context-Centric Matching your product or service offer closely to the visitors of an affiliate's site. Place the product or service in-context (closely related to the content it's next to) and more people will buy.

Contextual Link The integration of affiliate links with related text.

Contextual Merchandising Placing targeted products near relevant content.

Conversion Rate The percentage of clicks that result in a commissionable activity (sale or lead).

CPA (Cost Per Action) Cost metric for each time a commissionable action takes place.

CPC (Cost Per Click) Cost metric for each click of an advertising link.

CPM (Cost Per Thousand)   Cost metric for one thousand banner advertising impressions.

Customer Bounty   Pays the affiliate partner for every new customer that they direct to a merchant.

E-mail Link   An affiliate link to a merchant site in an e-mail newsletter, signature, or a dedicated e-mail blast.

E-mail Signature (or Sig File)   Signature option allows for a brief message to be imbedded at the end of every e-mail that a person sends.

e-Zine   Short for electronic magazine. Some e-zines are simply electronic versions of existing print magazines, whereas others exist only in their digital format.

FAQ (Frequently Asked Questions)   FAQs are documents that answer the most common questions on a particular subject.

HTML code   The lines of code that affiliates use to put links on their Web sites. Affiliate solution providers often provide a tool where affiliates can simply copy the code for an affiliate link and paste it into their own HTML pages.

Hybrid Model   Affiliate commission model that combines payment options (CPC & CPA).

Impression   Advertising metric that indicates how many times an advertising link is displayed.

In-House   The alternative to using an affiliate solution provider; building affiliate program architecture within a company.

Lifetime Value of a Customer   The amount of sales in dollars that a customer in his lifetime will spend with a particular company.

Manual Approval   The affiliate application approval process where all applicants are manually approved for an affiliate program.

Media Metrix   Measures traffic counts on all the Web sites and digital media properties on the Net. It regularly publishes the names of the Top 50 sites in the United States, the Global Top 50, and the Media Metrix Top 500.

Merchant   An online business that markets and sells goods or services. Merchants establish affiliate programs as a cost-effective method to get consumers to purchase a product, register for a service, fill out a form, or visit a Web site.

Mini-Site   A prefabricated HTML page for affiliates that displays new or specialized products with integrated affiliate links.

Onesie   Low-traffic sites that provide a degree of revenue and visibility for your program. These normally are sites that focus on original content or community niches, such as sports, movies, or rock stars. They might also focus on other areas of interest, or they may be community sites that host discussions on specific topics.

Pay-Per-Sale   A program where an affiliate receives a commission for each sale of a product or service that he or she refers to a merchant's Web site. Pay-per-sale programs usually offer the highest commissions and the lowest conversion ratio.

Pay-Per-Lead   A program where an affiliate receives a commission for each sales lead that he or she generates for a merchant Web site. Examples would include completed surveys, contest or sweepstakes entries, downloaded software demos, or free trials. Pay-per-lead generally offers midrange commissions and midrange-to-high conversion ratios.

Pay-Per-Click   A program where an affiliate receives a commission for each click (visitor) he or she refers to a merchant's Web site. Pay-per-click programs generally offer some of the lowest commissions (from $0.01 to $0.25 per click), and a very high conversion ratio because visitors need only click on a link to earn the affiliate a commission.

Residual Earnings   Programs that pay affiliates not just for the first sale a shopper from their sites makes, but all additional sales made at the merchant's site over the life of the customer.

ROI (Return on Investment)   This is what all marketing managers want to see from the money they spend on their marketing and advertising campaigns. The higher the sales, the large the number of shoppers and the greater the profit margin generated by sales—the better the ROI.

Spam (or Spamming)   Electronic junk mail or junk newsgroup postings, generally e-mail advertising for some product sent to a mailing list or newsgroup. A must to avoid if you treasure your company's reputation!

Storefront   A prefabricated HTML page for affiliates that displays new or specialized products with integrated affiliate links.

Super Affiliates   The small percentage of sites—the top 1% of affiliates, based on performance and earnings—that generate the lion's share of the revenue for your program. They are born marketers and are very successful with the affiliate program they promote from their sites.

Targeted Marketing   Offering the right offer to the right customer at the right time.

Tracking Method   The way a program tracks referred sales, leads, or clicks. The most common are by using a unique Web address (URL) for each affiliate, or by embedding an affiliate ID number into the link that is processed by the merchant's software. Some programs also use cookies for tracking.

Text Link   A link that is not accompanied by a graphical image.

Two-Tier   An affiliate marketing model that allows affiliates to sign up additional affiliates below themselves, so that when the second-tier affiliates earn a commission, the affiliate above them also receives a commission.

Up-and-Comer   Those affiliates that do not generate the types of revenues that super affiliates do, though they do show that kind of potential. With a little training and education about your product or service, they could join the ranks of your super affiliates.

Viral Marketing   The rapid adoption of a product or passing-on of an offer to friends and family through "word of mouth" (or "word of email") networks. Any advertising that propagates itself the way viruses do.

Dynamic Trade

participating online merchants, 203

payment thresholds, 203

set-up fees, 203

third-party solution provider, 203-204

tracking technology, 204

E

e-Base Interactive, 140, 241

e-commerce

networks, 24-25

products/services, growth forecasts, 36-38

e-mail

affiliates, contacting, 124-125

auto-responder programs, 163-165

discussion lists, feedback, 271-273

marketing lists, 28

eZines, 249-250

Mail Master Pro, 250-251

Postmaster General, 250-251

Sandy Bay Networks, 251

as marketing tool, 114-115

model

Barnes and Noble.com, 100

signatures, 100-101

spam warning, 99

SuperSig, 101

viral marketing, 101-102

opt-in lists, 290

promotional messages, 248

spam, 78

E-ZineZ.com Web site, 285

EasyCashMaker.com Web site, 315

eBags.com, embedded commerce example, 98

ebates.com, merchant affiliate program, 46-47

eBookstand.com, residual earnings model, 226

eBusiness

affiliate marketing, suitability for, 33

customer acquisition costs, 32

products/services

growth forecasts, 36-38

range of, 35-38

EchoFactor, affiliate program

details, 69

joining, 54

Edvardsson, Ova, consultant services, 72

eGroups Web site, free chat services, 306

elastic retailers, 24-25

eMarketer.com, daily e-mail statistics, 114

embedded commerce boutiques

Art.com, 97

eBags.com, 98

Site59.com, 99

Web Collage, 98

employees (programs), personnel requirements, 235

compensation, 237-238

locating, 236-237

outsourcing options, 238-243

EnContext (Commission Junction), 203

endorsements (creatives), 113-115

enrollment clauses in agreements, 170

Epinions, affiliate program details, 58

ePod.com, e-commerce network model, 25

escalating commissions, agreement terminology, 175-176

eSportsStuff, two-tier payment model, 225

eToys, customer acquisition payment model, 218

Evoy, Ken, consultant services, 72

exclusivity clauses in agreements, 171

eZines, 137, 249-250

BestEzines.com, 285

E-ZinesZ.com, 285

LifeStylesPub.com.com, 285

F

failed programs, reasons for, 82-83

FAQ (Frequently Asked Questions) pages, 251-252

affiliate support, 282

content thoroughness, 295

Federal Reserve Automated Clearing House (ACH), payment transfers, 197

Q - R